THE JEWISH COMMUNITY IN AMERICA

**BURT FRANKLIN
ETHNIC BIBLIOGRAPHICAL GUIDES**

GENERAL EDITORS:

Francesco Cordasco, *Montclair State College*
William W. Brickman, *University of Pennsylvania*

Francesco Cordasco
The Italian-American Experience:
An Annotated and Classified Bibliographical Guide,
With Selected Publications of the Casa Italiana Educational Bureau

William W. Brickman
The Jewish Community in America:
An Annotated and Classified Bibliographical Guide

Joseph M. Gowaskie
The Polish Community in America:
An Annotated and Classified Bibliographical Guide

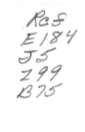

THE JEWISH COMMUNITY IN AMERICA

An Annotated and Classified Bibliographical Guide

by
WILLIAM W. BRICKMAN
Professor of Educational History
and Comparative Education
Graduate School of Education,
University of Pennsylvania

BURT FRANKLIN & COMPANY, INC.
NEW YORK

Library of Congress Cataloging in Publication Data
Brickman, William W.
The Jewish community in America.
(Ethnic bibliographical guides)
Includes index.
1. Jews in the United States—Bibliography.
2. United States—Bibliography. I. Title.
Z6373.U5B75 [E184.J5] 016.973'04'924 76-30284
ISBN 0-89102-057-8

To the Memory of My Parents,
Reb Sholem Dovid ben Reb Avrohom Ha-Levi,
Born in Friedrichshof, Germany
and
Chaya Soreh bas Reb Tsvi,
Born in Jedwabno, Russian Poland,
(David S. and Sarah)
Brickman,
Beneficiaries of American Freedom
and
Transmitters of a Spiritual Tradition

TABLE OF CONTENTS

Preface v
Introduction: The American Jewish Community
    in Historical Perspective vii
   I. General Histories 1
  II. Regional and Local History 15
 III. Specialized Historical Works 33
  IV. Sources and Collections of Documents 45
   V. Autobiographies, Memoirs, and Reminiscences . . . 59
  VI. Biographies 73
 VII. Social and Communal Life and Activity 101
VIII. Religious Life, Thought, and Affairs 129
  IX. Education 147
   X. Political, International, and Economic Activity . . . 169
  XI. Literature 181
 XII. Immigration 191
XIII. Intergroup Relations 201
XIV. Anti-Semitism 215
 XV. Periodicals, Yearbooks, and Encyclopedias 229
XVI. Bibliographies 251
    Appendix 263
    Main Entry Index 387

PREFACE

The objective of this volume is to present to scholars, teachers, and other interested persons a descriptively and, in part, critically annotated collection of over 800 basic and specialized writings in English, Hebrew, Yiddish, Ladino, German, French, Hungarian, Polish, and Russian. These publications and other materials throw light on the Jewish experience in America from the Colonial period to the present. The readers will be able to select from a variety of writings those which, in accordance with the background and experience they bring to their study, can extend their knowledge and understanding of well over 300 years of Jewish life, learning, and labor in the United States.

Stress is placed on the adjustment of Jews who migrated to American shores at various times from different countries. There is also a focus on the unique achievements of immigrant and native Jews in relation to the other inhabitants of the country. An effort has been made to present authentic data and to avoid ethnocentricism.

The annotated bibliography is classified according to several categories: general and specialized historical works, biographies, autobiographies and reminiscences, source collections, bibliographies, and recent monographs and other writings. The subject matter covers such topics as family life, society, religion, economics, industry, politics, education, literature, culture, and foreign relations.

The Jewish experience in America has been recorded in numerous documents, many of which have been published in newspapers, magazines, books, institutional and organizational records, and other works. There are also unpublished materials in the American Jewish Archives, the American Jewish Historical Society, the YIVO Institute for Jewish Research, and other repositories. A selection of significant source materials has been included.

It is to be hoped that this volume, along with the others in the Ethnic Bibliographical Guides series, will stimulate more substantial study of the American ethnic heritage.

Acknowledgment is made to Professor Francesco Cordasco for his initiative in the inauguration of the series of Ethnic Bibliographical Guides and for his encouragement in the preparation of the present volume; to Jill K. Moss and Carla P. Childs for aid in the checking of bibliographical details; and to Ms. Childs for the preparation of the index. The writer also thanks Dr. Lawrence Marwick, Head, and Myron M. Weinstein, Area Specialist, of the Hebraic Section of the Library of Congress, Dr. Nathan M. Kaganoff of the American Jewish Historical Society, and their assistants; and the staffs of the Jewish Section of the New York Public Library and of the Van Pelt and Hillel Libraries of the University of Pennsylvania for making the many books available and for other forms of assistance. Jeannette C. Weiss once again displayed her typing skill under, at times, trying circumstances.

William W. Brickman
June 1976

INTRODUCTION

THE AMERICAN JEWISH COMMUNITY IN
HISTORICAL PERSPECTIVE

The recent upsurge of interest in ethnic studies in the United States represents a reemergence of the movement of the 1930s that was called intercultural education. Professional educators, sociologists, and social workers were concerned with materials and methods that would enable elementary and high school pupils to appreciate the cultures of racial, religious, and national minorities and their contributions to American life. Social psychologists were beginning to stress the greater significance of the environment over heredity in the makeup of individuals and groups.

With events tending to move in a cyclical manner, the idea of studying the component groups was recently revived, but in a more acceptable, systematic, and profound form. Various colleges and universities have organized programs built around the history and culture of particular minorities in American society. One such program is called Jewish Studies, with instruction in the Hebrew language, literature, Jewish religious thought, history, and other areas. To a considerably lesser extent, elements of this program of study have been included in the curricula of schools below college level.

One branch of the Jewish Studies movement can be identified with the more than three centuries of Jewish life in America. The New World constitutes a distinctive geographical entity and the United States represents a unique sociopolitical system. Hence, there is ample justification for directing attention to what may be called American Jewish Studies. Without exhausting all the possible subdivisions of this subject, it is possible to list the content as comprising the history, sociology, religion, education, political and economic activity, literature, culture, and intergroup relations of the Jews in the United States. A reasonable appreciation of the nature, ideals, achievements, and goals of American Jewry would require a knowledge of the component elements of American Jewish Studies.

The Jewish experience in America has long been the subject of a variety of writings. Primary documents date from the seventeenth century. As individual Jews and groups grew in numbers and increased their activities, there emerged a literature of diaries, letters, reports, petitions, and organizational documents. The idea of an American Jewish history possibly originated in the form of a student's commencement oration in Hebrew at Columbia College in 1800. "As far as we know, that was the first sketch of American Jewish history by an American." [1] Since then, the literature and study of the history of American Jewry has proceeded at a rather slow pace. It was not until well into the twentieth century that scholarly works began to deal with the historical and other aspects of the life of Jews in the United States. More recently, there have appeared detailed monographs and collections of documents, all of which should make possible a more reliable knowledge and deeper comprehension of the past, present, and possible future of the American Jewish community.

There is no precise dating of the appearance of the first Jews within the present borders of the United States. As early as 1621, individual Jews are believed to have settled in Virginia, Maryland, and Massachusetts. Several colonial Americans may have taken seriously the argument advanced by Thomas Thorowgood in 1650 [2] and again in 1660 [3] that the North American Indians were the lost Ten Tribes of Israel. On the other hand, some may have been convinced by the contradictory argument of Hamon L'Estrange. [4] In any event, historians tend to agree that the first Jewish settlement as a group took place in the summer of 1654. Beginning with the arrival in New Amsterdam of Jacob Barsimson and Jacob Aboab on *de Pereboom*, which carried emigrants from the Netherlands, identifiable Jews began to make their home in the colonial areas. As Dutch citizens, they were received in the same way as their Christian countrymen. It was in September, 1654, that a group of twenty-three Jewish refugees from Brazil, recently wrested by Portugal from the Dutch, arrived on the *St. Charles* in New Amsterdam, and thus constituted the first Jewish community in colonial America. American Jewish history may be said to have begun at that time.

With this initial step on the record, it will be appropriate to pause for a moment to get an overall glimpse of American Jewish history before analyzing its component parts. One way to do this is to divide the totality of American Jewish experience into eras or periods of time in which one can identify particular characteristics and trends.

For some time, writers on the history of Jewish life in America have spoken of three "waves of immigration" of Jews to the United States: the Sephardic (of Spanish-Portuguese origin) in the seventeenth and eighteenth centuries; the German, chiefly during the first half of the nineteenth century; and the Russian or Eastern European, during the late nineteenth and early twentieth centuries. While this classification is still valid, it has been presented in a more sophisticated form by Jacob Rader Marcus. This distinguished scholar identifies the following eras: the "Rise and Decline of Sephardic Jewry," extending from 1654 through 1840; the "Age of the Rise and Dominance of the German Jew and Dominance of the German Jew and the Challenge to His Leadership, 1841-1920"; the "Age of the Advent and the Rise of the East European Jew and His Bid for Hegemony, 1852-1920"; and the period of "The Emerging American Jewish Community, The Age of Fusion, The Epoch of the Rise of the *American* Jew," 1921 to the present.[5] It is obvious that there is some overlapping between any two periods, but, in general, these periods are distinctly demarcated.

The central theme running through the more than three centuries of American Jewish history is that of polyethnic peregrination. Jews came to America from many countries and represented Spanish-Portuguese, Dutch, German, English, Russian, Eastern European, Middle Eastern, and North African origins. They brought with them their national languages plus Hebrew, Yiddish, and Ladino. All tried to make a fresh start, to survive, and to thrive in an atmosphere of freedom such as they had never experienced previously, whether in their native lands or in the areas of sojourn. In an encapsulated formula, one might sum up American Jewish history as arrival, adjustment, aspiration, activity, and achievement. The overall history of the Jewish community reveals growth, development, increase, and general improvement. This is not to claim that there were no difficulties, issues, and crises. Some of the contemporary problems, indeed, make one pause before indulging in optimism about specific aspects of the future.

Let us return to the early period of Jewish history in colonial America. Although the Jews were quite comfortable in the European Netherlands, the classic locale of religious and intellectual freedom, their initial reception in New Netherland was anything but hospitable. The testy governor, Peter Stuyvesant, looked with a jaundiced expression upon the Jewish refugees from Brazil who lacked passports and visible means of support. He appealed, therefore, to the body that controlled the colony, the Dutch West India Company in Amsterdam, to uphold his decision "to require them in a friendly way to depart." Although New Amsterdam was already a cosmopolitan community, in which no fewer than eighteen languages were spoken, Stuyvesant could not bring himself to extend the policy of pluralism to include the Jews, whom he identified as "the deceitful race—such hateful enemies and blasphemers of the name of Christ," and who, he implored the Amsterdam authorities, should "not be allowed further to infect and trouble this new colony. . . ." [6] The Jewish community of Amsterdam intervened in opposition to Stuyvesant's effort to close the door to their coreligionists beyond the Atlantic. In a petition to the Amsterdam Chamber of the Dutch West India Company, they enumerated four strong reasons why "the Jewish nation [should] be permitted, together with other inhabitants, to travel, live and traffic there, and with them enjoy liberty on condition of contributing like others. . . ." [7] This first crisis in colonial Jewish history was resolved by the reply by the Company to Stuyvesant's petition. Although the members of the Amsterdam Chamber shared some of the same sentiments as Stuyvesant regarding the Jews, they decided that "these people may travel and trade to and in New Netherland and live and remain there, provided the poor among them shall not become a burden to the company or to the community, but be supported by their own nation." [8]

With the danger of expulsion eliminated, the Jews of New Amsterdam continued their struggle to wrest civic rights, duties, and privileges from the intransigent Stuyvesant. In time, they won a status similar to the one enjoyed by the Jews of Amsterdam. They carried on a variety of vocations and occupations, among these handicrafts, trade, and banking. After the conquest of New Netherland by the British in 1664, the Jews continued their activity as heretofore in a similar environment of freedom. They organized their communal and religious life in an effort to carry on their inherited traditions. Although there are no documents extant with regard to the education of their children, we must assume that parents obeyed the Scriptural mandate that parents teach the commandments and other aspects of Judaism to their children. One can also assume that there were tutors who substituted for the parents as teachers or who supplemented their instruction. Records of formal school instruction cannot be found for the century between 1650 and 1750.

While there may have been a Jewish school in colonial America as early as 1731 (the Yeshibat Minhat Areb), the evidence seems to be stronger for 1755, when the Congregation Shearith Israel, the Spanish-Portuguese synagogue in New York City, opened a day school with a curriculum comprising religious and secular studies. The early minutes of the congregation indicate that there was instruction in Hebrew, English, Spanish, and arithmetic.[9] The successor to Yeshibat Minhat Areb, the Polónies Talmud Torah, which opened in 1802, declared that it aimed "to instill in the youthful mind a love of learning—a veneration for religion and morality—and an attainment of useful instruction. . . ."[10] To attain these goals, the school organized six hours of daily instruction, English in the morning and Hebrew in the afternoon. While this was not the prototype of the twentieth-century Jewish day school, it did constitute a pattern for the combined program of religious and secular studies which characterized the more rigorous type of Jewish education in the United States.

The next permanent Jewish settlement, after New Amsterdam, was in Newport, Rhode Island, a colony which preached and practiced freedom for religious minorities. Another favorable location was Pennsylvania, where Jews also enjoyed the blessings of religious freedom. Fewer numbers settled in the other New England and middle colonies, while a small number penetrated the deep South well into the eighteenth century. One discouraging factor was the apparent anomaly of hostility toward Jews in colonial Maryland, which had enacted a law of religious toleration in 1649. This famous legislative act, however, restricted the free exercise of religion to Catholics and Protestants who professed belief in the "holy Trinity the Father sonne and holy Ghost."[11] The penalties for any residents who disbelieved in Christianity or who were guilty of blasphemy could extend to execution. What gave colonial Jews everywhere the basic political rights was an act of Parliament in 1740 which specified that "such who profess the Jewish Religion" were eligible for naturalization and were exempt from reciting the phrase "upon the true Faith of a Christian" when taking an oath.[12]

Permanent Jewish settlements, usually organized in the form of a voluntary community (*Kehillah*), were established in New York, Newport, Philadelphia, Charleston (South Carolina), and Savannah. The colonial Jews were of Spanish-Portuguese, Dutch, English, German, and Polish origin. They were engaged in commerce, trade, manufacturing, and various forms of skilled craftsmanship. Not many enrolled in the colonial colleges, in part because of the fact that only few, Brown University in particular, made any effort to recognize the religious requirements of Judaism. The only person of Jewish origin identified with instruction at a colonial college was Judah Monis (1683-1764), who converted to Christianity in 1722 and served as instructor of Hebrew at Harvard College from that date until 1760. In 1735, he published *A Grammar of the Hebrew Tongue,* which became the standard textbook for the required course in Hebrew at Harvard.

There are no precise figures as to the number of Jews in colonial America. The estimate of 200-300 Jewish inhabitants by 1700 is reasonable. On the eve of the Revolution (1776), there were probably not more than 2,500 Jews in the thirteen colonies.

The advent of the Revolution found the vast majority of the Jews joining the struggle against England through participation in the armed forces, legislative action, and financial support. The most prominent activist in the area of finance was Haym Salomon (1740-1785), a Polish-born patriot. "His liberal advances of cash to officers of the government and his equally liberal investments in Revolutionary paper, *c.* 1780-84, constitute an outstanding example of devotion to the American cause; he contributed much in other ways to maintain the bankrupt government's credit." [13]

The birth of the New Republic led to a wider sphere of public activity on the part of the America Jew, but full political emancipation, particularly the right to hold government office, was not attained in all the states until some time afterward. The guarantees of religious freedom under the Northwest Ordinance of 1787 and the First Amendment to the Constitution were most significant for the Jews, but they did not result in the elimination of bias, prejudice, and discriminatory practices. President George Washington, it is true, stated the national policy of the United States government as one "which gives to bigotry no sanction, to persecution no assistance,"[14] but not all of his countrymen, contemporary or of posterity, lived up to this principle toward the Jew and others. By way of illustration, the "Jew Bill" of Maryland, "to consider the justice and expediency of extending to those persons professing the Jewish Religion, the same privileges that are enjoyed by Christians," introduced in 1819, did not pass until 1826.

Undaunted by the slow development of full equality and the persistence of prejudice in the press and in public affairs, the Jews extended their settlements and activities during the early decades of the nineteenth century. The new communities included Richmond, Baltimore, Cincinnati, St. Louis, New Orleans, Cleveland, Louisville, Chicago, and San Francisco. The total Jewish population of the United States rose from about 4,000 in 1820 to 6,000 in 1826, to 15,000 in 1840, and to 150,000 in 1860. As numbers began to accumulate in new centers, Jews established communal organizations—synagogues, religious schools, burial societies, and charitable institutions for the poor, the sick, and the orphaned. They began to play a more significant role in the federal and state legislatures, in the armed services, in the professions, and in industrial and commercial affairs. Periodicals with ideas and news of Jewish communal and religious interest made their appearance. Reform Judaism, imported from Germany, began to make inroads into the Orthodox communities. The influence of the Sephardic Jews waned as the nineteenth century progressed, and the German Jews replaced them as communal leaders, as philanthropists, and as spokesmen for their people.

An emerging new role for American Jews was increased by their interest in the welfare of Jews in other countries and by participation in the foreign affairs of the country. The most important individual in this respect during the first half of the nineteenth century was Mordecai Manuel Noah (1785-1851), editor, lawyer, New York City official, playwright, educational activist, and United States consul in Tunis during 1813-1815. In September, 1825, Noah sent out an invitation to Jewish communities all over the world to establish a refugee colony on Grand Island, in the Niagara River near Buffalo, New York. The intention was good, coming as it did at a time when persecution was prevalent in Germany and not unknown elsewhere. However, the proposal for a Jewish state under the protection of the United States government did not receive the approval of overseas Jews. The movement for a national Jewish homeland would have to wait until the advent of Zionism some seven decades later.

No doubt, the most important activity by American Jewry in foreign affairs prior to the Civil War was in connection with the false charges in Damascus in 1840 that a Jew had killed a Catholic priest to use the blood in the making of unleavened bread (matzah). The authorities, who represented the governor of Egypt, imprisoned and tortured many Jews— some died of the torment, some "turned Turks," and seventy-two others were sentenced to be hanged. In the words of the American consul, "The inquisition against the jews [sic] in that City (in which there may be 30000. Souls of that Nation) continues with much vigour and no jew [sic] can show his face out in the streets."[15] American Jews joined with their coreligionists in other countries, and with Christians, in a massive protest against the Damascus Blood Libel Affair. Letters of concern and protest were sent to President Martin Van Buren and the Secretary of State by the Jews of New York City, Philadelphia, Richmond, and other communities. The President was implored to "use every possible effort to induce the Pacha of Egypt to manifest more liberal treatment toward his Jewish subjects, not only from the dictates of humanity, but from the obvious policy and justice by which such a course is recommended by the intolerant spirit of the age in which we live."[16] The interposition of good offices of the United States, together with the efforts of other nations, led to the intervention by the Sultan of Turkey. This potentate declared that the blood libel was an "erroneous belief" and that the accusations against the Jews were "false and pure calumnies,"[17] thus bringing the persecution to an end.

The American Jewish community also reacted to other

incidents affecting Jews overseas: the Mortara affair in Italy (1858), in which a Jewish baby was secretly baptized and subsequently kidnapped from his family in Bologna; and the pogroms and discriminations against the Jews of Rumania (1870-1872) and of Russia (from 1881 onward).

Anti-Semitism proved to be closer to home than the Middle East and Eastern Europe. On December 17, 1862, Major-General U. S. Grant issued General Order No. 11 which expelled Jews from the area occupied by his troops for violating his trade regulations. This unjustified action, which singled out several Jews among many traders, evoked sharp protests to President Abraham Lincoln,[18] who objected to the sweeping condemnation of Jews and speedily issued an order of revocation. In the twentieth century, American Jewry was to have considerable experience in protesting against anti-Semitism, both native and foreign. Among such actions were the demonstrations against tsarist and Soviet Russia, the Nazis, Henry Ford, and various American fascist groups. The continuance of anti-Jewish activities brought about the establishment of such defense organizations as the American Jewish Committee, the American Jewish Congress, and the B'nai B'rith Anti-Defamation League.

Before the Civil War, Jews were generally ranged on opposite sides of the slavery issue, depending upon their geographic location. During the war, they served in the armed forces of the Union and the Confederacy. The recently arrived German Jewish immigrants supported the abolition of slavery and trooped to the colors of the "blue." Altogether, 10,000 Jews, 6,000 of them in the Northern forces, were engaged in military activities during the Civil War. Nine attained the rank of general officer, 18 that of colonel, and 9 that of lieutenant-colonel. On the Confederate side, the most prominent Jew was Judah P. Benjamin, born in the British West Indies of English and Portuguese Jewish parents, who was a member of the Louisiana state legislature and later the U. S. Senate. During the Civil War, he served the South successively as attorney general, secretary of war, and secretary of state.

In writing the history of the Jewry of America it is all too easy to highlight the roles, achievements, and impact of political, military, scientific, cultural, industrial, and commercial personalities, and to overlook leading individuals in the realm of religion. A brief essay, obviously, cannot do justice to any one category of accomplishment, let alone all of them. Since religion is intrinsic to Judaism, whereas other spheres of activity may not be, special attention is given to several spiritual figures who played a prominent part in American Jewish life prior to the arrival of the Russian refugees in the 1880s. Isaac Leeser (1806-1868), a native of Germany, served the American Jewish community as rabbi, founder of a congregational religious school (Mikveh Israel, Philadelphia) and Maimonides College and, most importantly, as editor of *The Occident and Jewish Advocate.* Although he is often credited with being a forerunner of Conservative Judaism in the United States, he strongly upheld the traditional religion in his preaching, teaching, and writing. A theological opponent, Isaac Mayer Wise (1819-1900), a Bohemian-born rabbi, became the founding father of Reform Judaism in America. Among Wise's lasting creations are the Union of American Hebrew Congregations (1873), the Hebrew Union College (1875), and the Central Conference of American Rabbis (1889). An opponent of Wise was the German-born Abraham Joseph Rice, or Reiss (1802-1862), who was the first rabbi with *Semichah* (Orthodox ordination) to serve in the United States. "A vigorous defender of Orthodoxy" as a rabbi in Baltimore, Rice established the German-Jewish day school there, attacked Reform, and organized emergency aid for the Jews in Palestine.[19]

As an exemplary philanthropist, Judah Touro (1775-1854) occupies an important place in American Jewish history. Born in Newport and prospering as a merchant in New Orleans, Touro provided support for synagogues, schools, hospitals, and cemeteries in many cities in the United States, as well as funds for the poor in Palestine. In his well-known will, Touro bequeathed funds to religious, educational, and charitable institutions, and to hospitals. Included among the recipients were St. Mary's Catholic Boys' Asylum, the Seamen's Home, the Alms House, and other non-Jewish establishments.[20]

As already indicated, the tsarist Russian government perpetrated and encouraged organized massacres, or pogroms, from 1881 until about World War I. While the condition of the Russians was actually intolerable under Nicholas I, it became impossible in the era of pogroms and the notorious anti-Jewish laws of May, 1882. With the articulation of an official policy of letting one-third of the Russian Jews starve to death, forcibly converting one-third to Christianity, and expelling the remainder, it became clear to most Jews that the only hope for survival was emigration. Although millions remained in a geographic ghetto, the Pale of Settlement, millions migrated to various countries in Europe, the Middle East, and the Western Hemisphere. As the Russian refugees arrived in the United States, the total Jewish population began to mount year by year. The number of American Jews, 251,000 in 1881, rose to 2,349,754 in 1910. The figure for immigration during 1881-1910 was 1,572,936 persons. An estimate for 1884-1905 revealed that 67.94 percent (or 551,708) of 811,936 Jewish immigrants from sixteen countries were Russians.[21] Some of the immigrants became farmers, but most settled in the larger cities, especially on the Lower East Side of New York City, where large numbers were engaged as workers in the clothing industries. Some Jews were active in manufacturing and other industrial activities, but most were laborers who soon organized trade unions to protect themselves against unfavorable working conditions and exploitation.

The immigrants became active in religious, educational, and cultural activities. Their common language, Yiddish, was represented in the synagogues, unions, theaters, and press, on the streets, and in the homes. To keep alive memories of their native villages (shtetls) of Eastern Europe, and also to maintain their friendships with fellow-townsmen, the erstwhile Russians organized a network of fraternal and charitable societies (*landsmanshaftn*), which met the demands of their social and often cultural requirements.

The Russian wave of immigration was accompanied by the establishment, growth, and development of Jewish schools and rabbinical seminaries. The Jewish Theological Seminary of America(1886) provided preparation for future Conservative rabbis. During the same year, the Orthodox founded in New York City the Yeshivah Etz Chaim, which became the Rabbi Isaac Elchanan Theological Seminary (1896), and subsequently expanded into the Yeshiva University (1945). The original curriculum of this pioneering Jewish day school consisted of six hours of daily instruction in religious studies, one hour of Hebrew and Yiddish, and two of English, "according to the strict Orthodox and Talmudical Law and custom of Poland and Russia."[22] This school was followed by the founding of the Rabbi Jacob Joseph School (1900), generally regarded as the mother of the *yeshivah ketanah*, the elementary Jewish day school, in the United States. Since then, well over 300 elementary and secondary day schools, the vast majority of them Orthodox, were established all over the United States and Canada. There were also afternoon schools, Sunday schools, and Yiddish-language secular schools throughout the country. In an effort at centralization of the afternoon schools of New York City, Jewish educators with secular higher educational training organized the Bureau of Jewish Education.[23]

The World War (1914-1918) slowed down the flow of immigrants and turned American Jews' attention to the relief of their unfortunate brethren in Eastern Europe and in Palestine. With the Balfour Declaration of 1917 came an increase of organizations devoted to Zionism and to the rebuilding of Palestine as a Jewish national homeland. The growth of isolationist and racist sentiment in the United States, in part because of the Bolshevik revolution of 1917 and other political changes in Europe, led to the growth of overt anti-Semitism and to the passing by Congress of the Johnson Act of 1924, which brought about the drying up of the sources of the Eastern European Jewish emigration.

The advent of Hitler and his Nazi Party to power in Germany in 1933 led to an exodus of German Jews, many of whom came to the United States and enriched its cultural, intellectual, scientific, and commercial resources. At the same time, the deeper development of the depression plus the inroads of Nazi and various forms of native American anti-Semitism brought about significant changes in the social, economic, philanthropic, and institutional life of the Jews. The needs of coreligionists everywhere—Eastern and Central Europe, Palestine, and the United States—were increasingly recognized even as Americans struggled to overcome the impact of the economic depression.

World War II heightened even more the consciousness and the activities of American Jewish organizations and individuals in behalf of their brethren in the shadow of death and destruction. With all their efforts and campaigns, however, they were unable to persuade their government to use its power and influence to rescue the endangered Jews of Central and Eastern Europe. The Holocaust with a toll of 6,000,000 Jewish victims constituted a reality which galvanized the Jews of America into activity in behalf of the establishment of a Jewish homeland to safeguard the remnant of European Jewry, the threatened hundreds of thousands in Arab lands, and others. The approval by the United Nations in 1948 of a State of Israel, owing to the initiative and support by the United States, the U.S.S.R., and other countries, acted as an incentive to the American Jewish community to magnify considerably its financial and other contributions to the perpetuation of the new republic.

Since 1945, the end of World War II, increasing numbers of Jews began to arrive in the United States. The newcomers were survivors of the Nazi German concentration and extermination camps in various parts of Europe. The postwar arrivals, unlike their predecessors who escaped Hitler's Germany, were not scientists and intellectuals for the most part. What they brought to the American Jewish community was the awareness of the Holocaust and loss in Hungary, Rumania, Poland, and other Eastern European Jewish communities. They also helped strengthen the use of the Yiddish language, as well as traditional Jewish religious observance and education.

With the death in 1953 of Joseph V. Stalin, the Soviet dictator who intensified the Jewish persecutions during "the black years" following 1945, American Jews increased their interest in, and concern for, their Soviet brethren and sisters. Slowly at first, but more concertedly in the late 1950s, rabbinical groups and individuals began to visit the Soviet Union and to try to lift the spirits of the Soviet Jews. Toward the end of the 1960s, American Jews organized activistic efforts in order to exert pressure on the Soviet government to ease restrictions upon its Jews and particularly to allow them to emigrate to Israel, the United States, and other countries. The American Conference on Soviet Jewry, the Academic Council on Soviet Jewry, and the Student Struggle for Soviet Jewry were the new groups which concentrated on the issue. Other organizations, too, joined in a mass effort to liberate Soviet Jews through demonstrations, publications, diplomatic steps, and economic pressure. By the mid-1970s, it was clear that American Jewry was concentrating its attention on Israel and the U.S.S.R. Less prominent, but also important, in the campaign to aid overseas Jews was the activity in behalf of the remaining Jews in Syria, Iraq, and other Arab countries, where, because of the anti-Israel atmosphere, they lived in constant danger of annihilation.

The review of American Jewish history in the previous pages is but a mere outline within restricted space. Justice cannot be done to the subject in an essay. There is a rich literature, in both narrative and documentary form, which aids toward a comprehension of specific developments, problems, and issues.

Before closing this survey, it is proper to take stock of the current status, situation, and prospects of the American Jewish community. It is eminently clear that the Jews in the

United States have been pouring their resources and exerting their energies to safeguard the survival and improve the lives of overseas Jews. What is less evident is their effort to ensure their own existence in their own country. There is no doubt that attention is being paid to various problems and challenges confronting American Jewry, but there is no certainty that it is adequate.

As of 1974, the total number of Jewish inhabitants in the United States was estimated by the *American Jewish Year Book* to be 5,731,685, or 2.7 percent of the total civilian population of 209,689,000. The major portion of the Jewish population was distributed regionally as follows: Middle Atlantic states, 53 percent; Pacific states, 12.1 percent; South Atlantic states, 11.8 percent; East North Central states, 10.1 percent; and New England states, 7.1 percent. Among the individual states, New York had 11.9 percent of the American Jews; New Jersey, 5.7 percent; Maryland, 5.6 percent; Massachusetts, 4.7 percent; the District of Columbia, 4.6 percent; Pennsylvania, 4 percent; Florida, 3.7 percent; California and Connecticut, 3.2 percent; Illinois, 2.4 percent; and Rhode Island, 2.4 percent. A few Jews lived in South Dakota (635), Alaska and Idaho (630), Montana (545), and Wyoming (345). [24]

Social analysts have recently observed the decline in the Jewish birthrate, especially in the suburban areas, which have been attracting large numbers of Jews. The vast majority lives in such metropolitan centers as New York City, Los Angeles, Chicago, Philadelphia, Miami, and the District of Columbia. The Jewish settlements in the small towns are diminishing and many will soon be reduced to zero inhabitants.

The American Jewish population constitutes about two-fifths of world Jewry. In 1850, the percentage was 1 percent; in 1900, 10 percent; and 1933, 28 percent. This growth is an indication of the rising significance of American Jewry in world Jewish affairs. In the United States, Jews have increasingly turned "from business and labor to the professions, free and salaried, and the managerial sectors." [25] About 85 to 90 percent of Jews in their upper teens and early twenties attend college. "American Jewry is becoming less and less a community of small or large businessmen and is becoming more and more a community of professionals, of the technically skilled and the managerially trained, a highly mobile group." [26]

The American Jewish community has over 300 national organizations, which deal with religion, education, culture, intergroup relations, social welfare, overseas assistance, and other communal affairs and interests. There are coordinating bodies, such as the National Jewish Community Relations Advisory Council in community relations, the Synagogue Council of America in religious and related matters, and the American Association for Jewish Education and Torah Umesorah in educational activities. However, these do not represent all Jewish groups in their respective spheres.

Although there is no single body that is authorized to speak for American Jewry as a whole, there are two organizations which encompass the activities of very large majorities of American Jews. The Council of Jewish Federations and Welfare Funds coordinates local federations in fund raising for national, international, and Israeli needs, plus communal and welfare requirements. The United Jewish Appeal represents the combined effort for aid to Jews in Israel and indeed everywhere. Its annual drive constitutes the major enterprise of a Jewish nature in most communities. The results are most impressive, since the campaigns collect contributions which have reached $300,000,000.

The federation and appeal organizations on the local and national levels tend to unite Jews of diverse backgrounds, interests, and beliefs in a common cause. However, there are strong reasons why American Jews do not agree on a single group as spokesman. For one thing, there is a powerful representation of secular sentiment in various organizations, so much so that religious values have been neglected if not indeed flouted. Another reason is that the federations, until relatively recently, have been more than cool to the Jewish day school movement. Even with the rise of some interest, the federation leadership cannot be accused of bias in behalf of the school system which has made a deep impact on the spiritual survival of American Jewry. In any event, it is true that "American Jewry is a community of organizations lacking organization." [27]

The Jewish school, which is essentially religious, along with the synagogue sponsors more intrinsically Jewish activities than any other institution in the community. Since World War I, theological and teachers' seminaries of various types have been founded. Pupil registration went up in all kinds of schools—Sunday, afternoon, and all-day. During the decade 1948-1958, the total enrollment more than doubled from 239,398 to 553,600. [28] But the numbers did not actually indicate knowledge. According to the American Association for Jewish Education, "the conditions prevailing in American Jewish education have often made for Jewish shallowness and know-nothingism. American Jewish education is likened to Mark Twain's characterization of the Platte River [29] as a 'monstrous big river—a mile wide and an inch deep.' " For the country at large, it is doubtful if the situation has changed perceptibly by 1975 in spite of the growth of centralized agencies on the local and national levels, the increasing availability of instructional materials, and the growing sophistication of teaching methodology.

Only in the area of intensive Jewish education has there been a dramatic reversal of the trend to Jewish "know-nothingism." That the Jewish day school has multiplied not only quantitatively, but also qualitatively has been conceded by all, including those who look upon it with skepticism or opposition. Although Orthodox in origin and preponderance, the idea of the day school has been adopted by Conservative Judaism and, most recently, by Reform. According to Torah Umesorah—the National Society for Hebrew Day Schools—the 30 Jewish day elementary schools and 9 high schools in 1944 increased to 289 and 138, respectively, in 1975. The 422 schools are located in 34 states, with 227 of them in communities outside of New York City. The pupil enrollment, which was 10,000 in 1945, was 82,200 in 1975. Of special significance is the increase in the number of high school pupils, from 10,200 in 1964 to 16,300 in 1975.[30] On the higher education (advanced yeshivah) level, well over 20 institutions of Talmudic study have been founded in the United States since 1940, as compared to the 9 in existence by that date. [31] These institutions prepare rabbis, teachers, administrators, and lay scholars for the United States, Latin America, Europe, and Israel. The Association of Advanced Rabbinical and Talmudic Schools, to which most of these institutions belong, is the coordinating body which is engaged in maintaining high standards of instruction, research, and publication through accreditation and other procedures.

The growth and development of the Jewish day schools and of the yeshivahs from the elementary to the postgraduate level also serves, as no other institution can, as insurance for the continued existence of Judaism and of the Jewish community. In recent years, there has taken place an alarming increase of intermarriage in the United States. Newspapers report, more and more frequently, weddings at which a Reform rabbi and a Christian clergyman perform the ceremonies. In many, possibly most, cases, the Jewish partner and the children become lost to the Jewish community. The success achieved by the American Jews in the intellectual, professional, and economic worlds loses its significance in the face of defection by intermarriage and, in the light of heightened Christian missionary activity, by conversion. The loss through indifference, ignorance, assimilation, and loss of identity is too large for comfort or complacency. In the words of a non-Jewish scholar, "The outlook for American Jews in maintaining their identity is . . . probably no more encouraging than the prospects for American Poles and other groups. Once the ancestral language (Hebrew, Yiddish) gives way to English, once the bonds of religious orthodoxy are loosed, the only unifying characteristic is tradition, which never fares very well in industrial, pragmatic society." [32]

The recent increase in summer camps emphasizing Jewish content and values, the Jewish Studies movement, the frequent trips to and study programs in Israel, and other educational developments have encouraged upholders of the Jewish identity even if they fall frequently short of achieving the depth, intensity, and commitment derived from study in Jewish day schools and advanced yeshivahs. The future of the American Jewish community cannot be ensured by business, culture, and philanthropy alone, but it can be perpetuated by the willingness of the individuals to identify themselves with Jewish religious values, traditions, practices, and education that, whatever its width, is a mile deep.

NOTES

1. Jacob R. Marcus, "The Periodization of American Jewish History." Reprint from *Publications of the American Jewish Historical Society* 47 (March 1958): 1.

2. Thomas Thorowgood, *Iewes in America.* (London: Slater, 1650).

3. Thomas Thorowgood, *Jews in America* (London: Brome, 1660).

4. Hamon L'Estrange, *Americans No Iewes* (London: Seile, 1652).

5. Marcus, "Periodization of American Jewish History," pp. 3-8.

6. Peter Stuyvesant to the Amsterdam Chamber of the Dutch West India Company, September 22, 1654, in *A Documentary History of the Jews in the United States, 1654-1875,* 3d ed., ed. Morris U. Schappes (New York: Schocken Books, 1971), pp. 1, 2.

7. Amsterdam Jews to the Directors of the Chartered West India Company, Chamber of the City of Amsterdam, January 1655, in ibid., p. 4.

8. Amsterdam Chamber of the West India Company to Peter Stuyvesant, April 26, 1655, in ibid., p. 5.

9. Minutes, September 5, 1756 and April 25, 1762, in Alexander M. Dushkin, Jewish Education in New York City (New York: Bureau of Jewish Education, 1918), p. 450.

10. "Constitution, Rules & Regulations of the Talmud Torah . . . 1808," in Schappes, *A Documentary History of the Jews in the United States,* p. 115.

11. "An Act Concerning Religion," 1649, in *The Archives of Maryland,* vol. 1, ed. W. H. Browne (Baltimore: Maryland Historical Society, 1883), pp. 244-47.

12. The text of the act is given in Simon W. Rosendale, "An Act Allowing Naturalization of Jews in the Colonies," *Publications of the American Jewish Historical Society,* no. 1, 2d ed. (New York: American Jewish Historical Society, 1905), pp. 94-98.

13. Joseph G. E. Hopkins, ed., *Concise Dictionary of American Biography* (New York: Scribner's, 1964), p. 906.

14. George Washington to the Hebrew Congregation in Newport, Rhode Island, 1790, in Morris A. Gutstein, *The Story of the Jews of Newport* (New York: Bloch, 1936), p. 213.

15. Jasper Chasseaud, Beirut, to John Forsyth, Secretary of State, March 24, 1840, in Schappes, *A Documentary History of Jews in the United States,* p. 203.

16. J. B. Kursheedt and Theodore J. Seixas to Martin Van Buren, August 24, 1840, in Jacob Ezekiel, "Persecution of the Jews in 1840," *Publications of the American Jewish Historical Society* 8, (1900): 142.

17. The Sultan's imperial edict, dated November 6, 1840, and transmitted by John P. Brown to the Secretary of State, is reproduced in Schappes, op. cit., pp. 214-15.

18. D. Wolff & Sons, C. J. Kaskel, and J. W. Kaskel to Abraham Lincoln, December 29, 1862, in Isaac Markens, *Abraham Lincoln and the Jews* (New York: The Author, 1909), p. 11.

19. I. Harold Sharfman, "Rice (Reiss), Abraham Joseph," *Encyclopaedia Judaica*, vol. 14, 1971, p. 156; Shmuel Singer, "From Germany to Baltimore: Rabbi Abraham Joseph Rice—the First Rabbi in America," Jewish Observer 10 (January 1975): 16-19.

20. The full text of the will, with a biographical introduction, is in Max J. Kohler, "Judah Touro, Merchant and Philanthropist," *Publications of the American Jewish Historical Society* 13 (1905): 93-111.

21. These data are from Joseph Jacobs, "Jewish Population in the United States," in *American Jewish Year Book 5675*, September 21, 1914, to September 8, 1915, ed. Herman Bernstein (Philadelphia: Jewish Publication Society of America, 1914), pp. 342, 346.

22. "Extracts from the Constitution of the Machzike Yeshibath Etz Chaim," in Dushkin, *Jewish Education in New York City*, p. 480.

23. S. Benderly, *Aims and Activities of the Bureau of Jewish Education of the Jewish Community (Kehillah) of New York City* (New York: The Bureau, 1912).

24. Morris Fine and Milton Himmelfarb, eds., *American Jewish Year Book, 1976*, vol. 76 (New York: American Jewish Committee and Philadelphia: Jewish Publication Society of America, 1976), pp. 230-32.

25. Abraham J. Karp, "American Jewry: 1954-1971," in Rufus Learsi, *The Jews in America: A History* (New York: KTAV, 1972), p. 365.

26. Ibid., 363.

27. Ibid., p. 366.

28. Alexander M. Dushkin and Uriah Z. Engelman, *Jewish Education in the United States: Report of the Commission for the Study of Jewish Education in the United States* (New York: American Association for Jewish Education, 1959), p. 45.

29. Ibid., pp. 3-4.

30. Samuel C. Feuerstein, *Torah Umesorah President's Report: 1975/5736* (New York: National Society for Hebrew Day Schools, [1975], pp. 3-5.

31. Charles S. Liebman, *Aspects of the Religious Behavior of American Jews* (New York: KTAV, 1974), pp. 183-87.

32. Thomas F. Magner, "The Rise and Fall of the Ethnics," *Journal of General Education* 25 (January 1974): 257.

I. GENERAL HISTORIES

I. GENERAL HISTORIES

1. ALEXANDER, HARTLEY B. *The Hebrew Contribution to the Americanism of the Future.* New York: Menorah Press, 1923.

   An appreciative address by a Christian on the historical role of Jews in civilization, with a conclusion that "in the future the Jews of America shall not be lost in finding themselves fully American" (p. 39).

2. BARON, SALO W. *Steeled by Adversity: Essays and Addresses on American Jewish Life.* Philadelphia: Jewish Publication Society of America, 1971.

   Documented essays by an outstanding scholar on various aspects of American Jewish history including education, scholarship, culture, immigration, and communal life, from 1654 to the twentieth century.

3. BUTWIN, FRANCES. *The Jews of America: History and Sources.* New York: Behrman House, 1973.

   A concise, illustrated survey of American Jewish history from the colonial era to the present time, plus supporting documentary extracts edited by Arthur C. Blecher. Useful as a junior high school textbook.

4. COHEN, GEORGE. *The Jews in the Making of America.* Boston: Stratford, 1924.

   Popular essays on the role of the Jew in American history, wars, economy, and culture.

5. *Critical Studies in American Jewish History: Selected Articles from American Jewish Archives.* 3 vols. Cincinnati, Ohio: American Jewish Archives and New York: Ktav Publishing House, 1971.

   Reprint of scholarly papers on religion, culture, society, and various other topics in the history of American Jewry.

6. DAVIS, MOSHE. *Beit Yisrael be-Amerikah: Mehkarim u-mekorot.* Jerusalem: Magnes Press, Hebrew University of Jerusalem, 1970.

   Studies in Hebrew and documents in Hebrew and English on various subjects dealing with American Jewish history, life, and foreign relations. Illustrations.

7. DAVIS, MOSHE. *Darkhei ha-Yahudut b'Amerikah.* Tel Aviv: Massadah Publishing House, 1953.

   A documented, illustrated account in Hebrew of the religious, communal, and educational history of the American Jews from the seventeenth to the twentieth century. Selected Hebrew bibliography. Based on the author's chapter in Louis Finkelstein, ed., *The Jews: Their History, Culture and Religion,* 2d edition (New York: Harper, 1955).

8. DAVIS, MOSHE, and ISIDORE S. MEYER, eds. *The Writing of American Jewish History.* New York: American Jewish Historical Society, 1957.

Reprint of the March, 1957, issue of the *Publications of the American Jewish Historical Society* (vol. 46) containing the proceedings of a conference of Jewish and non-Jewish historians in commemoration of the 300th anniversary of Jewish settlement in colonial America (1654). This collection of scholarly essays, focused on the writing of local and regional American Jewish history, economic and labor history, immigration and adjustment, and biography, is a helpful resource to research workers and students interested in the history of the Jews in the United States.

9. DAVIS-DUBOIS, RACHEL, and EMMA SCHWEPPE, eds. *The Jews in American Life.* New York: Nelson, 1935.

A detailed outline and syllabus, for the high-school student, of the contributions of the Jews to American culture, economy, and philanthropy. Chronologies, annotated chapter bibliographies, Hebrew-English glossary, and appended bibliography.

10. FISHMAN, JOSHUA A., comp. *Studies in Modern Jewish Social History.* New York: Ktav Publishing House, 1972.

Of the twenty-one scholarly papers reprinted from several issues of the *Yivo Annual of Jewish Social Science,* eight deal with historical aspects of American Jewish immigration, life, economy, identification, overseas relief, and military service.

11. FONER, PHILIP S. *The Jews in American History, 1654-1865.* New York: International Publishers, 1945.

A concise survey with quotations from sources. Documents and bibliography.

12. FREDMAN, J. GEORGE, and LOUIS A. FALK. *Jews in American Wars.* New York: Jewish War Veterans of the U.S., 1943.

   A brief overview of Jewish participation in the wars of the United States from the Revolution to World War II. Documents in the text.

13. FRIEDMAN, LEE M. *Jewish Pioneers and Patriots.* New York: Macmillan, 1943.

   Biographical and other essays, based on primary sources, concerning the experience and political, social, economic, cultural, and religious development of Jews in America from colonial times to the early twentieth century. Appendix of notes, documents, and supplementary bibliographical references. Illustrations and facsimiles.

14. FRIEDMAN, LEE M. *Pilgrims in a New Land.* New York: Farrar, Straus, 1948.

   A collection of twenty-seven interesting, scholarly essays on the social, religious, economic, and cultural aspects of American Jewish history. Particularly noteworthy are the chapters on the influence of Yiddish on American English and on American Jewish family names. Illustrations, facsimiles, and bibliographies.

15. GAY, RUTH. *Jews in America: A Short History.* New York: Basic Books, 1965.

   A popular, concise account from the seventeenth century to the 1960s, with special reference to recent and contemporary contributions, developments, and problems. Selected references.

16. GOLDEN, HARRY L., and MARTIN RYWELL. *Jews in American History: Their Contribution to the United States of America.* Charlotte, N.C.: Henry Lewis Martin Co., 1950.

A popular survey of American Jewish history from colonial times to World War II, with special attention to noted individuals and to their contributions to culture, learning, medicine, science, philanthropy, and sports. Selected references.

17. HANDLIN, OSCAR. *Adventure in Freedom: Three Hundred Years of Jewish Life in America.* New York: McGraw-Hill, 1954.

A concise, popular presentation of the social and communal development of American Jewry. Bibliographical essay, glossary, and illustrations.

18. HANDLIN, OSCAR. *American Jews: Their Story.* New York: Anti-Defamation League of B'nai B'rith, [1959].

A concise, illustrated historical overview. Glossary and selected, annotated references.

19. HARTSTEIN, JACOB I., ed. *The Jews in American History: A Resource Book for Teachers of Social Studies and American History.* New York: Anti-Defamation League of B'nai B'rith, [1955].

A concise overview of the Jewish past and community in the United States, specimen lesson outlines, outlines of the Jewish religion and history, and lists of published and audiovisual resource materials. Suggestive, but outdated in some respects.

20. HUHNER, LEON. *Essays and Addresses*. New York: Gertz, 1959.

    Four brief and undocumented, but informative statements on the historical Jewish role in American life, society, culture, and education.

21. KARP, ABRAHAM J., ed. *The Jewish Experience in America: Selected Studies from the Publications of the American Jewish Historical Society*. 4 vols. Waltham, Mass.: American Jewish Historical Society, and New York: Ktav Publishing House, 1969.

    Reprint of scholarly articles dealing with American Jewish social, economic, political, educational, and religious life primarily from the mid-seventeenth to the end of the nineteenth century. Photographs, facsimiles and full texts of documents, and updated bibliographies. A convenient and valuable reference work.

22. KOHN, EUGENE, ed. *American Jewry: The Tercentenary and After*. New York: Reconstructionist Press, 1955.

    Essays by specialists on the significance of three centuries of American Jewish experience in relation to communal life, culture, economy, Zionism, education, and religion.

23. LEARSI, RUFUS. *The Jews in America: A History*. New York: Ktav Publishing House, 1972.

    The 1954 edition (Cleveland: World Publishing) presented an overview of Jewish life in the United States from the colonial period to the mid-twentieth century. This reprinted edition includes a partially documented epilogue covering 1954-1971. Illustrations, maps, and a one-half-page bibliography.

24. LEBESON, ANITA L. *Pilgrim People.* New York: Harper, 1950.

An interesting, well-documented general history of American Jewry since colonial times. Illustrations, facsimiles of documents, and extensive bibliography.

25. LEVINGER, ELMA E. *Jewish Adventures in America: The Story of 300 Years of Jewish Life in the United States.* New York: Bloch Publishing Co., 1954.

An illustrated introduction to American Jewish history for junior high school students.

26. LEVINGER, LEE J. *A History of the Jews in the United States.* Cincinnati, Ohio: Union of American Hebrew Congregations, 1949.

Fourth revised edition of an illustrated high school textbook covering the colonial period to the mid-twentieth century, with particular reference to Jewish contributions to America. Chapter bibliographies.

27. MARCUS, JACOB R. *Studies in American Jewish History.* Cincinnati, Ohio: Hebrew Union College Press, 1969.

Reprint of addresses and essays on various topics in the history of Jews in the United States. Documents.

28. MARCUS, JACOB R., ed. *Essays in American Jewish History.* Cincinnati, Ohio: American Jewish Archives, 1958.

Scholarly papers on the social, educational, economic, religious, and cultural history of American Jewry. Bibliography of the writings of Dr. Marcus.

29. MARKENS, ISAAC. *The Hebrews in America: A Series of Historical and Biographical Sketches.* New York: The author, 1888.

Aspects of American Jewish history from the colonial period showing "the degree of prominence attained by the Hebrews in the United States" (p. v) in the armed services, commerce, public office, religion, and society.

30. MASSERMAN, PAUL, and MAX BAKER. *The Jews Come to America.* New York: Bloch Publishing Co., 1932.

A popular introduction to American Jewish history from the discovery by Columbus until after World War I, with special reference to Jewish contributions to literature, fine arts, entertainment, journalism, and other fields. Occasional documentation. No bibliography.

31. McCALL, SAMUEL W. *Patriotism of the American Jew.* New York: Plymouth Press, 1924.

An evaluation by the Governor of Massachusetts of the beneficial role of Jews in American history and life in their effort to combat the wave of anti-Semitism in the post-World War I years. Supporting foreword by President Charles William Eliot of Harvard University. Documents in the appendix.

32. MEISEL, A. *Geshikhte fun Yidn in di Fareinikte Shtatn*

fun Amerike. New York: Natsionaler Ump. Arbeter
Shul Organizatsie, 1929.

An illustrated, concise survey of American Jewish history, with particular emphasis on the economic activities and trade-union developments.

33. PETERS, MADISON C. *Justice to the Jew: The Story of
What He Has Done for the World.* 2d ed. New York:
McClure Co., 1908.

A Christian's appreciation of the historic and contemporary contributions of the Jew to the world and to
the United States in particular. The author called for
justice to Jews: "As America has given the Jew a
haven, let her do more, let her take him to her breast
and treat him as she does her other children, and she
will find that he will be just as dutiful, even more so"
(p. 243).

34. RAISIN, MORDECHAI ZEV. *Toldot ha-Yehudim
b'Amerikah.* Warsaw: Tushiah, 1902.

A Hebrew history of American Jewry from the colonial period to the end of the nineteenth century. Bibliographical footnotes.

35. RUDERMAN, JEROME L. *Jews in American History: A
Teacher's Guide.* New York: Anti-Defamation League
of B'nai B'rith, 1974.

An overview of American Jewish history from the
colonial period to the present, with pedagogical and
bibliographical aids for the high school teacher.

36. ST. JOHN, ROBERT. *Jews, Justice and Judaism: A Nar-*

rative of the Role Played by the Bible People in Shaping American History. Garden City, N.Y.: Doubleday, 1969.

A popular, balanced, sympathetic presentation of American Jewish history by a non-Jew. Selected references.

37. SCHAPPES, MORRIS U. *The Jews in the United States: A Pictorial History, 1654 to the Present.* New York: Citadel Press, 1958.

A valuable collection of drawings, facsimiles, and photographs with a supporting narrative, reference notes, and two indexes.

38. SEGAL, CHARLES M. *Fascinating Facts about American Jewish History.* New York: Twayne Publishers, 1955.

A compendium of factual data presented through questions and answers.

39. SLOAN, IRVING J., ed. *The Jews in America, 1621-1970: A Chronology & Fact Book.* Dobbs Ferry, N.Y.: Oceana Publications, 1971.

A listing of chronological data, followed by twenty-two historical documents, an appendix of statistics, selected book and audiovisual references, names of Jewish newspapers and periodicals, and organizational data.

40. SUHL, YURI. *An Album of the Jews in America.* New York: Franklin Watts, 1972.

Illustrations and texts related to the history of American Jewish life.

41. "Tercentenary Issue," *Jewish Quarterly Review* 45 (April 1955): 287-621. Philadelphia: Dropsie College, 1955.

Seventeen articles by various scholars on the history of the Jewish religion, culture, literature, education, scholarship, and immigration to the United States. Several articles are bibliographical surveys.

42. *The Two Hundred and Fiftieth Anniversary of the Settlement of the Jews in the United States.* New York: New York Cooperative Society, 1906.

Addresses and letters by Jewish and non-Jewish scholars, as well as newspaper editorials, concerning the value of the Jewish role in American history.

43. WIERNIK, PETER. *History of the Jews in America: From the Period of the Discovery of the New World to the Present Time.* New York: Hermon Press, 1972.

The third edition of an illustrated historical overview originally published in 1912 and revised in 1931. Special attention is given to Jewish religious, educational, and cultural activities. The period, 1932-1972, is covered by Irving J. Sloan in eighteen pages.

44. WISE, JAMES W., and LEE J. LEVINGER. *Mr. Smith Meet Mr. Cohen.* New York: Reynal and Hitchcock, 1940.

The past and current contributions of Jews to American life and culture. Critical bibliography.

45. WOLF, SIMON. *The American Jew as Patriot, Soldier and Citizen.* New York: Levytype, 1895.

A compendium of names, biographical sketches, and documents on Jewish contributors to America.

II. REGIONAL AND LOCAL HISTORY

II. REGIONAL AND LOCAL HISTORY

46. ABELOW, SAMUEL P. *History of Brooklyn Jewry.*
    Brooklyn, N.Y.: Scheba Publishing Co., 1937.

    An undocumented account of Jewish life and
    activities since the late nineteenth century. Bibli-
    ography and illustrations.

47. ADLER, SELIG, and THOMAS E. CONNOLLY. *From
    Ararat to Suburbia: The History of the Jewish Com-
    munity of Buffalo.* Philadelphia: Jewish Publication
    Society of America, 1960.

    A thoroughly documented study of the genesis and
    development of Jewish communal organization, main-
    ly since the mid-nineteenth century. Glossary and
    bibliography of manuscript and printed materials.

48. ALTFELD, E. MILTON. *The Jew's Struggle for Reli-
    gious and Civil Liberty in Maryland.* Baltimore:
    Curlander, 1924.

    A survey of the efforts to remove Jewish disabilities
    through legislation from the late eighteenth century
    through the passage of Maryland's "Jew Bill" of
    1826, with particular reference to the leadership of
    Thomas Kennedy, a non-Jewish legislator. The new

law mandated "a declaration of . . . belief in a future state of rewards and punishments" (p. 204) by office-holders to replace the oath "upon the true faith of a Christian" and similar statements. No footnotes. Documents in the text.

49. BAND, BENJAMIN. *Portland Jewry: Its Growth and Development.* Portland, Maine: Jewish Historical Society, 1955.

An historical account of the Jewish settlement in 1860, and life, communal organization, and activities in the largest city in Maine.

50. BRECK, ALLEN D. *A Centennial History of the Jews of Colorado, 1859-1959.* Denver, Colo.: University of Denver, 1960.

A detailed account of the Jewish settlement of the Colorado area and the development of the Jewish community.

51. BREGSTONE, PHILIP P. *Chicago and Its Jews: A Cultural History.* [Chicago] : Privately published, 1933.

A detailed, undocumented, somewhat subjective account of philanthrophy, reform, immigrants, literature, theater, and other aspects of Chicago Jewish life in the nineteenth and twentieth centuries.

52. BROCHES, S. *Jews in New England: Part I, Historical Study of the Jews in Massachusetts (1650-1750); Part II, Jewish Merchants in Colonial Rhode Island.* New York: Bloch Publishing Co., 1942.

A group of primary source materials preceded by historical sketches. Bibliography.

53. DINNERSTEIN, LEONARD, and MARY D. PALSSON, eds. *Jews in the South.* Baton Rouge: Louisiana State University Press, 1973.

Scholarly essays by Jewish and non-Jewish historians on Jewish life, society, and interreligious and interracial relations from the early eighteenth century to the 1960s. Informative introduction and bibliographical essay.

54. EHRENFRIED, ALBERT. *A Chronicle of Boston Jewry: From the Colonial Settlement to 1900.* n.p., 1963.

A detailed, popular treatment of the development of the various facets of Jewish life, with special reference to religion, philanthropy, culture, and charity. Some documentation.

55. ELOVITZ, MARK H. *A Century of Jewish Life in Dixie: The Birmingham Experience.* University: University of Alabama Press, 1974.

A documented account of the origins and development of the Jewish community of Birmingham, Alabama, from 1871 through the 1960s. The stress is on religious, economic, social, philanthropic, Zionist, and defense activities. Lists of officials and families, glossary, and bibliography.

56. ELZAS, BARNETT A. *The Jews of South Carolina from the Earliest Times to the Present Day.* Philadelphia: J. B. Lippincott Company, 1905.

A detailed account of Jewish religious, social, and communal life from the late seventeenth to the early twentieth century. Documents, lists of names, and bibliography of manuscript sources and printed works.

57. [ELZAS, BARNETT A.] *The Jews of South Carolina.* Charleston, S.C.: Daggett Printing Co., [1903].

A collection of brief essays and documents on Jewish settlement and life in South Carolina during the colonial and revolutionary periods.

58. EZEKIEL, HERBERT T., and GASTON LICHTEN-STEIN. *The History of the Jews of Richmond from 1769 to 1917.* Richmond, Va.: The authors, 1917.

A carefully documented historical work emphasizing biographies, synagogues, communal activities, and military participation by Richmond Jews in the Civil War. Epitaphs and documents.

59. EZEKIEL, HERBERT T., and GASTON LICHTEN-STEIN. *World War Section of the History of the Jews of Richmond.* Richmond, Va.: The authors, 1920.

A supplementary work recording the service of Jews residing or enlisting in Richmond in the United States military forces. Also includes a soldier's diary and details on service on the home front.

60. FEIBELMAN, JULIAN B. "A Social and Economic Study of the New Orleans Jewish Community." Ph.D. dissertation, University of Pennsylvania, 1941.

A study of a Southern Jewish community of the 1930s in terms of demography, family, education, economic activities, historical development, communal organization, and other aspects. The conclusion notes that "the New Orleans Jewish community has taken on the color of its surroundings with an avidity that is unknown in other sections of the country" and that there is no "distinct Jewish culture" in this city (p. 134). The author believes the process of assimilation "can only weaken the community" and "gradually disintegrated the institutions founded by more loyal forbears" (p. 135). Brief bibliography.

61. FEIN, ISAAC M. *The Making of an American Jewish Community: The History of Baltimore Jewry from 1773 to 1920.* Philadelphia: Jewish Publication Society of America, 1971.

A well-documented study of the social, religious, educational, and economic life of Baltimore's Jews until the formation, in 1920, of the Associated Jewish Charities—the first step in the organization of a united community. Glossary and comprehensive bibliography.

62. FRANK, FEDORA S. *Five Families and Eight Young Men (Nashville and Her Jewry, 1850-1861).* Nashville: Tennessee Book Co., 1962.

A detailed, documented account of the establishment and early development of the Jewish community of Nashville. Sizable bibliography.

63. FREEMAN, MOSES. *Fuftsig yor geshikhte fun Yiddishen leben in Philadelphia: 1879-1934.* 2 vols. Philadelphia: Mid-City Press and Farlag "Kultur," 1929-1934.

A detailed survey of a half-century of society, culture, religion, education, and other aspects of Jewish life in Philadelphia. Also included are the author's autobiography and reprints of his essays, and descriptions of Jewish organizations, schools, theatre, and medical institutions in the city.

64. FRIEDMAN, LEE M. *Rabbi Haim Isaac Carigal: His Newport Sermon and His Yale Portrait.* Boston: The author, 1940.

A scholarly analysis of aspects of the visit of Rabbi Carigal to Philadelphia, New York, and Newport in 1773. Texts of letters from and to Carigal.

65. GINSBERG, LOUIS. *Chapters on the Jews of Virginia, 1658-1900.* Petersburg, Va.: n.p., 1969.

Brief, documented, illustrated essays on Virginian Jewish life and society from the seventeenth to the end of the nineteenth century.

66. GINSBERG, LOUIS. *History of the Jews of Petersburg, 1789-1950.* Petersburg, Va.: n.p., 1954.

A documented account of the development of the Jewish community in a small Southern town. Lists of names, bibliography, and photographs.

67. GLANZ, RUDOLF. *The Jews in American Alaska (1867-1880).* [New York] The author, 1953.

A well-documented account of Jewish activities in the fur industry and other economic activities in Alaska.

68. GLANZ, RUDOLF. *The Jews of California: From the Discovery of Gold until 1880.* New York: The author, 1960.

A thoroughly documented account of the founding of the Jewish community from the 1840s through the

Gold Rush era. Considerable detail with many source quotations on economic, cultural, communal, social, political, and other Jewish activities.

69. GLUSHAKOW, A. D., ed. *A Pictorial History of Maryland Jewry*. Baltimore, Md., 1955.

Many photographs and illustrations depicting the history of the Jewish communities of Maryland, with special attention to individuals.

70. GOLDEN, HARRY. *The Greatest Jewish City in the World*. Garden City, N.Y.: Doubleday, 1972.

An anecdotal, informal history of the Jewish experience in New York City. Illustrations in black-and-white and color. Appended list of Jewish organizations includes the Jewish Reconstructionist Foundation among the Orthodox (p. 233).

71. GOREN, ARTHUR A. *New York Jews and the Quest for Community: The Kehillah Experiment, 1908-1922*. New York: Columbia University Press, 1970.

A carefully documented study, relying upon manuscript and published primary source materials, dealing with the history of Jewish communal organizations, educational activities, labor unions, and resistance to crime in the early decades of the twentieth century. The bibliography contains English, Hebrew, and Yiddish titles.

72. GRINSTEIN, HYMAN B. *The Rise of the Jewish Community of New York, 1654-1860*. Philadelphia: Jewish Publication Society of America, 1947.

A unique, scholarly study that traces, in detail, the

development of synagogue organization and religious practice, philanthropy and mutual aid, social and cultural life, education, and other themes in the early history of the Jews in New York City. The notes and the documentary appendix make use of English, Hebrew, and German archival and printed sources.

73. GUTSTEIN, MORRIS A. *A Priceless Heritage: The Epic Growth of Nineteenth Century Chicago Jewry.* New York: Bloch Publishing Co., 1953.

A competently documented analysis of the development of the Chicago Jewish community with emphasis on education and society. Documentary appendix, glossary, and bibliography.

74. GUTSTEIN, MORRIS A. *The Story of the Jews of Newport: Two and Half Centuries of Judaism, 1658-1908.* New York: Bloch Publishing Co., 1936.

A well-documented account of Jewish religious and social life from colonial times to the early twentieth century. Few details about education. The appendix contains documents, notes, a glossary, and a brief bibliography. Illustrations and facsimiles.

75. HUHNER, LEON. *Jews in America after the American Revolution.* New York: Gertz Bros., 1959.

Three documented essays, originally published in the *Publications of the American Jewish Historical Society,* on Jewish history in the South prior to the Civil War.

76. KATZ, IRVING I. *The Jewish Soldier from Michigan in the Civil War.* Detroit: Wayne State University Press, 1962.

An illustrated compendium of biographical and other information, drawn mainly from secondary works. Bibliography of manuscript and printed materials.

77. KOHN, S. JOSHUA. *The Jewish Community of Utica, New York, 1847-1948.* New York: American Jewish Historical Society, 1959.

A scholarly history of a Jewish community analyzing religious, social, communal, economic, educational, and other developments.

78. KORN, BERTRAM W. *Jews and Negro Slavery in the Old South, 1789-1865.* Elkins Park, Pa.: Reform Congregation Keneseth Israel, 1961.

A monographic study of Jews as slave owners and slave traders, together with an analysis of Jewish opinion about slavery. Facsimiles of documents and illustrations.

79. KORN, BERTRAM W. *The Early Jews of New Orleans.* Waltham, Mass.: American Jewish Historical Society, 1969.

An illustrated, scholarly study of Jewish life, work, and contributions from the French colonial period until about 1850. The notes occupy a substantial portion of the volume.

80. KORN, BERTRAM W. *The Jews of Mobile, Alabama, 1763-1841.* Cincinnati, Ohio: Hebrew Union College Press, 1970.

A documented, concise essay emphasizing the social and religious experience of Southern antebellum Jewry. Illustrations and facsimiles.

81. LANDESMAN, ALTER F. *Brownsville: The Birth, Development and Passing of a Jewish Community in New York.* New York: Bloch Publishing Co., 1969.

An interesting, comprehensive, well-documented account of the development and decline of two neighborhoods in Brooklyn—Brownsville and East New York—with special stress on social, communal, labor, cultural, religious, and educational activities and contributions. Bibliography of published and unpublished materials.

82. MARANS, HILLEL. *Jews in Greater Washington: A Panoramic History of Washington Jewry for the Years 1795-1960.* Washington: The author, 1961.

An historical survey of Jewish life, economy, religion, education, philanthropy, and communal life in Washington, D.C. and its suburbs.

83. MEITES, HYMAN L. *History of the Jews of Chicago.* Chicago: Jewish Historical Society of Illinois, 1924.

A considerably detailed, comprehensive history of the Jewish settlement, communal organization, social and economic activity, education, and culture in Chicago.

84. MORAIS, HENRY S. *The Jews of Philadelphia: Their History from the Earliest Settlements to the Present Time.* Philadelphia: Levytype Co., 1894.

A detailed account, including biographical and other data. Much stress on cultural and military activities.

85. PLAUT, W. GUNTHER. *The Jews in Minnesota: The First Seventy-Five Years.* New York: American Jewish Historical Society, 1959.

A scholarly account of the origins and development of Jewish life, religion, education, and intergroup relations. Glossary and bibliography.

86. REZNIKOFF, CHARLES, and URIAH Z. ENGELMAN. *The Jews of Charleston: A History of an American Jewish Community*. Philadelphia: Jewish Publication Society of America, 1950.

A scholarly study of Jewish life, with special emphasis on social and religious development, from the eighteenth to the twentieth century. Documentary appendix and illustrations.

87. RISCHIN, MOSES. *The Promised City: New York's Jews, 1870-1914*. Cambridge, Mass.: Harvard University Press, 1962.

A thoroughly documented monograph on the development of Jewish community, economy, and social relations in the metropolis. Illustrations.

88. ROSENBACH, HYMAN P. *The Jews in Philadelphia Prior to 1800*. Philadelphia: Edward Stern, 1888.

An historical sketch which emphasizes religious life from the 1740s to the end of the century.

89. ROSENBERG, STUART E. *The Jewish Community in Rochester, 1843-1925*. New York: Columbia University Press, 1954.

A published Ph.D. dissertation covering the early settlement, the Eastern European migration, and the Rochester Jews' participation in the community, society, religion, culture, and other activities. Full documentation, glossary, and bibliography.

90. ROSENTHAL, FRANK. *The Jews of Des Moines: The First Century.* Des Moines, Iowa: Jewish Welfare Federation, 1957.

An informative history of the Jewish community from the earliest settlement in 1845, with special stress on religious, economic, social, and cultural activities.

91. SCHINDLER, SOLOMON. *Israelites in Boston.* [Boston: Berwick & Smith, 1890].

An illustrated sketch of the "history of the development of Judaism in Boston" by a Reform rabbi.

92. SHINDELING, ABRAHAM I. *History of the Los Alamos (New Mexico) Jewish Center (1944 to 1957).* Albuquerque, N.M.: The author, 1968.

An account of the genesis and growth of a unique Jewish community by atomic and nuclear research scientists.

93. SHINDELING, ABRAHAM I. *West Virginia Jewry: Origins and History—1850-1938.* 3 vols. Philadelphia: [Press of M. Jacob], 1961.

A detailed, fully indexed presentation of the history of the various Jewish communities in West Virginia.

94. SHPALL, LEO. *The Jews in Louisiana.* New Orleans, La.: Steeg Printing & Publishing Co., 1936.

An overview of Jewish personalities and institutions in the development of Louisiana.

95. SWICHKOW, LOUIS J., and LLOYD P. GARTNER. *The History of the Jews of Milwaukee*. Philadelphia: Jewish Publication Society of America, 1963.

A well-balanced, thoroughly documented analysis of Jewish communal organization; religious and philanthropic activities; Jewish educational experience, society, and economic status; and other phases of the life of Milwaukee's Jewry from the mid-nineteenth to the mid-twentieth century. Illustrations, facsimiles, bibliography, documentary appendix, statistics, and lists of personalities.

96. TRACHTENBERG, JOSHUA. *Consider the Years: The Story of the Jewish Community of Easton, 1752-1942*. Easton, Pa.: Temple Brith Sholom, 1944.

An illustrated, appropriately documented report on the historical development of a "small and unimportant community" (p. xiii) which, however, is interesting and exemplary for larger local communities. Illustrations, documents, lists of rabbis and laymen, and a note on primary sources in Yiddish, German, and English.

97. VORSPAN, MAX, and LLOYD P. GARTNER. *History of the Jews of Los Angeles*. San Marino, Calif.: Huntington Library, 1970.

An interesting, reliably documented account of the social, religious, economic, educational, and communal development of Los Angeles Jewry from 1850 to the late 1960s. Documentation from English and Yiddish sources. Appendix of population data and of officers of major institutions of the Jewish community. Illustrations.

98. WATTERS, LEON L. *The Pioneer Jews of Utah.* New York: American Jewish Historical Society, 1952.

A monograph, drawing upon manuscript and other primary sources, recounting the earliest Jewish settlement and religious, social, commercial, and other activities in Utah from 1854 to 1884. "Of great historical interest is the relationship of the Jews to the Mormons who were, for the most part, very sympathetic to the developing Jewish community in Utah" (p. 102). Biographical appendix, illustrations, facsimiles, and bibliography.

99. WESSEL, HENRY N. *History of the Jewish Hospital Association of Philadelphia.* Philadelphia: n.p., 1915.

An account of the Philadelphia Jewish contribution to the health care of Jews and non-Jews. Appendix of names and photographs.

100. WIEDER, ARNOLD A. *The Early Jewish Community of Boston's North End.* Waltham, Mass.: Brandeis University, 1962.

A "sociologically oriented" study of East European Jewish immigrants in a Boston neighborhood, 1870-1900. The author concludes that the fifty families who settled in the North End in 1870 "left their mark on the history of Boston Jewry" (p. 70). The appendix contains a Hebrew and Yiddish glossary, the facsimile of a Hebrew document with an English translation, and two newspaper articles on local Jewish history.

101. WOLF, EDWIN, II, and MAXWELL WHITEMAN. *The History of the Jews of Philadelphia from Colonial*

Times to the Age of Jackson. Philadelphia: Jewish Publication Society of America, 1957.

A detailed, extensively documented study dealing with communal organization and functions, patriotism, religious life, economy, sociopolitical activities, philanthropy, culture, and science. Very little on religious education. Illustrations and comprehensive index.

102. WOLFE, JACK. *A Century with Iowa Jewry: As Complete a History as Could Be Obtained of Iowa Jewry from 1833 to 1940.* Des Moines: Iowa Printing & Supply Co., 1941.

An account of the historical development, chiefly of the Des Moines Jewish community, but including information on others as well.

III. SPECIALIZED HISTORICAL WORKS

III. SPECIALIZED HISTORICAL WORKS

103. ADLER, CYRUS, and AARON M. MARGALITH. *With Firmness in the Right: American Diplomatic Action Affecting Jews, 1840-1945.* New York: American Jewish Committee, 1946.

An analysis of actions by the United States government with regard to the interests of American Jews abroad and humanitarian treatment of Jews in foreign countries. The role of American Jewish organizations is mentioned. Documents in the text and appendix. An important work.

104. BAUER, YEHUDA. *My Brother's Keeper: A History of the American Jewish Joint Distribution Committee, 1929-1939.* Philadelphia: Jewish Publication Society of America, 1974.

A thoroughly documented, detailed analysis of a decade of philanthropic activity in Eastern Europe and especially in connection with the Jewish emigration from Nazi Germany. Brief bibliography.

105. CHAIKIN, J. *Yiddishe bleter in Amerike.* New York: The author, 1946.

An account of the Yiddish press in the United States

and Canada from the late nineteenth to the mid-twentieth century.

106. COHEN, NAOMI W. *Not Free to Desist: The American Jewish Committee, 1906-1966.* Philadelphia: Jewish Publication Society of America, 1972.

A detailed, appropriately documented historical analysis of "the oldest Jewish defense organization" in America, including activities in education and intergroup and international relations.

107. DALY, CHARLES P. *The Settlement of the Jews in North America.* New York: Philip Cowen, 1893.

Essays on Jewish settlements in six colonies and biographical sketches of Mordecai M. Noah and other New York Jews. Edited by Max J. Kohler, who also supplied a preface, introduction, notes, and a documentary appendix.

108. DAVIDSON, GABRIEL. *Our Jewish Farmers: The Story of the Jewish Agricultural Society.* New York: L. B. Fischer, 1943.

A popular survey of the founding of the Jewish Agricultural and Industrial Aid Society in 1900 and its development, activities, and impact during the following four decades written by the managing director of the Society. A useful account of the American Jew as farmer.

109. FEINSTEIN, MARNIN. *American Zionism, 1884-1904.* New York: Herzl Press, 1965.

A documented account of the early development of Zionist thought and organizational activity in the

United States. The author concludes that, by 1904, "Zionism was undeniably a weak and relatively small movement within American Jewry," but the movement, however modest, "became a part of the American scene" (p. 286).

110. FELDMAN, ABRAHAM J. *The American Jew: A Study of Backgrounds.* New York: Bloch Publishing Co., 1937.

An outline of the European backgrounds of the Spanish-Portuguese, German, and Russian-Polish Jews of America. The author concludes that "the 'melting pot' theory which in general American life failed, within American *Jewry* has worked and still works successfully" (p. 49). The groups have blended into "the American Jew." Chronological tables and extensive bibliography.

111. FREUND, MIRIAM K. *Jewish Merchants in Colonial America: Their Achievements and Their Contributions to the Development of America.* New York: Behrman House, 1939.

A study of the commercial activities of the Jews throughout the English colonies. Bibliography.

112. FRIEDMAN, LEE M. *Early American Jews.* Cambridge, Mass.: Harvard University Press, 1934.

Eight of the eleven essays deal with Jewish life and personalities in colonial Massachusetts and New York. Of particular interest is the essay on Judah Monis, first Hebrew instructor at Harvard College. Thorough documentation from primary sources. Original documents in the text and in the appendix. Bibliography and illustrations.

113. GLADSTONE, J., S. NIGER, and H. ROGOFF, eds.
*Finf un zibetsik yor Yiddishe presse in Amerike,
1870-1945.* New York: I. L. Peretz Shreiber Farein
(Yiddish Writers Union), 1945.

A broad overview of seventy-five years of Yiddish
newspapers in the United States, followed by
sketches of six daily newspapers and essays on various
other related aspects of Yiddish journalism and literature. Illustrations, facsimiles, and a listing of Yiddish
newspapers and magazines.

114. GOODMAN, ABRAM V. *American Overture: Jewish
Rights in Colonial Times.* Philadelphia: Jewish Publication Society of America, 1947.

An appropriately documented analysis of "the interaction of Jewish forces with the early American scene
as manifested in the expanding rights of the Jewish
minority" (p. vii). Bibliography of primary sources
and secondary works.

115. GRUSD, EDWARD E. *B'nai B'rith: The Story of a
Covenant.* New York: Appleton-Century-Crofts,
1966.

A popular history since 1843 of "America's largest,
oldest, and most representative national Jewish
organization . . . [and] the nation's oldest native-born
service organization" (p. xvii).

116. GUMPERTZ, SYDNEY G. *The Jewish Legion of Valor:
The Story of Jewish Heroes in the Wars of the Republic.* New York: The author, 1941. Supplement for
1941-1945.

A popular history of Jewish participation in Amer-

ican armed services, from the Revolutionary War
through World War II. Biographical sketches, documents, and photographs. The author, an infantry
captain, won a Congressional Medal of Honor.

117. HECKELMAN, A. JOSEPH. *American Volunteers and
Israel's War of Independence.* New York: Ktav Publishing House, 1974.

A well-documented study of the role of Americans
who were paid and those who volunteered, because of
"ideology, conscience, and a zest for adventure" (p.
xiv) to help the Palestinian Jews in the war of 1948
to fight for the establishment of a Jewish state.

118. HUHNER, LEON. *Jews in America in Colonial and
Revolutionary Times.* New York: Gertz Bros., 1959.

Thirteen documented papers, originally published in
the *Publications of the American Jewish Historical
Society,* on Jewish participation in government, education, professions, revolutionary activities, and
other aspects of early American history.

119. HURWITZ, MAXMILIAN. *The Workmen's Circle: Its
History, Ideals, Organization and Institutions.* New
York: Workmen's Circle, 1936.

An account of the Arbeiter Ring, or Workingmen's
Circle, a Yiddish-speaking organization founded in
1892 for "the furtherance of education among the
members" and various social purposes. Photographs.

120. KAYSERLING, M. *Christopher Columbus and the Participation of the Jews in the Spanish and Portuguese
Discoveries.* New York: George Dobsevage, 1928.

An account of the Jewish associates of Columbus in the discovery of the New World. Based on archival sources and other materials in several languages. Documentary appendix in Latin and Spanish.

121. KOHLER, MAX J. *The United States and German Jewish Persecutions—Precedents for Popular and Governmental Action.* New York: Jewish Academy of Arts and Sciences, 1933.

An historical review, including documents, of efforts by the American government to persuade foreign governments to give up policies of anti-Jewish discrimination and persecution. It presents the rationale for the request for action against Nazi German anti-Semitism.

122. KORN, BERTRAM W. *American Jewry and the Civil War.* 1951. Reprint. Cleveland, Ohio: World Publishing Co., 1961.

A "group biography" of American Jewry, North and South, as it experienced the Civil War. The focus is on rabbinical attitudes toward slavery, the chaplaincy controversy, General U. S. Grant's notorious General Order No. 11 (1862) expelling Jews "as a class" from his area of jurisdiction, and Lincoln's relations with Jews. Thorough documentation, facsimiles, excellent bibliography, and documentary appendix. Originally published in 1951, this reprint edition adds an additional and substantial preface. The illustrations of the original edition are lacking in the reprints.

123. KORN, BERTRAM W. *Eventful Years and Experiences: Studies in Nineteenth Century American Jewish History.* Cincinnati, Ohio: American Jewish Archives, 1954.

Eight scholarly essays on the life, work, sociopolitical relations, education, and philanthropy of American Jews from the middle to the end of the nineteenth century.

124. KORN, BERTRAM W. *The American Reaction to the Mortara Case: 1858-1859.* Cincinnati, Ohio: American Jewish Archives, 1957.

A careful study, based on primary sources, of American Jewish and non-Jewish press comment on the kidnapping and conversion of a Jewish child in mid-nineteenth century Italy. Illustrations.

125. LEBESON, ANITA L. *Recall to Life—The Jewish Woman in America.* New York: Thomas Yoseloff, 1970.

An informative, suitably documented study of the role of women in the history of Jewish welfare, culture, religion, education, and society in the United States.

126. LIFSON, DAVID S. *The Yiddish Theatre in America.* New York: Thomas Yoseloff, 1965.

A detailed, thoroughly documented history of the Yiddish theater, mainly in New York City, with particular reference to the impact of Maurice Schwartz, Jacob Ben-Ami, and other leading actor-directors. Illustrations, chronological lists of productions, and comprehensive bibliography in English and Yiddish.

127. MARCUS, JACOB R. *The Colonial American Jew, 1492-1776.* 3 vols. Detroit, Mich.: Wayne State University Press, 1970.

A competently documented study of the life, society, education, work, and other activities of the Jews in the thirteen colonies and other colonial areas in the Western hemisphere. The most detailed work of its kind.

128. MEYER, ISIDORE S., ed. *Early History of Zionism in America.* New York: American Jewish Historical Society and Theodor Herzl Foundation, 1958.

Scholarly papers on various aspects of Zionism in the United States in the nineteenth and early twentieth centuries.

129. PETERS, MADISON C. *The Jews Who Stood by Washington.* New York: Trow Press, 1915.

Addresses on the services donated to the American Revolution by Jews, especially Haym Salomon, who "brought not only all his wealth to the aid of his adopted country, but a financial insight which, for clearness and depth, was not surpassed by Alexander Hamilton nor equalled by Robert Morris" (p. 16). This work also includes an address by President William Howard Taft on Haym Salomon.

130. RABINOWITZ, BENJAMIN. *The Young Men's Hebrew Associations (1854-1913).* New York: National Jewish Welfare Board, 1948.

A fully documented account of the origins and development of the YMHA and the beginning of the Jewish Community Center movement. Chronologies and bibliography.

131. ROGOFF. ABRAHAM M. "Formative Years of the Jewish Labor Movement in the United States

(1890-1900)." Ph.D. thesis, Columbia University, 1945.

A study of the early development of the Jewish labor unions. By the first decade of the twentieth century, "most of the present powerful Jewish labor unions were founded and well established" (p. 111).

132. RUBINGER, NAPHTALI J. *Abraham Lincoln and the Jews*. New York: Jonathan David, 1962.

A concise, popular summary of facts regarding Lincoln's Jewish friends and his actions in problems affecting Jews. Quotations in the text.

133. SACHS, A. S. *Di geshikhte fun Arbeiter Ring, 1892-1925*. 2 vols. [New York]: Natsionaler Ekzekutiv Comiteh fun Arbeiter Ring, 1925.

A detailed account of the development of the Workmen's Circle and its social, educational, and other activities. Documents and photographs.

134. SCHACHNER, NATHAN. *The Price of Liberty: A History of the American Jewish Committee*. New York: American Jewish Committee, 1948.

An unofficial, popular account by a staff member of the activities at home and abroad of a leading American Jewish defense organization from the beginning of the twentieth century to the end of World War II. The author concludes that "the American Jewish Committee has never believed in a defeatist philosophy, and will go on to fight for freedom, liberation, dignity and equal rights, and that democracy without which the others are mere hollow shams" (p. 214).

135. SHATZKY, YAKOV, ed. *Zaml-bukh zu der geshikhte fun der Yiddisher presse in Amerika.* New York: Yiddisher Kultur Gezelshaft, 1934.

Thirteen essays, twelve in Yiddish and one in English, concerning the history of the Yiddish press in the United States.

136. SILVERBERG, ROBERT. *If I Forget Thee O Jerusalem: American Jews and the State of Israel.* New York: William Morrow & Co., 1970.

A detailed account of the role of American Jewry in the genesis and growth of Israel from the early twentieth century until 1967. Illustrations and bibliography.

137. SIMONHOFF, HARRY. *Jewish Participants in the Civil War.* New York: Arco Publishing Co., 1963.

An account of the role of Jews in the armed forces of the North and South. Illustrations, documents, and bibliography.

138. TELLER, JUDD L. *Strangers and Natives: The Evolution of the American Jew from 1921 to the Present.* New York: Delacorte Press, 1968.

A well-informed journalist's interpretative analysis of the development of American Jewish community, culture, and religion.

IV. SOURCES AND COLLECTIONS
OF DOCUMENTS

IV. SOURCES AND COLLECTIONS OF DOCUMENTS

139. ADLER, CYRUS, ed. *The Voice of America on Kishineff.* Philadelphia: Jewish Publication Society of America, 1904.

     A compilation of editorials, sermons, resolutions, petitions, and other documentary materials giving expression to protests by American Jews and non-Jews against the pogrom inflicted upon the Jews of Southwestern Russia in 1903.

140. *Annual Reports of the Hebrew Sheltering and Immigrant Aid Society of America.* New York, 1909 to date.

     Valuable source material on the Jewish immigration to the United States.

141. BELTH, NATHAN C., ed. *Fighting for America: An Account of Jewish Men in the Armed Forces—From Pearl Harbor to the Italian Campaign.* New York: National Jewish Welfare Board, 1944.

     The activities of, and awards to, Jewish members of the American armed services during World War II.

142. BENJAMIN, I. J. *Three Years in America, 1859-1862.*
      2 vols. Philadelphia: Jewish Publication Society of
      America, 1956.

      Observations and commentary on life and culture in
      the United States at the time of the Civil War by the
      traveler, Israel Joseph Benjamin, known also as
      Benjamin II (1818-1864). Special attention is given to
      "the history of the Jews in North America; the devel-
      opment of their religious and communal conditions;
      their charitable institutions . . ." (p. 42). In his edify-
      ing introduction, Oscar Handlin points out that this
      report is "the only coherent account by a Jewish
      traveler of American life in the period before 1870"
      (p. 8). Translated from the German, *Drei Jahre in
      Amerika.* 2 vols. (Hannover, 1862).

143. BLAU, JOSEPH L., and SALO W. BARON, eds. *The
      Jews of the United States, 1790-1840: A Documen-
      tary History.* 3 vols. New York: Columbia University
      Press, 1963.

      A collection of 334 documents: government papers,
      constitutional provisions, court decisions, letters,
      newspaper accounts and editorials, advertisements,
      addresses, sermons, circulars and handbills, reports,
      poetry, wills, and miscellaneous primary source mate-
      rials on Jewish life in the early Republic. The subject
      matter includes politics, religion, interreligious rela-
      tions, anti-Semitism, legal status, economic activities,
      family and social life, international relations, culture,
      immigration, and education. Informative introduc-
      tion, scholarly notes, a chronological listing of the
      documents, and a complete index. An indispensable
      aid to research.

144. BLOCH, JOSEF S. *Ein Besuch beim Judenthum in New York und Umgebung: Drei Vortrage.* Vienna: Verlag der "Oesterreichischen Wochenschrift," 1912.

An Austrian Jewish visitor's impressions of Jewish life in New York City and vicinity in the early twentieth century.

145. BLUMENTHAL, L. ROY, *et al. Fighting for America: A Record of the Participation of Jewish Men and Women in the Armed Forces during 1944.* New York: National Jewish Welfare Board, [1945].

A compilation of data on the military services of American Jews, including lists of the dead and wounded and award winners.

146. BYARS, WILLIAM V., ed. *B. and M. Gratz: Merchants in Philadelphia, 1754-1798.* Jefferson City, Mo.: Hugh Stephens Printing Co., 1916.

Most of this volume comprises a large number of letters and other papers reflecting the business activities of this noted American Jewish family. Also included are documents, especially those of Rebecca Gratz, dealing with social and educational matters. The appendix, the editorial introduction, and chronology in the appendix are valuable.

147. FIERMAN, FLOYD S. *Sources of Jewish Education in America prior to 1881.* El Paso, Texas: Temple Mt. Sinai, 1960.

Contains data on congregational, communal, and private schools in America, 1654-1881, selected English documents and facsimiles, and a comprehensive bibliography.

148. FINK, REUBEN, ed. *America and Palestine.* New
York: Herald Square Press, 1945.

The second revised edition of a collection of documents on "the attitude of official America and the
American people toward the rebuilding of Palestine as
a free and democratic Jewish commonwealth" (sub-
title), past and recent. Historical backgrounds by the
editor.

149. GARTNER, LLOYD P., ed. *Jewish Education in the
United States: A Documentary History.* New York:
Teachers College Press, 1969.

A collection of thirty-nine documents and statements
illustrating the development of Jewish religious and
secular education from 1760 to 1960. The introduction places the subject in religious-historical context,
while the bibliography offers basic references which
aid further research.

150. GOODMAN, PHILIP, comp. *A Documentary Study of
a Century of the Jewish Community Center,
1854-1954.* New York: National Jewish Welfare
Board, 1953.

Facsimiles and transcriptions of source materials il-
lustrating the origins and development of the Young
Men's Hebrew Literary Associations, the Young
Men's Hebrew Associations, and the Jewish
Community Centers. Two documents are in German
and one is in Hebrew. Some are secondary in nature.

151. HERSHKOWITZ, LEO. *Wills of Early New York Jews
(1704-1799).* New York: American Jewish Historical
Society, 1967.

Facsimiles and transcribed texts of the wills of forty-one Jews, four of them women. Informative introduction and notes. A useful source for social and religious history. Comprehensive bibliography and index.

152. HERSHKOWITZ, LEO, and ISIDORE S. MEYER, eds. *The Lee Max Friedman Collection of American Jewish Colonial Correspondence: Letters of the Franks Family (1733-1748).* Waltham, Mass.: American Jewish Historical Society, 1968.

The texts of thirty-seven letters written by Mrs. Jacob (Bilhah Abigail) Franks to her son Naphtali in London. The letters, as well as the scholarly introductory notes, shed light on colonial Jewish society and family life. Illustrations, facsimiles, comprehensive bibliography, and thorough index.

153. HERTZ, EMANUEL, ed. *Abraham Lincoln: The Tribute of the Synagogues.* New York: Bloch Publishing Co., 1927.

Sermons, eulogies, and other statements of appreciation in English and German by American rabbis and laymen, from 1865 to 1927, of the personality, ideals, and significance of the Great Emancipator. Photographs and facsimiles.

154. HINDUS, MILTON, ed. *The Old East Side: An Anthology.* Philadelphia: Jewish Publication Society of America, 1969.

Selections from autobiographical, fictional, and other writings by American Jews and non-Jews throwing light on the experience of Jewish immigrants and their children in New York City.

155. KOHUT, GEORGE A. *Ezra Stiles and the Jews: Selected Passages from His Literary Diary Concerning Jews and Judaism.* New York: Cowen, 1902.

An analysis of, with frequent quotations from, the diary of the president of Yale College.

156. MARCUS, JACOB R. *American Jewry: Documents, Eighteenth Century.* Cincinnati, Ohio: Hebrew Union College Press, 1959.

A compilation of 196 letters and other documents illustrating the family and social life, religious and educational activities, economic pursuits, and communal organization of Jews in colonial America and in the early years of the Republic. Enlightening introductions by Dr. Marcus.

157. MARCUS, JACOB R. *Early American Jewry.* 2 vols. Philadelphia: Jewish Publication Society of America, 1951-1953.

The first volume combines historical narrative with primary documents on Jewish history, 1649-1794, in New York, New England, and Canada. The second volume covers, in a similar fashion, the history of the Jewish experience in Pennsylvania and the Southern colonies, 1655-1790. Illustrations, notes, and index.

158. MARCUS, JACOB R. *Mavoh l'toldot Yahadut Amerikah bitkufat reshitah.* Jerusalem: Magnes Press, Hebrew University, 1971.

Survey and documents, in Hebrew, of American Jewish history, 1654-1800. Illustrations and bibliography, mainly in English.

159. MARCUS, JACOB R., ed. *On Love, Marriage, Children . . . and Death, Too.* n.p.: Society of Jewish Bibliophiles, 1965.

An illustrated collection of "intimate glimpses into the lives of American Jews in a bygone age as told in their own words." The source materials comprise letters of the eighteenth century.

160. MARKENS, ISAAC. *Abraham Lincoln and the Jews.* New York: The author, 1909.

A commentary on Lincoln's attitude, together with the texts of letters to and from the president.

161. METZKER, ISAAC. *A Bintel Brief: Sixty Years of Letters from the Lower East Side to the Jewish Daily Forward.* Garden City, N.Y.: Doubleday, 1971.

Translations from the Yiddish of letters and editorial replies on personal problems, as well as on political and social issues. Interpretative foreword and notes by Harry Golden. Illustrations.

162. PHILIPSON, DAVID. *Max Lilienthal: American Rabbi; Life and Writings.* New York: Bloch Publishing Co., 1915.

The biography of a German-born rabbi (1815-1882) who was active in Russia and influential in the United States. Over three-fourths of the volume consists of Lilienthal's letters, essays, and addresses.

163. PHILIPSON, DAVID, ed. *Letters of Rebecca Gratz.* Philadelphia: Jewish Publication Society of America, 1929.

Letters, 1808-1866, by an eminent American Jewish woman, founder of the Hebrew Sunday School Society. Genealogical introduction and index.

164. PLAUT, W. GUNTHER, [ed.]. *The Growth of Reform Judaism: American and European Sources until 1948.* New York: World Union for Progressive Judaism, 1965.

A compilation of documents and extracts illustrating the religious and social development of the Reform movement in the United States in the nineteenth and twentieth centuries. Helpful editorial introduction and epilogue.

165. POLIER, JUSTINE W., and JAMES W. WISE, eds. *The Personal Letters of Stephen Wise.* Boston: Beacon Press, 1956.

Letters, 1899-1949, to the Jewish leader's family and friends, with insight into Jewish and general issues. Illustrations.

166. *Reports of the Educational Alliance.* New York: Educational Alliance, 1890-1917.

Important sources of data on the activities and adjustment of Eastern European Jewish immigrants on the Lower East Side of New York City.

167. REZNIKOFF, CHARLES, ed. *Louis Marshall: Champion of Liberty.* 2 vols. Philadelphia: Jewish Publication Society of America, 1957.

Essays, addresses, legal brief, and letters by an outstanding American Jewish lawyer and leader. The subject matter, which is mainly concerned with Jews, covers sociopolitical problems, international affairs, immigration, discrimination and bigotry, minority rights overseas, Zionism, religion, education, constitutional freedom, conservation, and other matters. Autobiographical material and a chronology. Perceptive introduction by Oscar Handlin. A valuable resource for research.

168. ROGOW, ARNOLD A., ed. *The Jews in a Gentile World.* New York: Macmillan, 1961.

An anthology of statements by non-Jews concerning Jews, with a substantial section on American Jews from the colonial era to the twentieth century (pp. 219-385).

169. ROSENFELD, LEONORA C. *Portrait of a Philosopher: Morris R. Cohen in Life and Letters.* New York: Harcourt, Brace & World, 1962.

A daughter's biographical commentary on the distinguished philosopher. The many letters in this volume reveal Dr. Cohen's views on philosophical, legal, and Jewish questions. Notes and full index.

170. SCHABER, WILL, ed. *Aufbau, Reconstruction: Dokumente einer Kultur im Exil.* New York: Overlook Press, and Cologne, Germany: Kiepenheuer & Witsch, 1972.

Reprint of German-language essays, reports, and other writings by German-Jewish refugees published in Aufbau between 1939 and 1971. Useful source on the adjustment of this group of immigrants to American life.

171. SCHAPPES, MORRIS U., ed. *A Documentary History*

of the Jews in the United States, 1654-1875. 3d ed. New York: Schocken Books, 1971.

A valuable and convenient compilation of 159 documents of various types dealing with the various facets of Jewish life and activity in America prior to the mass emigration from Russia. Pertinent introductions and extensive notes, not without politically ideological interpretations.

172. SCHAPPES, MORRIS U., ed. *The Letters of Emma Lazarus, 1868-1886.* New York: New York Public Library, 1949.

Letters by the American Jewish poet to Ralph Waldo Emerson, Rabbi Gustav Gottheil, Henry George, Philip Cowen, and others. Introduction and notes by the editor.

173. SCHOENER, ALLON, ed. *Portal to America: The Lower East Side, 1870-1925.* New York: Holt, Rinehart and Winston, 1967.

Reproductions of photographs, accompanied by contemporary newspaper and magazine articles and editorials, and translations of Yiddish letters published in the "Bintel Brief" section of the *Jewish Daily Forward.* These materials afford an insight into the life of immigrant Jews in New York City.

174. SELZER, MICHAEL, ed. *"Kike!" A Documentary History of Anti-Semitism in America.* New York: World Publishing Co., 1972.

Primary source materials on past and present anti-Jewish attitudes in the United States. Notes and bibliography.

175. "The Hebrew Union College—Jewish Institute of Religion: A Centennial Documentary." Special Issue, *American Jewish Archives* 26 (November, 1974): 100-276.

Documents with a brief introduction and comments illustrating the genesis, growth, and development of the first rabbinical seminary in the United States. Thoroughly indexed.

176. VOSS, CARL H., ed. *Stephen S. Wise: Servant of the People.* Philadelphia: Jewish Publication Society of America, 1969.

A collection of letters, 1896-1949, by the Reform rabbinical and Zionist leader on general and Jewish problems and issues. Chronology, editorial notes, biographical register, and illustrations.

V. AUTOBIOGRAPHIES, MEMOIRS, AND REMINISCENCES.

V. AUTOBIOGRAPHIES, MEMOIRS,
AND REMINISCENCES.

177. ADLER, CYRUS. *I Have Considered the Days.* Philadelphia: Jewish Publication Society of America, 1941.

Autobiography of a leader in Jewish higher education and international affairs. Illustrations.

178. ANTIN, MARY. *The Promised Land.* Boston: Houghton Mifflin, 1912.

An autobiography by a young immigrant, with a comparison of Jewish life in Russia and in America. Illustrations.

179. BAILIN, I. B. *Perzenlekhkeitn in der geshikhte fun Yidn in Amerike.* New York: YKUF, 1955.

Biographical sketches in Yiddish of many personalities, including some non-Jews, in American Jewish history. Illustrations.

180. BARUCH, BERNARD M. *Baruch: My Own Story.* New York: Holt, 1957.

An illustrated autobiography of a South Carolina born descendant of German and Spanish-Portuguese

Jews who made his mark as a business leader and adviser to United States presidents. "Until after graduation from college, I kept every Jewish holy day and fasted scrupulously on the Day of Atonement" (p. 51), but his "two daughters were brought up in the Episcopalian faith of their mother" (p. 52), a fact which did not shield them from social discrimination as Jews.

181. BERNHEIMER, CHARLES S. *Half a Century in Community Service.* New York: Association Press, 1948.

The autobiography of a leader in Jewish social work and observations on social-communal activities in New York City. A list of the author's writings in the appendix.

182. BISGYER, MAURICE. *Challenge and Encounter: Behind the Scenes in the Struggle for Jewish Survival.* New York: Crown Publishers, 1967.

Historical and autobiographical reminiscences by an American Jewish leader concerning the important events and conflicts involving Jews in the United States and abroad. Illustrations.

183. BLOOM, SOL. *The Autobiography of Sol Bloom.* New York: G. P. Putnam, 1948.

Reminiscences of a prominent congressman from New York City, who was brought up as an Orthodox Jew by his Russian-Polish immigrant parents. One chapter is devoted to the author's special concerns and activities as a Jew, particularly to the equal treatment of Jewish displaced persons after World War II and to the establishment of the State of Israel.

184. BOGEN, BORIS D. *Born a Jew*. New York: Macmillan, 1930.

Reminiscences by a Russian-born Jewish community leader of his experiences in Russia, America, Poland, and the Netherlands.

185. CAHAN, Ab. *Bleter fun maya leben*. 5 vols. New York: Forverts Association, 1926-1931.

Autobiography of the well-known Yiddish writer and editor who also published in English. Covers his childhood in Lithuania and his life and work in America. Illustrations.

186. CARVALHO, SOLOMON NUNES. *Incidents of Travel and Adventure in the Far West; with Col. Fremont's Last Expedition. . . . Edited by Bertram W. Korn. Philadelphia: Jewish Publication Society of America, 1954.*

To the student of American Jewish history, the most pertinent parts of the reprint of the record of Colonel Frémont's fifth Western expedition, originally published in 1857, are Bertram W. Korn's informative account of Carvalho as a Jew and artist, and the contemporary reproductions of the paintings and portraits of Jewish personalities and themes.

187. CELLER, EMANUEL. *You Never Leave Brooklyn*. New York: John Day, 1953.

Reminiscences by an influential congressman of his political, legislative, and Jewish activities.

188. CHYET, STANLEY F., ed. *Lives and Voices: A Collec-*

tion of American Jewish Memoirs. Philadelphia:
Jewish Publication Society of America, 1972.

Memoirs by ten American Jews (including one
woman) depicting Jewish life in the nineteenth and
early twentieth centuries. Illustrations.

189. COHEN, MORRIS RAPHAEL. *A Dreamer's Journey.*
Boston: Beacon Press, 1949.

The life of a renowned philosopher and professor at
the College of the City of New York (1880-1947).
Dr. Cohen describes his childhood in Russia, adolescence and youth on the East Side, and his educational activities. He also outlines his philosophical development and expresses his views on American
Jewish issues and the meaning of life. Bibliography of
Dr. Cohen's published works.

190. COWEN, PHILIP. *Memories of an American Jew.* New
York: International Press, 1937.

Autobiography of the first editor of the *American
Hebrew* and an account of his Jewish communal activities. Documents in the text.

191. DAVID, JAY, ed. *Growing Up Jewish.* New York:
William Morrow & Co., 1969.

Extracts from the autobiographies of twenty-five
Jews, thirteen of them Americans, from the sixteenth
to the twentieth century.

192. EISENSTEIN, JUDAH D. *Otzar Zikhronotai.* New
York: The author, 1929.

Hebrew autobiography, reminiscences since 1872,

outline of American Jewish history, and miscellaneous materials. Illustrations.

193. FLEXNER, ABRAHAM. *An Autobiography.* New York: Simon and Schuster, 1960.

The life of an American Jew (1866-1959) who exercised a profound influence on medical and higher education in the United States during the twentieth century. A revision of *I Remember* (1954).

194. GOLD, HERBERT. *My Last Two Thousand Years.* New York: Random House, 1972.

Autobiography, reminiscences, and experiences of an American Jewish novelist.

195. GOMPERS, SAMUEL. *Seventy Years of Life and Labor: An Autobiography.* New York: E. P. Dutton & Co., 1957.

The recollections of a London-born descendant of Dutch Jews, the founder of the American Federation of Labor. Apart from details on his Jewish upbringing in London, there is very little about Jews. Gompers acknowledges that the study of the Talmud "develops the more subtle qualities of mind; the student learns to deal with abstract problems, to make careful discriminations, to follow a line of reasoning from premise to conclusion. This legal training given to Jewish boys is fundamental in explaining the intellectual quality of many of the Jewish people" (p. 49).

196. HABER, JULIUS. *The Odyssey of an American Zionist: A Half-Century of Zionist History.* New York: Twayne Publishers, 1956.

Reminiscences by an early Zionist leader in the United States.

197. HECHT, BEN. *A Child of the Century: The Autobiography of Ben Hecht.* New York: Simon and Schuster, 1954.

An illustrated autobiography of an American-Jewish writer who worked for the establishment of a Jewish state.

198. HILLQUIT, MORRIS. *Loose Leaves from a Busy Life.* New York: Macmillan, 1934.

Autobiography of a Russian-born Jewish immigrant who became a leader in the labor movement and in the Socialist Party.

199. HINDUS, MAURICE. *Green Worlds: An Informal Chronicle.* New York: Doubleday, Doran, 1938.

Reminiscences of an immigrant Jew who became a well-known foreign correspondent and author of works on the Soviet Union.

200. HORWICH, BERNARD. *My First Eighty Years.* Chicago: Argus Books, 1939.

Autobiography of a Russian immigrant who became a founder of the Zionist Organization of America.

201. KAZIN, ALFRED. *A Walker in the City.* New York: Grove Press, 1951.

A noted literary critic's reminiscences of his childhood and adolescence in the Brownsville (Brooklyn, N.Y.) Jewish community.

202. KOHLER, KAUFMANN. *Personal Reminiscences of My Early Life*. Cincinnati, Ohio: Hebrew Union College, 1918.

A brief, illustrated autobiographical essay by a nineteenth-century leader of American Reform Judaism.

203. KOHUT, REBEKAH. *My Portion (An Autobiography)*. New York: Thomas Seltzer, 1925.

Reminiscences of the wife of the scholarly Alexander Kohut, especially of her participation in American Jewish life and overseas activities, and in education and social work.

204. KROCK, ARTHUR. *Myself When Young: Growing Up in the 1890's*. Boston: Little, Brown, 1973.

The early life of the well-known and influential columnist of the *New York Times*. His grandfather "came from largely Jewish stock in rural Prussia and Alsace-Lorraine," as did his grandmother, while he identified himself as "a Caucasian with even quarterings of Hebrew blood . . . a Jew by the world's definition" (p. 22).

205. LEWISOHN, LUDWIG. *Mid-Channel: An American Chronicle*. New York: Harper & Bros., 1929.

Autobiography of an American Jew covering the period of his recognition as a novelist and literary critic.

206. LEWISOHN, LUDWIG. *Up Stream: An American Chroncile*. New York: Boni and Liveright, 1922.

The early life, education, and work of a German-born, American Jewish novelist and literary critic.

207. LISITZKY, EPHRAIM E. *In the Grip of Cross-Currents.* New York: Bloch Publishing Co., 1959.

An interesting autobiography, translated from the Hebrew, of an immigrant poet and teacher in the United States and Canada.

208. MARCUS, JACOB R. *Memoirs of American Jews, 1775-1865.* 3 vols. Philadelphia: Jewish Publication Society of America, 1955.

Reminiscences by Jewish soldiers, politicians, educators, merchants, workers, religious leaders, and other personalities in the United States until the Civil War. The well-known and the lesser known are included. Illustrations and full index. A unique collection.

209. MASLIANSKY, H. *Maslianskys zichroines: Firtsig yor leben un kemfen.* New York: Farlag "Zerubabel," 1924.

Memoirs of forty years of life and struggle in Eastern Europe and the United States by the outstanding preacher in the Yiddish language during the early decades of the twentieth century.

210. MAYERBERG, SAMUEL S. *Chronicle of an American Crusader.* New York: Bloch Publishing Co., 1944.

Reminiscences of a Reform rabbi's religious, communal, and political activities.

211. NEWMARK, MAURICE H., and MARCO R. NEW-MARK, Eds. *Sixty Years in Southern California,*

1853-1913: Containing the Reminiscences of Harris Newmark. Los Angeles, Calif.: Zeitlin & Ver Brugge, 1970.

Fourth edition, revised, of a lengthy volume of "frank and honest" recollections by a Los Angeles Jewish merchant who arrived from East Prussia in 1853—it includes an introduction and notes by W. W. Robinson. While most of the book is of general interest, it contains interesting information on Jewish communal life and activities.

212. PHILIPSON, DAVID. *My Life as an American Jew: An Autobiography.* Cincinnati, Ohio: John G. Kidd, 1941.

An interesting autobiography of a distinguished Reform rabbi and scholar.

213. PODHORETZ, NORMAN. *Making It.* New York: Random House, 1967.

Autobiography of a writer who "made it," at a very young age, as the editor of *Commentary.*

214. PROSKAUER, JOSEPH M. *A Segment of My Time.* New York: Farrar, Straus, & Cudahy, 1950.

Autobiography of a judge who also served as president of the American Jewish Committee.

215. RIBALOW, HAROLD U., comp. *Autobiographies of American Jews.* Philadelphia: Jewish Publication Society of America, 1965.

Autobiographical accounts covering the early lives of twenty-five Jews from 1880 to 1920. Among the writers are rabbis, writers, educators, philanthropists, and representatives of other callings.

216. ROSENBAUM, JEANETTE W. *Myer Myers, Goldsmith, 1723-1795.* Philadelphia: Jewish Publication Society of America, 1954.

A well-illustrated analysis of the skill of an early American Jewish craftsman who worked with religious and secular objects. Biographical data and facsimiles. Bibliography of printed works and manuscript sources.

217. ROSKOLENKO, HARRY. *The Time That Was Then: The Lower East Side, 1900-1914, an Intimate Chronicle.* New York: Dial Press, 1971.

Reminiscences by the son of Russian immigrants of Jewish life and culture during his childhood in New York City.

218. SHILOH, AILON, ed. *By Myself I'm a Book!: An Oral History of the Immigrant Jewish Experience in Pittsburgh.* Waltham, Mass.: American Jewish Historical Society, 1972.

Reminiscences, including direct quotations, by Jewish immigrants concerning life in Eastern Europe; the trans-Atlantic trip; and life, education, society, religion, and other aspects of the Jewish experience in America. The appendix contains an overview of Pittsburgh Jewish history and a bibliography of published and unpublished materials. Photographs and facsimiles.

219. STEIN, LEON, ABRAHAM P. CONAN, and LYNN DAVISON, trans. *The Education of Abraham Cahan.*

Philadelphia: Jewish Publication Society of America, 1969.

Translation of the first two volumes of Cahan's five-volume Yiddish autobiography. The content covers life in Russian Lithuania and the immigrant's adjustment to America and development as a teacher, lawyer, journalist, Socialist leader, and labor union activist. A documented introduction by Leon Stein, photographs, cartoons, and a glossary of names.

220. STERN, ELISABETH G. *I Am a Woman—and a Jew.* New York: Arno Press, 1969.

Autobiography of "Leah Morton," originally published in 1926 (New York: J. H. Sears & Co.).

221. STRAUS, OSCAR S. *Under Four Administrations: From Cleveland to Taft; Recollections.* Boston: Houghton Mifflin, 1922.

Autobiography of an American Jewish statesman, diplomat, and member of the presidential cabinet. Mention is made of the author's defense of Russian Jews and of his role in the founding of the Young Men's Hebrew Association.

222. THOMASHEFSKY, BORIS. *Mein Lebens-geshikhte.* New York: The author, 1937.

An illustrated autobiography, in Yiddish, of a leading star of the Yiddish theater in the early decades of the twentieth century. Glossary of Anglicisms in Yiddish.

223. WALD, LILLIAN D. *Windows on Henry Street.* Boston: Little, Brown and Company, 1934.

Illustrated reminiscences, by an influential public health nurse, of life on the East Side of New York in the early twentieth century.

224. WIENER, NORBERT. *Ex-Prodigy: My Childhood and Youth.* Cambridge, Mass.: M.I.T. Press, 1953.

Autobiography of an eminent American mathematician and expert on cybernetics, who was "about seven-eighths Jewish in ancestry," but "neither I myself nor my father nor . . . his father has been a follower of the Jewish religion" (p. 8). The volume contains references to Dr. Wiener's Jewish awareness and identification.

225. WISE, ISAAC M., ed. *Reminiscences.* Cincinnati, Ohio: Leo Wise, 1901.

Autobiography of the nineteenth-century leader of Reform Judaism in America, the founder of the Union of American Hebrew Congregations, the Hebrew Union College, and the Central Conference of American Rabbis. Introduction by David Philipson, obituaries in prose and verse, and a glossary of Hebrew and Yiddish words and expressions.

226. WISE, STEPHEN. *Challenging Years.* New York: G. P. Putnam, 1949.

Autobiography of a Reform rabbi-educator and a leader in the struggle for Jewish rights. Illustrations.

VI. BIOGRAPHIES

VI. BIOGRAPHIES

227. ADLER, CYRUS. *In Memory of Edward Wolf.* Philadelphia: n.p., 1917.

A brief appreciation of a German-born merchant and manufacturer who was very active in Jewish education in Philadelphia.

228. ADLER, CYRUS. *Jacob H. Schiff: His Life and Letters.* 2 vols. Garden City, N.Y.: Doubleday, Doran, 1928.

The life and correspondence of an outstanding Jewish philanthropist and communal leader of the late nineteenth and early twentieth centuries, who was born in Germany. A descendant of eminent rabbis, Schiff became a railroad magnate and banker, and played a notable role in all phases of general and Jewish activities in the United States, including education. The letters are incorporated into the text.

229. AGRESTI, OLIVIA R. *David Lubin: A Study in Practical Idealism.* Berkeley: University of California Press, 1941.

The second edition of a detailed biography of a Russian-born, American Jewish expert in agriculture.

"David Lubin was a prophet who foretold the needs of the agricultural world with astonishing accuracy and devoted his whole life without reserve to the development of his ideals" (p. xiii), thus benefiting the farmers of the world. Letters are included in the text.

230. *American Jews: Their Lives and Achievements: A Contemporary Biographical Record.* Vol. 2. New York: American Jewish Literary Foundation, 1958.

Biographical sketches arranged by specialties, e.g., arts, clergy, education, law, literature, medicine, philanthropy, etc. Lists of organizations, brief essays, and photographs.

231. BAKER, LIVA. *Felix Frankfurter.* New York: Coward-McCann, 1969.

An appropriately documented biographical study of the associate justice of the United States Supreme Court with focus on his educational, legal, and judicial career. Frankfurter, an immigrant who descended from "a long line of rabbis," was proud of his heritage even if "he abandoned formal Judaism as a very young man" (p. 18). He "identified deeply with Jews as a people" (p. 83) and was active in Zionist causes. Bibliography and photographs.

232. BENTWICH, NORMAN. *For Zion's Sake: A Biography of Judah L. Magnes, First Chancellor and First President of the Hebrew University of Jerusalem.* Philadelphia: Jewish Publication Society of America, 1954.

The life of an American-born rabbinical, communal, and educational leader (1877-1948), with stress on his activities and contributions in Palestine: "Few men in our time have left a nobler memorial" (p. 317). Photographs and a list of Dr. Magnes' publications.

233. BENTWICH, NORMAN. *Solomon Schechter: A Biography.* Philadelphia: Jewish Publication Society of America, 1938.

A detailed biography of the Rumanian-born scholar who made significant documentary discoveries in the Cairo Genizah (synagogue repository), and who became the leading influence on Conservatism through his presidency of the Jewish Theological Seminary of America and other activities. Illustrations, documentation, bibliography, and a Hebrew-English glossary.

234. BIRMINGHAM, STEPHEN. *"Our Crowd": The Great Jewish Families of New York.* New York: Harper & Row, 1967.

Interesting portrayals of the Guggenheim, Lehman, Schiff, Loeb, Warburg, and other nationally prominent Jewish families who made significant contributions to banking, industry, government, and philanthropy, and also supported education, the arts, and the sciences. Illustrations.

235. BIRMINGHAM, STEPHEN. *The Grandees: America's Sephardic Elite.* New York: Harper & Row, 1971.

A popular, illustrated account of prominent American Jewish families of Spanish-Portuguese descent. Genealogical insert and bibliography.

236. CHYET, STANLEY F. *Lopez of Newport: Colonial American Merchant Prince.* Detroit, Mich.: Wayne State University Press, 1970.

An illustrated, scholarly biography of a Jewish immigrant who became an outstanding merchant in eighteenth-century Newport, Rhode Island, and who was active in synagogue affairs.

237. CLARK, RONALD W. *Einstein: The Life and Times.* New York: World Book Co., 1971.

A thoroughly scholarly biography of the eminent scientist, with accounts of his Jewish background and activities. Photographs and bibliography.

238. COHEN, HARRY, and ITZHAK J. CARMIN, eds. *Jews in the World of Science: A Biographical Dictionary of Jews Eminent in the Natural and Social Sciences.* White Plains, N.Y.: Monde Publishers, 1956.

This reference work contains 3,000 biographies, many of them of American Jews.

239. COHEN, NAOMI W. *A Dual Heritage: The Public Career of Oscar S. Straus.* Philadelphia: Jewish Publication Society of America, 1969.

An illustrated, scholarly biography of an American Jewish philanthropist who served as a diplomat and secretary of commerce and labor, and who defended Jewish rights in tsarist Russia. Extensive bibliography.

240. COIT, MARGARET L. *Mr. Baruch.* Boston: Houghton Mifflin Company, 1957.

A detailed, thoroughly documented biography of the financier and presidential adviser (born in 1870) who had "reverence for the traditions of his ancestors and a tolerance for the beliefs of others" (p. 44). The author concludes that, "oddly enough, the admiration which Baruch has aroused in the American people has not been shared by a vocal minority of the Jewish population" (p. 671)—the Orthodox, the Zionists, the political liberals, and the intellectuals. Illustrations and bibliography.

241. DeHAAS, JACOB. *Louis D. Brandeis: A Biographical Sketch, with Special Reference to His Contributions to Jewish and Zionist History.* New York: Bloch Publishing Co., 1929.

The first half of this volume is a biographical account of the eminent Zionist who served as a United States Supreme Court justice, while the second part contains twenty of Brandeis' addresses, essays, and statements on Zionism, Palestine, and Jewish rights.

242. DRACHMAN, BERNARD. *The Unfailing Light: Memoirs of an American Rabbi.* New York: Rabbinical Council of America, 1948.

Autobiography of an American-born Orthodox rabbi and educator (1861-1945). Illustrations.

243. DUFFUS, ROBERT L. *Lillian Wald.* New York: Macmillan, 1938.

An interesting biography of a leader in nursing who was active in health and social work among Jewish immigrants on New York City's Lower East Side.

244. EPSTEIN, MELECH. *Profiles of Eleven.* Detroit: Wayne State University Press, 1965.

Profiles of eleven Jewish labor leaders, journalists, and others "who guided the destiny of an immigrant society and stimulated social consciousness among the American people," e.g., Abraham Cahan, Meyer London, Sidney Hillman. Documentation and glossary.

245. FELS, MARY. *The Life of Joseph Fels.* New York: Doubleday, Doran, 1940.

A popular biography by the widow of a noted American Jewish merchant of the late nineteenth and early twentieth centuries who promoted the single tax, educational experiments, and Jewish colonization in Palestine. He respected the synagogue "as a conservator of a magnificent tradition, but it seemed to him a force for the maintenance of dogma" (p. 12).

246. FELSENTHAL, EMMA, ed. *Bernhard Felsenthal: Teacher in Israel.* New York: Oxford University Press.

Biography of a nineteenth-century American Reform rabbi and educator, with a selection of his writings in German and English on religious subjects. A well-annotated, indexed bibliography.

247. FISH, SIDNEY M. *Aaron Levy: Founder of Aaronsburg.* New York: American Jewish Historical Society, 1951.

A concise biography, based on primary source materials, of the founder of "Jewstown" (ca. 1742-1815) who, in the words of Felix Frankfurter, realized that "faith without works is sterile" and who "proved by deed . . . [his] belief in the common humanity" (p. 55). Illustrations.

248. FITZPATRICK, DONOVAN, and SAUL SAPHIRE. *Navy Maverick: Uriah Phillips Levy.* Garden City, N.Y.: Doubleday, 1963.

A popular, illustrated biography of a pioneering Jewish officer in the nineteenth-century American navy. Explanatory notes and selected bibliography.

249. GINZBERG, ELI. *Keeper of the Law: Louis Ginzberg.* Philadelphia: Jewish Publication Society of America, 1966.

A son's interesting and not really filiopietistic biography of his father, who was born in Russian Lithuania and who became an outstanding Biblical scholar and influential professor at the Jewish Theological Seminary. Letters in the text, photographs, and a list of writings on Louis Ginzberg.

250. GLASSMAN, LEO M., ed. *Biographical Encyclopaedia of American Jews.* New York: Biographical Encyclopaedia of American Jews, 1935.

A volume intended "as an historical record of participation by American citizens of Jewish origin in every phase of contemporary American civilization" (preface).

251. GOLDBERG, ABRAHAM. *Pioneers and Builders: Biographical Studies and Essays.* New York: Abraham Goldberg Publication Committee, 1943.

Brief treatments of sixty-five thinkers, poets, statesmen, scholars, philanthropists, novelists, and other leaders in Jewish life in Europe and the United States during the nineteenth and twentieth centuries.

252. GOLDBERG, ISAAC. *Major Noah: American-Jewish Pioneer.* New York: Alfred A. Knopf, 1937.

An interesting biography, drawn from primary source

materials, of a colorful nineteenth-century Jewish figure, with particular references to his activities in politics, journalism, diplomacy, the theater, education, and Jewish affairs. Documents in the text. Illustrations, comprehensive bibliography.

253. GOLDSTEIN, HERBERT S., ed. *Forty Years of Struggle for a Principle: The Biography of Harry Fischel.* New York: Bloch Publishing Co., 1928.

The life of a Russian-born immigrant who became a philanthropist and active leader in Jewish communal, charitable, religious, and educational causes, and, especially, a supporter of Orthodox Judaism.

254. GREEN, BER. *Yiddishe shreiber in Amerike.* New York: YKUF, 1963.

Thirty-eight reprinted essays on Yiddish writers in America, including Morris Rosenfeld, Yehoash, Reuben Brainin, Leon Kobrin, and Sholem Asch. Photographs.

255. GUTSTEIN, MORRIS A. *Aaron Lopez and Judah Touro: A Refugee and a Son of a Refugee.* New York: Behrman's Jewish Book House, 1939.

A concise presentation of the lives and contributions of two Jews during the colonial and early Republican eras. Two documents in the appendix.

256. HELLER, JAMES G. *Isaac M. Wise: His Life, Work and Thought.* New York: Union of American Hebrew Congregations, 1965.

A thoroughly documented biography of a founding father of American Reform Judaism, as well as an exposition of his viewpoint on theology, Zionism, and other issues. Bibliography, five-language glossary, and full index.

257. HELLMAN, GEORGE S. *Benjamin N. Cardozo: American Judge.* New York: Whittlesey House, 1940.

A biography of an associate justice of the United States Supreme Court who was a member of the Spanish-Portuguese Congregation in New York and was associated with Jewish cultural and philanthropic organizations.

258. HOENIG, SIDNEY B. *Solomon Zeitlin: Scholar Laureate.* New York: Bitzaron, 1971.

Appreciations by students and colleagues of the contributions of the renowned professor of Dropsie University to many branches of Jewish scholarship. The main part of the volume consists of excellent annotations of 406 publications from the pen of Dr. Zeitlin, 1915-1970. Thorough indexes.

259. HOFFMANN, BANESH. *Albert Einstein: Creator and Rebel.* New York: Viking Press, 1972.

An illustrated account of the life, education, thought, and influence of the eminent scientist who spent the last part of his life in America. There are references to his Jewish identification and associations. Written in collaboration with Helen Dukas.

260. HUHNER, LEON. *The Life of Judah Touro (1775-1854).* Philadelphia: Jewish Publication Society of America, 1946.

A thoroughly documented biography of a prominent

nineteenth-century American Jew. Illustrations, documents, and glossary.

261. JACOB, H. E. *The World of Emma Lazarus.* New York: Schocken Books, 1949.

The life and writings of the nineteenth-century American Jewish poet, with generous samplings of her poetry.

262. KAGAN, SOLOMON R. *American Jewish Physicians of Note: Biographical Sketches.* Boston, Mass.: Boston Medical Publishing Co., 1942.

An illustrated biographical directory which includes younger physicians. Medical chronology with abundant bibliographical references in all specialties, 1887-1942.

263. KAGAN, SOLOMON R. *Jewish Contributions to Medicine in America from Colonial Times to the Present.* Boston, Mass.: Boston Medical Publishing Co., 1939.

The second edition of a compendium of data about American Jewish physicians, from the eighteenth to the twentieth century, and their activities, discoveries, and publications in all the specialties of medicine. Illustrations, chronology, documentation, lists of Jewish medical institutions, and bibliographical references.

264. KARP, DEBORAH. *Heroes of American Jewish History.* New York: Ktav Publishing House, 1972.

A concise textbook for junior high schools with many illustrations and facsimiles of value to more advanced readers. Glossary.

265. KARPMAN, I. J. CARMIN, chief ed. *Who's Who in World Jewry: A Biographical Dictionary of Outstanding Jews.* New York: Pitman Publishing Corporation, 1972.

A collection of about 10,000 biographies, preponderately of persons in Israel and the United States. The first edition was published in 1965.

266. KNOX, ISRAEL. *Rabbi in America: The Story of Isaac M. Wise.* Boston: Little, Brown and Company, 1957.

A concise account of the life, thought, and influence of the founder of Reform Judaism in the United States. "It was his conviction that Judaism as monotheism—both ethical and rational—would before long, indeed, by the beginning of the twentieth century, become the universal religion of mankind" (p. 160). A helpful essay on sources.

267. KOHLER, MAX J. *Rebecca Franks: An American Jewish Belle of the Last Century.* New York: Philip Cowen, 1894.

A biographical sketch of "a descendant of a very influential and prominent American Jewish family" who lived during the Revolutionary era, but who was, at most, a marginal Jew.

268. KORN, BERTRAM W. *Benjamin Levy: New Orleans Printer and Publisher, with a Bibliography of Benjamin Levy Imprints, 1817-1841.* Portland, Maine: Anthoensen Press, 1961.

A brief, documented biography, lists of imprints, illustrations, and facsimiles.

269. LANDAU, DAVID. *Kissinger: The Uses of Power.* Boston: Houghton Mifflin Company, 1972.

A critical study of the ideas on foreign policy and international activity of Dr. Kissinger, "a man who fled from Hitler Germany as a Jewish refugee, a victim of the greatest ideological holocaust of all time" (p. 7). Documentation and bibliography.

270. LESSER, ALLEN. *Weave a Wreath of Laurel: The Lives of Four Jewish Contributors to American Civilization.* New York: Coven Press, 1938.

Popular biographical sketches of Francis Salvador, Adah Isaacs Menken, Aaron Lopez, and Emma Lazarus. Illustrations and selected references.

271. LEVIN, ALEXANDRA L. *The Szolds of Lombard Street: A Baltimore Family, 1859-1909.* Philadelphia: Jewish Publication Society of America, 1960.

A biography of the family that produced Henrietta Szold and Marcus and Joseph Jastrow. Genealogical table, biographical appendix, bibliography, and illustrations.

272. LEVIN, ALEXANDRA L. *Vision: A Biography of Friedenwald.* Philadelphia: Jewish Publication Society of America, 1964.

A detailed, documented life of Harry Friedenwald, a prominent physician and historian of medicine who was very active in Zionist and Jewish communal affairs.

273. LEVITAN, TINA. *Jews in American Life.* New York: Hebrew Publishing Co., 1969.

Illustrated biographical sketches of American Jewish
educators, merchants, craftsmen, rabbis, soldiers,
philanthropists, writers, artists, statesmen, scientists,
and other prominent figures from colonial times to
the present.

274. LEVITAN, TINA. *The Firsts of American Jewish History*. Brooklyn, N.Y.: Charuth Press, 1957.

The second edition of a collection of concise historical sketches of events, persons, institutions, and
things constituting "firsts" in all aspects of the Jewish
experience in the United States from colonial times
to the mid-twentieth century. Illustrations and a useful bibliography.

275. LITMAN, SIMON. *Ray Frank Litman: A Memoir*. New
York: American Jewish Historical Society, 1957.

The life, activities, ideas, and writings of the first
woman student (ca.1864-1948) of Isaac Mayer Wise,
("Maiden in the Temple," "Later-Day Deborah") and
a journalist active in Jewish causes. This de facto
woman rabbi gave up her career in favor of being the
"helpmate" of her husband, a professor at the University of Illinois, and author of this biography. Mrs.
Litman became an adviser to Jewish students and an
active community worker. Documentary extracts and
photographs.

276. LONDON, HANNAH R. *Miniatures of Early American
Jews*. Springfield, Mass.: Pond-Ekberg Co., 1953.

A biographical essay of eighteenth- and nineteenth-
century Jews followed by reproductions of their miniature portraits. Supplementary listing of miniatures
and bibliography.

277. LONDON, HANNAH R. *Portraits of Jews by Gilbert Stuart and Other Early American Artists*. New York: William Edwin Rudge, 1927.

Reproductions of portraits with an explanatory text. A list of additional portraits and a short bibliography.

278. LONDON, HANNAH R. *Shades of My Forefathers*. Springfield, Mass.: Pond-Ekberg Co., 1941.

Reproductions of profiles and silhouettes of Americans of the eighteenth and nineteenth centuries. Interpretive essays and selected references.

279. LOTZ, PHILIP H., ed. *Distinguished American Jews*. New York: Association Press, 1945.

Biographical sketches of twelve American Jews in various fields—Adolph S. Ochs, Yehudi Menuhin, Felix Adler, Lillian Wald, Charney Vladeck, Stephen S. Wise, Charles P. Steinmetz, Fannie Hurst, Paul Muni, Joseph Goldberger, Carl Laemmle, Louis D. Brandeis. Suggested readings.

280. LOWENTHAL, MARVIN. *Henrietta Szold: Life and Letters*. New York: Viking Press, 1942.

A biographical portrait of an outstanding Jewish leader of the American Zionist movement. Many letters in the text.

281. LOZOWICK, LOUIS. *One Hundred Contemporary American Jewish Painters and Sculptors*. New York: Art Section, YKUF, 1947.

Biographical sketches of, and statements by, American Jewish artists. Illustrations.

282. LYONS, EUGENE. *David Sarnoff: A Biography.* New York: Harper & Row, 1966.

A popular, detailed, illustrated life of a Russian-born Jew who made outstanding contributions to the development of radio, motion pictures, and television in the United States, and who maintained an active identification with Judaism.

283. MADISON, CHARLES A. *Eminent American Jews: 1776 to the Present.* New York: Frederick Ungar, 1970.

Brief, but enlightening, biographical essays on Haym Salomon, Mordecai Manuel Noah, Jacob H. Schiff, Oscar S. Straus, Felix Adler, Stephen S. Wise, Judah Philip Benjamin, Louis D. Brandeis, Adolph S. Ochs, Julius Rosenwald, Abraham Flexner, Herbert H. Lehman, Felix Frankfurter, Sidney Hillman, and J. Robert Oppenheimer, all of whom made a lasting impact in politics, economics, education, law, journalism, labor, and science. Illustrations and bibliography. No footnotes.

284. MAKOVER, A. B. *Mordecai M. Noah: His Life and Work from the Jewish Standpoint.* New York: Bloch Publishing Co., 1917.

A brief account of the life and work of the nineteenth-century personality who sought to establish a city of refuge for the Jews of the world ("Ararat") on Grand Island, N.Y., near Buffalo.

285. MAKOVSKY, DONALD I. *The Philipsons: The First Jewish Settlers in St. Louis, 1807-1858.* St. Louis, Mo.: Judaism Sesquicentennial Committee of St. Louis, 1958.

A brief account of the first Jewish family in St. Louis. Documentation and facsimiles.

286. MASON, ALPHEUS T. *Brandeis: A Free Man's Life.* New York: Viking Press, 1946.

A thoroughgoing, fully documented, illustrated biography of the associate justice of the United States Supreme Court, including his activities in behalf of justice to the Jews.

287. MAY, MAX B. *Isaac Mayer Wise: The Founder of American Judaism.* New York: G. P. Putnam, 1916.

A biography of the founder of American Reform Judaism. Notes, illustrations, and a bibliography of Rabbi Wise's writings by Adolph S. Oko.

288. MEADE, ROBERT D. *Judah P. Benjamin, Confederate Statesman.* New York: Oxford University Press, 1943.

A detailed, competently documented biography of a Sephardic Jew who served as a lawyer, United States senator from Louisiana, and secretary of state and of war and attorney-general of the Confederacy. Illustrations and bibliography.

289. MENDELSON, WALLACE, ed. *Felix Frankfurter: A Tribute.* New York: Reynal & Co., 1964.

Documented statements by American and foreign scholars, statesmen, lawyers, and others on the significance of the work of United States Supreme Court Associate Justice Frankfurter for humanity, society, and law. Rare references to his Jewish activities ("he was a stouthearted Zionist"—Sir Isaiah Berlin).

290. MERRIAM, EVE. *Emma Lazarus: Woman with a Torch.* New York: Citadel Press, 1956.

A popular biography of the noted American Jewish poet. The text includes several poems.

291. MOISE, L. C. *"Biography of Isaac Harby, with an Account of the Reformed Society of Israelites of Charleston, S.C., 1824-1833."* Master's thesis, University of South Carolina, [1931].

A short life of a journalist and dramatist who was "the gifted moral leader of his people" and "the soul of the first great reform effected in America" (p. 45). Documents, facsimiles, and selected references.

292. MONSKY, MRS. HENRY, and MAURICE BISGYER. *Henry Monsky: The Man and His Work.* New York: Crown Publishers, 1947.

A popular, illustrated biography of a leader of B'nai B'rith who raised his voice repeatedly "in moral indignation against the heavy injustices visited upon his people by a callous world" (p. x).

293. MORAIS, HENRY S. *Eminent Israelites of the Nineteenth Century: A Series of Biographical Sketches.* Philadelphia: Stern, 1880.

One hundred short biographies of Jewish spiritual and cultural leaders in Europe and the United States.

294. OSHEROWITCH, M. *Dovid Kessler und Muni Weisenfriend: Tsvei Doiros Yiddish Teater.* New York: n.p., 1930.

A comparison by a noted Yiddish writer of two leading actors of the Yiddish stage. The younger star, Weisenfriend, became known as Paul Muni on the screen.

295. OSTERWEIS, ROLLIN G. *Rebecca Gratz: A Study in Charm.* New York: G. P. Putnam, 1935.

An illustrated, popular biography of a leader of early nineteenth-century Jewry in Philadelphia and a founder of the Hebrew Sunday School. The bibliographical note includes references to primary sources.

296. PARZEN, HERBERT. *Architects of Conservative Judaism.* New York: Jonathan David, 1964.

A documented account of the development of the Conservative movement in American Judaism, mainly in terms of the lives and activities of outstanding scholars and spiritual leaders—Solomon Schechter, Cyrus Adler, Louis Ginzberg, Issac Friedlaender, and Moredecai M. Kaplan.

297. PERLMUTTER, SHOLEM. *Yiddishe dramaturgn un teater-kompozitors.* New York: Yiddisher Kultur Farband (YKUF), 1952.

Biographies in Yiddish of Yiddish dramatists in Eastern Europe and in the United States, and of composers for the Yiddish theater.

298. POOL, DAVID DE SOLA. *Portraits Etched in Stone: Early Jewish Settlers, 1682-1831.* New York: Columbia University Press, 1952.

A study of early Jewish cemeteries in New York City, together with biographies of prominent and lesser-known persons. Documents in text, glossary, bibliography, and indexes.

299. RAISIN, MORDECHAI A. *Yisrael b'Amerikah.* Jerusalem: Achiever, 1928.

Essays in Hebrew of Jewish leaders and life in the Unites States, past and contemporary with the author.

300. RIBALOW, HAROLD U. *The Jew in American Sports.* New York: Bloch Publishing Co., 1966.

Revised edition of a collection of illustrated biographies of Jewish stars, past and recent, in baseball, boxing, football, tennis, basketball, golf, and chess.

301. ROGOFF, HARRY. *An East Side Epic: The Life and Work of Meyer London.* New York: Vanguard Press, 1930.

A popular biography of a Jewish member of the United States Congress, who represented the Lower East Side of New York City earlier in the century.

302. ROGOFF, HILLEL. *Meyer London: A biografie.* New York: Meyer London Memorial Fund, 1930.

Life of a Jewish Socialist congressman written in Yiddish. Illustrations.

303. ROGOW, SALLY. *Lillian Wald: The Nurse in Blue.* Philadelphia: Jewish Publication Society of America, 1966.

An illustrated account, for young people, of the life

and social work of Lillian Wald in the Lower East Side of New York City. Selected references.

304. ROSENBLATT, SAMUEL. *Yossele Rosenblatt: The Story of His Life as Told by His Son.* New York: Farrar, Straus and Young, 1954.

A popular biography of a Russian-born American cantor of worldwide reputation for his singing and piety. Glossary of Hebrew and Yiddish terms.

305. ROSENBLOOM, JOSEPH R. *A Biographical Dictionary of Early American Jews: Colonial Times through 1800.* [Lexington:] University of Kentucky Press, 1960.

Brief identifications with bibliographical references.

306. ROSENSTOCK, MORTON. *Louis Marshall, Defender of Jewish Rights.* Detroit, Mich.: Wayne State University Press, 1965.

A well-documented biography of a leading American Jewish lawyer's activities against anti-Semitism. Bibliography.

307. ROSS, B. JOYCE. *J. E. Spingarn and the Rise of the NACCP, 1911-1939.* New York: Atheneum Publishers, 1972.

A scholarly work stressing the role of Joel Elias Spingarn, "of Jewish lineage," to the growth and development of the National Association for the Advancement of Colored People.

308. RUSSELL, CHARLES E. *Haym Salomon and the Revolution.* New York: Cosmopolitan Book Corp., 1930.

A documented biography of the Polish-Jewish immigrant, which includes considerable detail on his contribution to the American Revolution. Texts of documents and illustrations.

309. SIMONHOFF, HARRY. *Jewish Notables in America,
1776-1865: Links of an Endless Chain.* New York:
Greenberg, 1956.

Illustrated biographical accounts of many Jews who
became prominent in a variety of fields from the Revolutionary to the Civil War. This compilation includes
personalities who are not usually included in biographical works, e.g., Lorenzo da Ponte—librettist of
Mozart's Italian operas, instructer of Italian at Columbia University, and a convert to Christianity—and
Warder Cresson—author, agriculturist, first United
States consul to Palestine, and a convert from Christianity. Glossary and bibliography.

310. SIMONHOFF, HARRY. *Saga of American Jewry,
1865-1914: Links of an Endless Chain.* New York:
Arco Publishing Co., 1959.

Illustrated, biographical essays on prominent Jews in
all branches of activity, from the Civil War to World
War I. Glossary and selected references.

311. SIMONS, JOHN, ed. *Who's Who in American Jewry: A
Biographical Dictionary of Living Jews of the United
States and Canada.* New York: National News Associ-
ation, 1938.

The third edition of this compilation contains 8,477
biographies and 400 photographs of rabbis, government and military officials, social and communal lead-

ers, educators, industrialists, businessmen, scientists, and persons active in the arts. Geographical index.

312. Entry cancelled.

313. STERN, MALCOLM H., comp. *Americans of Jewish Descent: A Compendium of Genealogy.* New York: KTAV Publishing House, 1971.

A unique compendium of genealogical tables, with indication of sources, of Jewish families that had established themselves in North America by 1840. In several instances, descent is traced from the Middle Ages. The compiler points out that, prior to 1840, Sephardic and Ashkenazic Jews intermarried, that over 15 percent of the marriages involved Jews and Christians, and that about 8 percent resulted in the conversion of the non-Jew. Bibliography and thorough index. A valuable resource for research.

314. *The Israel Honorarium.* 5 vols. Jerusalem: Israel Publishing Institute, and New York: B. M. Educational Publishing Institute, 1968.

A collection of illustrated biographical sketches of persons (from Abraham David Ben Gurion), who contributed greatly to Jewish history, especially to the development of Israel; brief biographies of notable Jews in American history; an annotated list of Jewish organizations in the United States; and general historical essays. Volumes 2-5 contain an alphabetically arranged, illustrated who's who of contemporary Jews, mostly Americans, active in various aspects of life, education, science, business, society, etc.

315. THOMAS, HELEN S. *Felix Frankfurter: Scholar on the Bench.* Baltimore, Md.: Johns Hopkins Press, 1960.

A fully documented monograph on the judicial contributions by the Vienna-born son of a rabbi who
distinguished himself as a professor at the Harvard
Law School and as associate justice of the United
States Supreme Court.

316. TRUAX, RHODA. *The Doctors Jacobi.* Boston: Little,
Brown and Company, 1952.

A popular biography of Dr. Mary Corrina (Minnie)
Putnam and her husband, Dr. Abraham Jacobi, a
Prussian-born Jewish immigrant—two important pedi-
atricians of the late nineteenth and early twentieth
centuries. The Jewish references in the volume are
occasional and incidental. Explanatory notes.

317. UROFSKY, MELVIN I. *A Mind of One Piece: Brandeis
and American Reform.* New York: Charles Scribner's
Sons, 1971.

A well-documented analysis of the thought and activity of the outstanding lawyer and associate justice of
the United States Supreme Court who was a partici-
pant in Zionist and other Jewish affairs.

318. VORSPAN, ALBERT. *Giants of Justice.* New York:
Union of American Hebrew Congregations, 1960.

Biographical essays on fourteen American Jewish personalities—rabbis, philanthropists, social workers, labor leaders, and others.

319. WEINSTEIN, JACOB J. *Solomon Goldman: A Rabbi's
Rabbi.* New York: KTAV Publishing House, 1973.

A sympathetic biography of a Conservative rabbi and

Biblical scholar who made great contributions to education, preaching, literature, and Zionism.

320. WERNER, M. R. *Julius Rosenwald: The Life of a Practical Humanitarian.* New York: Harper, 1939.

A biography of a Reform Jew who made notable contributions to philanthropic causes involving Jews and Christians, Blacks and whites. Bibliography.

321. WHITEMAN, MAXWELL. *Copper for America: The Hendricks Family and a National Industry, 1755-1939.* New Brunswick, N.J.: Rutgers University Press, 1971.

A scholarly history of a prominent family of merchants and industrialists who played a significant part in the nation's economy and who made notable contributions to traditional Judaism in America. Documents, facsimiles, and illustrations.

322. *Who's Who in American Jewry: 1926.* New York: Jewish Biographical Bureau, 1927.

Biographical data on "those Jews in American life who have, in some way or another, made important contributions to the life and thought of contemporary America."

323. *Who's Who in American Jewry: 1928.* New York: Jewish Biographical Bureau, 1928.

The second, revised edition lists "contemporary Jewish contributions to America's literature, drama, music, art, science and public service," as well as Jewish communal, religious, educational, and philanthropic fields of activity and service.

324. WISE, JAMES W. *Jews Are Like That!* Freeport, N.Y.:
Books and Libraries Press, 1969.

A reprint of brief biographies of nine leading American Jewish figures, including Louis Lipsky, Ludwig
Lewisohn, and Aaron Sapiro. Illustrations.

VII. SOCIAL AND COMMUNAL LIFE AND ACTIVITY

VII. SOCIAL AND COMMUNAL LIFE AND ACTIVITY

325. ADLER, CYRUS. *Lectures, Selected Papers, Addresses.* Philadelphia: Privately printed, 1933.

Most of the essays are concerned with the personalities and intellectual developments of the Jewish community in the United States.

326. ALT, HERSCHEL. *Forging Tools for Mental Health: Highlights in the Work of the Jewish Board of Guardians, 1944-1954.* New York: Jewish Board of Guardians, 1955.

A survey of the guidance, protective, preventive research, and other services performed for Jewish delinquents and other troubled children and adolescents. Bibliography and informative appendix.

327. BERNARD, JACQUELINE. *The Children You Gave Us: A History of 150 Years of Service to Children.* New York: Jewish Child Care Association of New York, 1973.

A popular, illustrated account of the origins and development of the Jewish orphanages and other agencies that took care of "the orphaned, the destitute, the neglected" in the Jewish community of New York City. Well-organized bibliography.

328. BIGMAN, STANLEY K. *The Jewish Population of Greater Washington in 1956: Report of an Interview Survey of Size, Social Characteristics, Residential Mobility, Community Participation, and Observance of Some Traditional Jewish Practices.* Washington, D.C.: The Jewish Community Council of Greater Washington, 1957.

Statistical tables and concise interpretations of a variety of data, including religious membership, Jewish education, and intermarriage. Indexed. Mimeographed, but disseminated to libraries.

329. BOGEN, BORIS D. *Jewish Philanthropy: An Exposition of Principles and Methods of Jewish Social Service in the United States.* New York: Macmillan, 1917.

A presentation of charitable procedures with some historical background. Study questions and bibliography.

330. BRAV, STANLEY R. *Jewish Family Solidarity: Myth or Fact?* Vicksburg, Miss.: Nogales Press, 1940.

A questionnaire study with pertinent statistics on a small Jewish community (Vicksburg) in relation to a phase of the sociology of Jewish life in America. The author's conclusion is that the study "gives definite credence to the popular assumption of strength in Jewish family solidarity," but that strength is "more relative than is real" (p. 68).

331. CAMPBELL, MONROE, JR., and WILLIAM WIRTZ.

The First Fifty Years: A History of the National Council of Jewish Women, 1893-1943. New York, 1943.

An historical account of the genesis and development of an organization offering social and educational services to the Jewish community.

332. COHEN, MORRIS R. *Reflections of a Wondering Jew.* Boston: Beacon Press, 1950.

Essays and book reviews by the influential philosopher of Jewish problems and issues, both in general and in the United States.

333. *Di Yiddishe landsmanshaftn fun New York.* New York: I. L. Peretz Yiddish Writers' Union, 1938.

Essays in Yiddish on the Jewish associations of fellow townsmen in the old country, directories of various organizations, bibliography, poems about many Eastern European cities, and illustrations.

334. DOROSHKIN, MILTON. *Yiddish in America: Social and Cultural Foundations.* Rutherford, N.J.: Fairleigh Dickinson University Press, 1969.

A documented study of the role of the Yiddish language in the development of the Jewish community and culture in the United States. Education, inexplicably, is omitted. Statistical and documentary appendix. Extensive bibliography in English and Yiddish.

335. EDIDIN, BEN M. *Jewish Community Life in America.* New York: Hebrew Publishing Co., 1947.

An introduction to the organization of the Jewish

community center, school, synagogue, and other institutions, with special reference to their activities in
the community, the nation, and in other countries
(including Palestine). Bibliography.

336. *Fifty Years of Social Service: The History of the Unit-
ed States Hebrew Charities of the City of New York,
Now the Jewish Social Service Association, Inc.* New
York, 1926.

An historical account of the development of economic aid to Russian Jewish immigrants, particularly
since 1881.

337. FISHMAN, PRISCILLA, ed. *The Jews of the United
States.* New York: Quadrangle/The New York Times
Book Co., 1973.

An informative, up-to-date survey of the historical
background and various contemporary aspects of the
American Jewish community, including relations with
world Jewry and several current concerns and issues.
This volume "is based on comprehensive research . . . conducted by a staff of scholars in various
areas of specialization." These scholars are not identified. Illustrations and bibliography.

338. FRANK, WALDO. *The Jew in Our Day.* New York:
Duell, Sloan and Pearce, 1944.

Thoughts by an American Jewish man of letters on
the situation and problems of the Jew in various parts
of the world, including America. The introduction by
Reinhold Niebuhr supports Frank's view that "the
fact that the Jew has survived over many centuries is
undoubtedly an achievement of the religious quality
of the Jewish culture" and that "the Jew distin-

guishes himself primarily by this religious overtone of his culture" (p. 7).

339. FREID, JACOB, ed. *Jews in the Modern World*. 2 vols. New York: Twayne Publishers, 1962.

A compilation of twenty-eight essays on Jewish life, problems, culture, society, and philosophy in various parts of the world. About half of the contents deal with American Jewry.

340. FREID, JACOB, ed. *Judaism and the Community: New Directions in Jewish Social Work*. New York: Thomas Yoseloff, 1968.

A collection of twenty brief essays on the relations of Judaism to communal and social welfare, inter-marriage and philanthropy. A symposium on the significance of Judaism to mental health is also included.

341. FRIEDLAENDER, ISRAEL. *Past and Present: A Collection of Jewish Essays*. Cincinnati, Ohio: Ark Publishing Co., 1919.

This volume includes essays on the culture and problems of the Jewish community in the United States.

342. FRIEDMAN, THEODORE, and ROBERT GORDIS, eds. *Jewish Life in America*. New York: Horizon Press, 1955.

Eighteen essays by rabbis and other specialists on the contemporary status of the American Jewish religion, culture, education, scholarship, labor, and communal relations with reference to the past.

343. GALE, JOSEPH, ed. *Eastern Union: The Development of a Jewish Community.* Elizabeth, N.J.: Jewish Culture Council of Eastern Union County, 1958.

An historical overview of the Jewish settlement, organization, and activities of Jewish communities in Elizabeth, Rahway, and other cities in the Eastern part of Union County, N.J.

344. GINZBERG, ELI. *Agenda for American Jews.* New York: King's Crown Press, 1950.

An economist's assessment of the potential contributions of the social sciences toward "the effective solution of the complex problems that confront American Jews" (p. v) in the areas of community, religion, education, welfare, the Gentile world, Israel.

345. GINZBERG, ELI. *Report to American Jews on Overseas Relief, Palestine and Refugees in the United States.* New York: Harper, 1942.

A report, with statistical tables, of the fund-raising activities of the United Jewish Appeal and of its constituent organizations—the Joint Distribution Committee, the United Palestine Appeal, and the National Refugee Service.

346. GLAZER, NATHAN, JOSEPH L. BLAU, HERMAN D. STEIN, and OSCAR and MARY F. HANDLIN. *The Characteristics of American Jews.* New York: Jewish Education Committee Press, 1965.

Scholarly studies of American Jewish society, religion, social work, and sociopolitical rights from an historical perspective. Reprint of a section of *The Jews: Their History, Culture, and Religion,* Vol. 2

(New York: Harper, 1960), edited by Louis Finkelstein.

347. GOLDBERG, S. P. *The American Jewish Community:
Its Structure, Role & Organizations.* New York: Women's American ORT, 1968.

An introduction to religious, educational, cultural,
welfare, and other organizations in American Jewish
life.

348. GOLDEN, HARRY. *Our Southern Landsman.* New
York: G. P. Putnam's Sons, 1974.

The editor of the *Carolina Israelite* (Charlotte, N.C.)
writes interestingly of the life, characteristics, activities, and intergroup relations of Southern Jews, past
and present.

349. GOLDEN, HARRY, and RICHARD GOLDHURST.
Travels through Jewish America. Garden City, N.Y.:
Doubleday, 1973.

Journalistic descriptions of Jewish life in ten American cities.

350. GOLDSTEIN, SIDNEY, and CALVIN GOLDSCHEID-
ER. *Jewish Americans: Three Generations in a Jewish
Community.* Englewood Cliffs, N.J.: Prentice-Hall,
1968.

A sociological study of generation change in the Jewish community of greater Providence, Rhode Island,
with special reference to intermarriage, culture, and
religion. The authors infer that "in three generations
Jews have become integrated into the general com-

munity" (p. 243). Statistical appendix and brief bibliography.

351. GORDON, ALBERT I. *Jews in Suburbia.* Boston: Beacon Press, 1959.

A rabbi-anthropologist's informative analysis of Jewish life in eighty-nine urban communities in ten states from New York to California.

352. GORDON, ALBERT I. *Jews in Transition.* Minneapolis: University of Minnesota Press, 1949.

An occasionally subjective study of religious, communal, social, and cultural change in a midwestern Jewish community with reference to the historical background. Bibliographical notes, list of name changes, and glossary.

353. HENDRICK, BURTON J. *The Jews in America.* Garden City, N.Y.: Doubleday, Page, 1923.

A not always felicitously phrased interpretation of Sephardic and German Jewish contributions to American life and business. While trying to be objective, the author concluded that "there is only one way in which the United States can be protected from the anti-Semitism which so grievously afflicts the eastern sections of Europe. That is by putting up bars against these immigrants until the day comes when those already here are absorbed" (p. 171).

354. HERTZ, J. S. *Fuftsig yor Arbete Ring in Yiddishn lebn.* New York: National Executive Committee, Workmen's Circle, 1950.

A survey of a half-century (1900-1950) of the social,

welfare, educational, and political activities carried on the Jewish community by the Socialistic Workmen's Circle. Photographs, facsimiles, list of officials, and selected references in Yiddish and English.

355. HIRSH, JOSEPH, ed. *The Hadassah Medical Organization: An American Contribution to Medical Pioneering and Progress in Israel.* New York: Hadassah, the Women's Zionist Organization of America, 1956.

A record of American Jewish women's activity in behalf of public health and medical and nursing education in Palestine and Israel. Chronology.

356. HIRSH, JOSEPH, and BEKA DOHERTY. *The First Hundred Years of the Mount Sinai Hospital of New York, 1852-1952.* New York: Random House, 1952.

A detailed centennial account of a hospital founded and supported by Jews in New York City.

357. HURWITZ, SAMUEL J., and MOSES RISCHIN, eds. *A Liberal in Two Worlds: The Essays of Solomon F. Bloom.* Washington: Public Affairs Press, 1968.

Reprint of nineteen general essays by Dr. Bloom (1903-1962), a journalist and professor of history at Brooklyn College. Born in Rumania, the author throws light on Jewish life in Europe and America.

358. JANOWSKY, OSCAR I. *The JWB Survey.* New York: Dial Press, 1948.

A comprehensive report on the history, aims, functions, and program of the National Jewish Welfare Board. The "most important conclusion" of this document, based on questionnaires, interviews, and field visits, is that "the Jewish center should have a Jewish purpose—that it should be an agency with which the Jew might identify himself in order to satisfy his specialized Jewish needs." The logical inference is that "the program of the Jewish center should devote primary attention to Jewish content, without, of course, excluding or ignoring the general activities which are essential to a well-rounded center program" (p. xxiii).

359. JANOWSKY, OSCAR I., ed. *The American Jew: A Composite Portrait.* New York: Harper, 1942.

A dozen essays by academic and religious scholars, including one non-Jew, on the history, religion, education, culture, communal structure, economic activity, and ideologies of the Jews of America. A reliable picture of Jewish life around 1940. Annotated bibliography.

360. JANOWSKY, OSCAR I., ed. *The American Jew: A Reappraisal.* Philadelphia: Jewish Publication Society of America, 1964.

Essays by specialists on the history, society, economy, religion, education, culture, communal services, intergroup and international relations, and problems of the Jewish people in the United States. Documentary and bibliographical notes. Although outdated in various respects, this volume is still a significant source of knowledge about America's Jews.

361. *Jewish Communal Survey of Greater New York: Report of Executive Committee.* New York: Bureau of Jewish Social Research, 1929.

A factual and statistical report on the status of Jews

in relation to welfare, health, education, philanthropy, and other communal areas of activity.

362. KAHN, ROGER. *The Passionate People: What It Means to Be a Jew in America.* New York: William Morrow & Co., 1968.

A journalist's portraits of contemporary Jewish society and religion in the United States.

363. KALLEN, HORACE M. *Of Them Which Say They Are Jews: And Other Essays on the Jewish Struggle for Survival.* New York: Bloch Publishing Co., 1954.

Essays by a noted thinker on the status of American Jewish communal and educational organization and activities.

364. KAPLAN, BENJAMIN. *The Eternal Stranger: A Study of Jewish Life in a Small Community.* New York: Bookman Associates, 1957.

A sociological analysis of the impact of the small-town environment on Jewish communal, social, economic, and religious life in three Louisiana communities. Documentation, lists of persons and organizations, and bibliography.

365. KAPLAN, BENJAMIN. *The Jew and His Family.* Baton Rouge: Louisiana State University Press, 1967.

A professor of sociology's appreciation of the significance of the Jewish family in history and in contemporary America. The author concludes that "in the case of the Jewish family, a religiously motivated home can bring a sense of belonging to its members, its group, and its faith . . . [and] can strengthen the

ethnic foundations of the Jewish community. . . ."
(p. 189). Selected references.

366. KARPF, MAURICE J. *Jewish Community Organization in the United States: An Outline of Types of Organizations, Activities, and Problems.* New York: Bloch Publishing Co., 1938.

Descriptions and analyses of American Jewish communal and central organizations in religion, education, defense, health, and welfare serving the Jews in the United States and other countries. Documentation and bibliography.

367. KERTZER, MORRIS N. *Today's American Jew.* New York: McGraw-Hill, 1967.

A popular portrayal of American Jewish personalities, perceptions, and problems.

368. KIELL, NORMAN, ed. *The Psychodynamics of American Jewish Life: An Anthology.* New York: Twayne Publishers, 1967.

An unusual compilation of essays by psychologists, sociologists, psychoanalysts, and psychiatrists on American Jewish family dynamics, personality problems, child and youth identification, and rituals.

369. KIRSHENBOIM, YAKOW. *Amerike--Dos Land fun vunder: Reportazhen.* Warsaw: Brzoza, 1939.

A Polish Jew's impressions, written in Yiddish, of America, especially of Jewish life in the East.

370. KOPELYOV, Y. *Amol un shpeter: Di letzte yorn fun vorikn yorhundert biz di zvantzikste yorn fun*

haintikn yorhundert in Amerike. Wilno: Farlag "Altnai," 1932.

Reminiscences and reports in Yiddish of various aspects of American Jewish life and problems from the late nineteenth century to the 1920s.

371. KRAFT, LOUIS. *A Century of the Jewish Community Center Movement (1854-1954): With Biographical Sketches of the National Leaders.* New York: Jewish Community Center Centennial Committee, 1953.

Historical overview of the development of the Young Men's Hebrew Association and the Jewish Community Center.

372. KRAFT, LOUIS, and CHARLES S. BERNHEIMER, eds. *Aspects of the Jewish Community Center.* New York: National Jewish Welfare Board, 1954.

Essays by specialists on the Jewish Community Center movement and its various activities.

373. KRAMER, JUDITH R., and SEYMOUR LEVENTMAN. *Children of the Gilded Ghetto: Conflict Resolutions of Three Generations of American Jews.* New Haven, Conn.: Yale University Press, 1961.

A sociological analysis of Jewish life, communal organization, and problems in a midwestern community ("North City"). Interesting contrast of "lodgniks" and "clubniks." Bibliography.

374. KRANZLER, GEORGE. *The Face of Faith: An American Hassidic Community.* Baltimore, Md.: Baltimore Hebrew College Press, 1972.

An original, richly illustrated photographic collection, with accompanying text, presenting a clear conception of life, education, religion, and society among the Hasidic groups in the Williamsburg section of Brooklyn. Glossary.

375. KRANZLER, GEORGE. *Williamsburg: A Jewish Community in Transition.* New York: Philip Feldheim, 1961.

A sociological analysis of the Hasidic community with case studies, a glossary, illustration, and a bibliography.

376. LEVITAN, TINA. *Islands of Compassion: A History of the Jewish Hospitals of New York.* New York: Twayne Publishers, 1964.

An illustrated survey of the thirteen Jewish hospitals from the time of the Jews' Hospital (1852), now Mount Sinai Hospital, to the 1960s. Extensive bibliography.

377. LEWISOHN, LUDWIG. *The American Jew: Character and Destiny.* New York: Farrar, Straus, 1950.

Reflections and opinions by a novelist and literary critic on American Jewish life, with a plea for "Jewish faith and form."

378. LINFIELD, HARRY S. *The Communal Organization of the Jews in the United States, 1927.* New York: American Jewish Committee, 1930.

An analysis of the scope and work of Jewish communal, religious, educational, cultural, philanthropic, and other organizations. Abundant statistical data ob-

tained with the cooperation of the Jewish organizations and the United States Bureau of the Census. A
useful source for the 1920s. Some of the interpretations of the educational scene are narrow and subjective.

379. LINFIELD, HARRY S. *The Jews in the United States,
1927: A Study of Their Numbers and Distribution.*
New York: American Jewish Committee, 1929.

Statistical data in tabular form on Jews in urban and
rural settlements. A helpful source for historical and
sociological analysis.

380. LIPTZIN, SOL. *Generation of Decision: Jewish Rejuve-
nation in America.* New York: Bloch Publishing Co.,
1958.

Essays by a scholar in comparative literature on "the
impact of the Jew upon the American mind and the
repercussions of that impact on the Jew" (p. 1.).
Liptzin discusses the history, culture, society, and
problems of the American Jew. He concludes that.
"neither optimism nor pessimism with regard to ultimate survival of Jewishness in America beyond the
purely religious sphere is as yet justified" (p. 299),
but he sees the possibility of a "Golden Age of
Jewishness" in America and Israel.

381. LURIE, HARRY L. *A Heritage Affirmed: The Jewish
Federation Movement in America.* Philadelphia: Jewish Publication Society of America, 1961.

A documented study of communal welfare organization and its impact on American Jewish life from
1895 to 1960. A valuable source of information on
the development of communal responsibility for and

subsidization of various welfare services. "The principle of federation responsibility for Jewish education, however, was not accepted easily" (p. 74). Illustrations and bibliography.

382. MASLOW, WILL. *The Structure and Functioning of the American Jewish Community.* New York: American Jewish Congress, 1974.

A concise, illustrated introduction to the nature and activities of American Jewish organizations.

383. McCALL, SAMUEL W., et al. *For the Honor of the Nation.* New York: Plymouth Editions, 1939.

Non-Jewish statements on Jewish contributions to civilization and to American life and culture.

384. MORRIS, ROBERT, and MICHAEL FREUND, eds. *Trends and Issues in Jewish Social Welfare in the United States, 1899-1952.* Philadelphia: Jewish Publication Society of America, 1966.

Essays by specialists on various aspects of the historical development of charitable and welfare work, especially among Jewish immigrants from Eastern Europe. Special note is taken on the proceedings and reports of the National Conference of Jewish Communal Service. Documentary appendix. A comprehensive, valuable work in its field.

385. PENN, ASCHER. *Yiddish in Amerike in likht fun Medinas Yisroel.* New York: The author, 1948.

The writer bewails the decline of the status of Yiddish in America and urges that the Jewish community encourage its youth to strength Yiddish culture.

386. POLL, SOLOMON. *The Hasidic Community of Williamsburg.* New York: Free Press, 1962.

A socioeconomic analysis of "an ultrareligious group" in Brooklyn. Long glossary and brief bibliography. Documents included in the text.

387. RAWIDOWICZ, SIMON, ed. *The Chicago Pinkas.* Chicago: College of Jewish Studies, 1952.

Scholarly essays in English and Hebrew on Jewish life, demography, and culture in Chicago. Comprehensive bibliography of Hebrew and Yiddish publications issued in Chicago and a listing of references to Chicago in European Jewish periodicals.

388. ROBISON, SOPHIA M., ed. *Jewish Population Studies.* New York: Conference on Jewish Relations, 1943.

Demographic analyses of the Jewish populations of Buffalo, Pittsburgh, Detroit, Chicago, Minneapolis, San Francisco, and other communities during the 1930s.

389. ROSE, PETER I., ed. *The Ghetto and Beyond: Essays on Jewish Life in America.* New York: Random House, 1969.

Essays on the sociology, religion, politics, literature, and intergroup relations of American Jews.

390. ROSENZWEIG, GERSHON. *Talmud Yankai.* New York: Druckerman, 1909.

Parody in Hebrew and Aramaic, in the Talmudic style of exposition and commentary, satirizing American

Jewish life. Of the six "tractates," the longest is "Maseches Amireika."

391. RUBIN, ISRAEL. *Satmar: An Island in the City.* Chicago: Quadrangle Books, 1972.

An analytical study of the structure and changes in a Hasidic community in the Williamsburg district of Brooklyn in New York. Attention is given to religion, the family, education, economic and political activity, and sociological processes.

392. SCHNEIDERMAN, HARRY, ed. *Two Generations in Perspective: Notable Events and Trends, 1896-1956.* New York: Monde Publishers, 1957.

A compilation of essays on aspects of twentieth-century European and American Jewish life, community, religious development, and labor and race relations. Appreciative statements, a biographical sketch, extracts from writings, and an annotated list of the published works of Rabbi Israel Goldstein, a Conservative leader, to whom the volume is dedicated.

393. *Selected Addresses and Papers of Simon Wolf: A Memorial Volume, Together with a Biographical Sketch.* Cincinnati, Ohio: Union of American Hebrew Congregations, 1926.

Statements by a Jewish leader on historical, communal, and other aspects of Jewish life in the United States.

394. SHERMAN, C. BEZALEL. *The Jew within American Society: A Study in Ethnic Individuality.* Detroit, Mich.: Wayne State University Press, 1961.

A documented sociological analysis of Jewish immigration, isolation, assimilation, community life, and upward economic mobility in the United States. Selected references.

395. SHINDELING, ABRAHAM I., and MANUEL PICKUS. *History of the Beckley (West Virginia) Jewish Community and of Congregation Beth El (The Beckley Hebrew Association) (Including Raleigh and Fayette Countries, West Virginia, 1895-1955).* Beckley, W. Va., 1955.

An historical account of a community of some 200 Jews (1955) from the earliest settlement, with special stress on biographical data and on social, economic, and organizational activities.

396. SIDORSKY, DAVID, ed. *The Future of the Jewish Community in America.* New York: Basic Books, 1973.

Essays by Jewish scholars in the social sciences, philosophy, religion, and education on the status and prospects of the American Jewish community.

397. SIMONHOFF, HARRY. *Under Strange Skies.* New York: Philosophical Library, 1953.

Descriptions of Jewish social and communal life in various parts of the South.

398. SKLARE, MARSHALL. *America's Jews.* New York: Random House, 1971.

An insightful sociological analysis of the American Jewish people, their families, communities, education, and relations with Gentiles and Israel. Notes and statistics.

399. SKLARE, MARSHALL, ed. *The Jews: Social Patterns of an Ammerican Group.* Glencoe, Ill.: Free Press, 1958.

Scholarly studies of American Jewish demography, communal organization, religion, identification, and culture.

400. SKLARE, MARSHALL, and JOSEPH GREENBLUM. *Jewish Identity on the Suburban Frontier: A Study of Group Survival in the Open Society.* New York: Basic Books, 1967.

A careful sociological analysis of a suburban Jewish community ("Lakeville")—synagogues and their activities, Jewish home rituals, Jewish voluntary societies, and social relations with fellow Jews. The authors conclude that "the Lakeville Jew remains considerably more Jewish in action than in thought" (p. 329) and that "in spite of the best of intentions . . . only a minority of Lakeville parents have been able to provide their children with substantial materials for developing . . . a pattern of strong Jewish identification" (p. 331).

401. SKLARE, MARSHALL, JOSEPH GREENBLUM, and BENJAMIN B. RINGER. *Not Quite a Home: How an American Jewish Community Lives with Itself and Its Neighbors.* New York: Institute of Human Relations Press, American Jewish Committee, 1969.

A summary of two long sociological analyses ("The Lakeville Studies") of a suburban Jewish community. The authors conclude that the "Lakeville" Jews "illustrate a unique paradox of American society: The very freedom which permits groups to maintain their distinctive cultural traits also permits group identity to be washed out" (p. 85).

402. SNYDER, CHARLES R. *Alcohol and the Jews: A Cultural Study of Drinking and Sobriety.* Glencoe, Ill.: Free Press, 1958.

A research study of New Haven, Connecticut, which concluded that, inasmuch as drinking is associated with religious rituals and ceremonies, "Orthodox Jews clearly demonstrate that virtually every member of a group can be exposed to drinking alcoholic beverages with negligible departure from a norm of sobriety and without the emergence of drinking pathologies such as alcoholism" (p. 202).

403. SOLOMON, BARBARA S. *Pioneers in Service.* Boston: Court Square Press, 1956.

An historical account of the Federated Jewish Charities of Boston in the areas of health, education, and social service.

404. SOLTES, MORDECAI. *The Yiddish Press: An Americanizing Agency.* New York: Ph.D. dissertation, Teachers College, Columbia University, 1924.

An analysis of the content of the editorials of the Yiddish daily newspapers, with a focus on their contribution "toward the civic education" of their immigrant readers. The newspapers "have consciously employed direct means and have endeavored to give their readers an American education, acquainting them with the English language, with American history, geography, and so forth" (p. 178). The author foresaw, on the basis of his reader questionnaire, "the gradual decline of the Yiddish press in this country" (p. 174). Illustrations, translated editorials, and bibliography.

405. STERN, HORACE. *The Spirtual Values of Life: Occasional Addresses on Jewish Themes.* Philadelphia: Jewish Publication Society of America, 1953.

Speeches by the chief justice of the Supreme Court of Pennsylvania on Jewish religion and culture, philanthropy and social service, and Palestine, plus memorial appreciations of Louis Marshall, Cyrus Adler, and other prominent American Jews.

406. STROBER, GERALD S. *American Jews: Community in Crisis.* Garden City, N.Y.: Doubleday, 1974.

A critical assessment of contemporary Jewish communal life and leadership, intergroup relations, and social problems in the United States.

407. SULMAN, ESTHER, and LEONARD J. GOLDSTEIN. *A Goodly Heritage: The Story of the Jewish Community of New London, 1860-1955.* New London, Conn.: n.p., 1957.

An historical account, with some documentation, of the religious, social, communal, and educational activities of New London Jewry.

408. *The Future of the Jewish Community in America: A Task Force Report.* New York: American Jewish Committee, 1972.

A statement by Jewish scholars and communal leaders that seeks to interpret the possible outcomes of the current demographic, sociological, psychological, educational, cultural, and religious status and problems.

409. *The Jewish Communal Register of New York City, 1917-1918.* 2d ed. New York: Kehillah (Jewish Community) of New York City, [1918].

An encyclopedic work of historic significance containing the history and activities of the Kehillah; statistical data; information on Jewish communal, religious, educational, recreational, cultural, economic, mutual aid, philanthropic, research, and other agencies; central and national religious, educational, *Landsmanschaft* (immigrant hometown societies), Zionist, international, and other organizations. The bibliography mainly in English, also includes titles in Hebrew, Yiddish, German, and Russian. Many photographs. Fully indexed.

410. UCHILL, IDA L. *Pioneers, Peddlers, and Tzadikim.* Denver, Colo.: Sage Books, 1957.

A comprehensive account, with some documentation, of the social, communal, religious, and economic development of the Jewish community of Denver.

411. VAN DEN HAAG, ERNEST. *The Jewish Mystique.* New York: Stein and Day, 1969.

An attempt to explain the thoughts, attitudes, and behaviors of American and other Jews.

412. WALDMAN, MORRIS D. *Not by Power.* New York: International Universities Press, 1953.

This volume contains "neither history nor autobiography yet a little of both in an impressionistic picture of the broader issues in American Jewish life and their relation to the community at large" (p. vii). The content covers Nazism, Palestine, and the social, communal, cultural, and economic life of Jews in the United States.

413. WIRTH, LOUIS. *The Ghetto.* Chicago: University of Chicago Press, 1928.

A sociological and historical study of the cultural life of the Jews of Europe and the United States in areas segregated by compulsion or by voluntary action, with special attention to the Chicago ghetto.

414. YAFFE, JAMES. *The American Jews.* New York: Random House, 1968.

A critique of American Jewish life by a self-informed creative writer. Far from flawless and by no means free from subjectivity and narrow vision. Selected references.

415. ZAGAT, SAMUEL. *Jewish Life on New York's Lower East Side, 1912-1962.* New York: Rogers Book Service, 1972.

Reproductions of paintings and Yiddish-language cartoons reflecting Jewish social, economic, and religious life in New York City, as well as of political cartoons which appeared in Yiddish- and English-language newspapers. Of special interest in the cartoon series, "Gimpel Beinish der Shadchan" (The Matchmaker).

416. ZARCHIN, MICHAEL M. *Glimpses of Jewish Life in San Francisco: History of San Francisco Jewry.* San Francisco: n.p., 1952.

Origins and development of the San Francisco Jewish community from the nineteenth century, with particular reference to cultural, religious, and social activities.

VIII. RELIGIOUS LIFE, THOUGHT, AND AFFAIRS

VIII. RELIGIOUS LIFE, THOUGHT, AND AFFAIRS

417. ADLER, FRANK J. *Roots in a Moving Stream: The Centennial History of Congregation B'nai Jehudah of Kansas City, 1870-1970.* Kansas City, Mo.: the Temple, Congregation B'nai Jehudah, 1972.

A detailed, fully documented history of a Reform Temple. Illustrations, facsimiles, and membership lists.

418. BERNSTEIN, PHILIP S. *Rabbis at War: The CANRA Story.* Waltham, Mass.: American Jewish Historical Society, 1971.

A brief account of the activities of the Committee on Army and Navy Religious Activities of the National Jewish Welfare Board (CANRA) during World War II. Many photographs of Jewish chaplains on active service. The appendix contains letters, religious responsa, and other documentary materials.

419. BLAKE, PETER, ed. *An American Synagogue for Today and Tomorrow.* New York: Union of American Hebrew Congregations, 1954.

Essays by Reform rabbis, architects, historians, and other specialists on the history of the synagogue, the various steps in the construction, remodeling, and maintenance of such structures, and relation of art and music to worship. Illustrations and glossary.

420. BLAU, JOSEPH, ed. *Reform Judaism: A Historical Perspective.* New York: KTAV Publishing House, 1973.

A collection of twenty-four scholarly inspirational essays, reprinted from the Yearbooks of the Central Conference of American Rabbis, on the philosophy and program of the Reform movement in the United States, as well as on theological, legal, and other themes. The authors represent the nineteenth and twentieth centuries. Of particular significance is the essay by Rabbi William G. Braude (1942) suggesting that "a few students" from the Hebrew Union College be sent "to one of the better *yeshivahs* for a year" (p. 120) and that Reform rabbis and laymen study more Torah and practice more of its commandments.

421. *David Einhorn Memorial Volume.* New York: Bloch Publishing Co., 1911.

A collection of 48 sermons and addresses in German (1847-1876) by a German-born rabbi who served in Baltimore, Philadelphia, and New York. Also included, in English, are a biographical essay by Kaufmann Kohler and a memorial oration by Emil G. Hirsch.

422. DAVIS, MOSHE. *The Emergence of Conservative Judaism: The Historical School in 19th Century America.* Philadelphia: Jewish Publication Society of America, 1963.

A carefully documented study of the origins and development of the Conservative religious movement, 1840-1902, with emphasis on education, the community, and the synagogue. Illustrations, biographical sketches, documents, and a good bibliography in English, Hebrew, Yiddish, and German.

423. DAVIS, MOSHE. *Yahadut Amerika be-hitpathutah.* New York: Jewish Theological Seminary of America, 1951.

This detailed Hebrew monograph treats the development of American Jewish religious life and organization from 1840 to 1902, with stress on the Conservative and Reform communities. The appendix contains biographical sketches, documentary texts, and an extensive bibliography in Hebrew, English, German, and Yiddish.

424. DRESNER, SAMUEL H. *The Jew in American Life.* New York: Crown Publishers, 1963.

A Conservative rabbi's experiences and thoughts in relation to theological questions and to Jewish life and problems in the United States.

425. EISENSTEIN, IRA, and EUGENE KOHN, eds. *Mordecai M. Kaplan: An Evaluation.* New York: Jewish Reconstructionist Foundation, 1952.

Essays by religious leaders and scholars on the role of Dr. Kaplan and the Reconstructionist movement he inaugurated in the Jewish community in the United States.

426. ELZAS, BARNETT A. *The Reformed Society of Israelites of Charleston, S.C.* New York: Bloch Publishing Co., 1916.

A brief historical sketch of the genesis of this congregation with the full text of the constitution of 1825 and later documents.

427. GLAZER, NATHAN. *American Judaism.* 2d ed. Chicago: University of Chicago Press, 1972.

An historical interpretation of the factors of the growth, development, and change in the Jewish religion from the seventeenth century to the present. The treatment of religious education is rather compressed. A few notes, but very useful chronology and bibliographical essay.

428. GOLDMAN, ALEX J. *Giants of Faith: Great American Rabbis.* New York: Citadel Press, 1964.

Biographical accounts of eighteen Oxthodox, Conservative, and Reform leaders of the nineteenth and twentieth centuries, including Bernard L. Levinthal, Aaron Kotler, Solomon Schechter, and Kaufmann Kohler. Illustrations and bibliographies.

429. GOLDSTEIN, ISRAEL. *A Century of Judaism in New York: B'nai Jeshurun, 1825-1925, New York's Oldest Ashkenazic Congregation.* New York: Congregation B'nai Jeshurun, 1930.

An account of the development of the congregation in the context of changing times in New York City. Illustrations, documents, reference sources, bibliography, and lists of officers and members.

430. GOLDSTEIN, MARGARET F., ed. *American Jewish Organizations Directory.* New York: American Jewish Organizations Directory (Frenkel Mailing Service), 1973.

Eighth edition of a geographically classified compilation of basic data about congregations and various Jewish organized groups. Formerly known as the American Synagogue Directory. The first edition was published in 1957.

431. GUTSTEIN, MORRIS A. *To Bigotry No Sanction: A Jewish Shrine in America, 1658-1958.* New York: Bloch Publishing Co., 1958.

A description and documented story of the role of the Touro Synagogue in Newport, R.I., in American history, chiefly until the end of the eighteenth century. Illustrations, facsimiles, and selected bibliography.

432. KAMPF, AVRAM. *Contemporary Synagogue Art: Developments in the United States, 1945-1965.* Philadelphia: Jewish Publication Society of America, 1966.

Photographs exemplifying the external and internal art of American synagogues. Explanatory text and notes.

433. KAPLAN, MORDECAI M. *Judaism as a Civilization: Toward a Reconstruction of American-Jewish Life.* New York: Schocken Books, 1967.

Originally published in 1934, this is the standard work on beliefs and practices of the Reconstructionist religious community in America by the founder-ideologist of the movement.

434. KAPLAN, MORDECAI M. *The Future of the American Jew.* New York: Macmillan, 1948.

A wide-ranging, extended argument in behalf of the idea that the future of the American Jew depends on the actualization of the principles of Reconstructionism—Judaism is a religious civilization, rather than a religion—in life, religion, society, and education.

435. KARP, ABRAHAM J. *A History of the United Synagogue of America, 1913-1963.* New York: United Synagogue of America, 1964.

A brief record of the development of the central organization of Conservative temples, including educational and recreational activities. Illustrations and documents.

436. KATZ, IRVING I. *The Beth El Story with a History of the Jews in Michigan before 1850.* Detroit, Mich.: Wayne University Press, 1955.

A richly-illustrated, popular centennial history of a Reform Temple against the background of early Jewish history in Michigan. Also included is a brief historical essay on American Jewry by Jacob R. Marcus. Numerous documentary facsimiles and a bibliography.

437. KOHLER, K[AUFMANN]. *Studies, Addresses, and Personal Papers.* New York: Bloch Publishing Co., 1931.

A collection of theological and historical writings in English and German by an eminent American Reform rabbi. Of particular pertinence are the essays on the Hebrew Union College and on contemporary Reform rabbis. Bibliography of Dr. Kohler's works and scholarly notes.

438. KOHUT, ALEXANDER. *The Ethics of the Fathers.*
New York: Privately printed, 1920.

Edited and revised by Barnett A. Elzas, the first half
contains memorial essays on the noted American Jewish rabbi and especially on his contributions to Jewish
scholarship and religion, while the remainder consists
of a commentary on the ancient ethical treatise.

439. KORN, BERTRAM W. *German-Jewish Intellectual Influences on American Jewish Life, 1824-1972.* Syracuse, N.Y.: Syracuse University Press, 1972.

A documented essay tracing the contributions to the
Jewish religion, scholarship, and thought in the United States.

440. LEISER, JOSEPH. *American Judaism: The Religion
and Religious Institutions of the Jewish People in the
United States.* New York: Bloch Publishing Co.,
1925.

An historical overview and critical analysis of American Jewish consciousness and community from a Reform point of view.

441. LENN, THEODORE I., *et al. Rabbi and Synagogue in
Reform Judaism.* [Cincinnati, Ohio:] Central Conference of American Rabbis, 1972.

A descriptive study by two psychologists, two psychiatrists, two sociologists, and one Conservative rabbi
of the backgrounds, beliefs, and activities of American Reform rabbis, as well as of the characteristics,
beliefs, and affiliations of Reform congregants, seminary students, and youth.

442. LEVINGER, LEE J. *Jews and Judaism in the United States: A Syllabus.* Cincinnati, Ohio: Union of American Hebrew Congregations, 1925.

An outline, with bibliographical references, of American Jewish history from colonial times to the twentieth century, with special stress on the development of the Reform movement.

443. LEVINTHAL, ISRAEL H. *Point of View: An Analysis of American Judaism.* New York: Abelard-Schuman, 1958.

A well-known Conservative rabbi's analysis of American Jewish religious movements.

444. LEVY, BERYL H. *Reform Judaism in America: A Study in Religious Adaptation.* New York: Bloch Publishing Co., 1933.

A reliably documented study of the Reform movement in relation to changes in prayer, ritual, observance, and theology in historical perspective. Bibliography in German, Hebrew, and English.

445. LIEBMAN, CHARLES. *Aspects of the Religious Behavior of American Jews.* New York: Ktav Publishing House, 1974.

This volume includes a new introduction and three previously published essays describing the religious organization and activities of American Jews. The first essay, on Orthodoxy, explores the emergence of Orthodox, Judaism as a major force on the American Jewish scene. It discusses the divisions within Orthodoxy, its major institutions, and the different types of Orthodox Jews.

446. LIEBMAN, CHARLES S. *The Ambivalent American Jew: Politics, Religion, and Family in American Jewish Life.* Philadelphia: Jewish Publication Society of America, 1973.

Documented, penetrating essays on the relation of Jewish roots in Europe to the development of American Judaism, communal and educational issues, and Jewish political liberalism. The author concludes that "Jewish peoplehood is threatened by cosmopolitanism and universalism, by the vision of an undifferentiated and diffuse love and the desire to destroy all that separates men . . . [and] by contemporary currents in Jewish life . . . literature, art, scholarship, politics—all seems to undermine . . . the essentials of Judaism. . . . Jewish survival requires a turning against the integrationist response" (p. 197).

447. MANN, ARTHUR, ed. *Growth and Achievement of Temple Israel, 1854-1954.* Cambridge, Mass.: Temple Adath Israel, 1954.

A centennial history of a congregation with particular emphasis on four rabbis.

448. MENKUS, BELDEN, ed. *Meet the Amerian Jew.* Nashville, Tenn.: Broadman Press, 1963.

Essays by rabbis, sociologists, and other Jewish leaders regarding the American Jewish religion, social life, and relations with Israel and non-Jews. Compiled by a Protestant with the assistance of Rabbi Arthur Gilbert.

449. MILLER, ALAN W. *God of Daniel S.: In Search of the American Jew.* New York: Macmillan, 1969.

Portraits of several types of American Jews: the Hasid, the Orthodox, the Conservative, the Reform, the Zionist, the agnostic, and the social activist. Bibliography.

450. NEUSNER, JACOB. *American Judaism: Adventure in Modernity.* Englewood Cliffs, N.J.: Prentice-Hall, 1972.

Essays on the nature and status of Jewish religion in America pointing out the "central dilemma facing American Judaism: Its commitment to the rationality, respectability, and worldliness of middle-class life to which Jews aspire, and in large part have achieved seems to conflict with the vision contained in the holy books and deeds, indeed, with the whole symbolic structure of the Judaic inheritance" (p. 152). Short bibliographical essay and glossary.

451. ,NEUSNER, JACOB, ed. *Contemporary Judaic Fellowship in Theory and in Practice.* New York: Ktav Publishing House, 1972.

Informative essays on the historical background and status of recent Jewish religious-cultural communes in various parts of the United States.

452. NODEL, JULIUS J., and ALFRED APSLER. *The Ties Between: A Century of Judaism on America's Last Frontier.* Portland, Ore.: Temple Beth Israel, 1959.

An account of the origin and development of Temple Beth Israel, Portland (Oregon), a pioneering house of worship in the area.

453. PENN, ASCHER. *Yiddishkeit in Amerike: A vegveizer zu dem geistikn Yiddishn lebn in Amerike in der*

tsveiter helft fun 20tn yorhundert. New York: The author, 1958.

An illustrated introduction, in Yiddish, to "the spiritual and cultural status of the American Jewish community within the specific framework of educational activities among the youth and the wide network of religious and lay movements in this country" (p. vii). Essays on religious, cultural, and educational leaders, institutions, and organizations. Of special interest is the section of Hasidic groups and yeshivahs in New York. Foreword and table of contents in English.

454. PHILIPSON, DAVID. *The Oldest Jewish Congregation in the West (B'ne Israel, Cincinnati).* Cincinnati, Ohio: Krehbriel, 1894.

The origins and development of the synagogue that developed into an influential Reform temple. Illustrations, documents, and lists of officers and members.

455. POOL, DAVID, and TAMAR DE SOLA. *An Old Faith in the New World: Portrait of Shearith Israel, 1654-1954.* New York: Columbia University Press, 1955.

A valuable history, based on primary sources, of the first American Jewish synagogue. Illustrations, facsimiles, documents, glossary, and bibliography.

456. POSTAL, BERNARD, and LIONEL KOPPMAN. *Jewish Landmarks in New York: An Informal History and Guide.* New York: Hill and Wang, 1964.

Convenient descriptions of historic synagogues, shops, restaurants, various institutions, and points of interest.

457. ROSEN, BERNARD C. *Adolescence and Religion: The Jewish Teenager in American Society.* Cambridge, Mass.: Schenkman Publishing Co., 1965.

A questionnaire and inteview study of the formation of the religious attitudes and practices of American Jewish adolescents. The results of the research "clearly indicated that most adolescents were opposed to assimilation and that in general they were oriented positively toward religion. Yet this positive orientation lacked enthusiasm and coexisted with marked confusion in the area of religious belief and practice" (p. 203). The author concluded that "the average adolescent in this study was neither a traditionalist nor a non-traditionalist" (p. 192) and that "minority group pressures, for the most part, tend to strengthen the adolescent ties with the ethnic group" (p. 201). Bibliography.

458. ROSENBERG, STUART E. *America Is Different: The Search for Jewish Identity.* London: Nelson, 1964.

A perceptive, critical analysis, in historical perspective, of the interrelationship of the American and the Jewish traditions, with particular reference to religious development and to secularist thought. The author notes the change in policy of "the myraid of secular Jewish organizations . . . from their earlier preoccupations with programs of community relations, political action, or civic defense, and are recognizing the need to expand their efforts in the direction of cultural enterprises" (p. 259).

459. ROSENTHAL, GILBERT S. *Four Paths to God: Today's Jew and His Religion.* New York: Bloch Publishing Co., 1973.

A documented, analytical survey of the historical development and ideology of American Orthodox, Reform, Conservative, and Reconstructionist Judaism. Rabbi Rosenthal concludes that "for all its flaws and failings, its superficialities and shoddiness, American Jewry is an imposing edifice, rich in promise and ripe in achievements" (p. 275). Glossary and selected references.

460. ROUTTENBERG, MAX J. *Decades of Decision.* New York: Bloch Publishing Co., 1973.

A Conservative rabbi's statements on religion, the role of the rabbi, education, and social problems in American Jewish life.

461. SILBERMAN, LOU H. *American Impact: Judaism in the United States in the Early Nineteenth Century.* [Syracuse, N.Y.: Syracuse University, 1964.]

A brief, documented essay on the beginnings of Reform Judaism in 1824 in Charleston, S.C.

462. SILVER, SAMUEL M., ed. *The Quotable American Rabbis.* Anderson, S.C.: Droke House, and New York: Grosset and Dunlap, 1967.

A collection of concise statements, classified by topic, by Orthodox, Conservative, and Reform rabbis.

463. SKLARE, MARSHALL. *Conservative Judaism: An American Religious Movement.* New York: Schocken Books, 1972.

A suitably documented study, originally published in 1955, on the development of the Conservative synagogue, religious worship, social and educational activities, rabbinical role, and theology. This new edition, which adds a chapter on recent developments, points out that "the drop in Conservative morale at the very zenith of Conservative influence" is due to "the emergence of Orthodoxy, the problem of Conservative observance, and the widespread alienation among Conservative young people from the American culture to which their movement has been strongly attached" (p. 281).

464. SLEEPER, JAMES A., and ALAN L. MINTZ, eds. *The New Jews*. New York: Random House, 1971.

A collection of essays by young American Jews of various backgrounds, views, and professions on the meaning of Jewish tradition and spirituality in contemporary America.

465. WASKOW, ARTHUR T. *The Bush Is Burning! Radical Judaism Faces the Pharaohs of the Modern Superstate*. New York: Macmillan, 1971.

The "awakening to Judaism and . . . wrestlings with the Jewish communities in America and Israel" (p. 8) by a leader of the radical Jewish movement in the United States. the book is "personal, political, and religious all at once, Most of all it is communal and collective" (p. 7).

466. WAXMAN, MORDECAI, ed. *Tradition and Change: The Development of Conservative Judaism*. New York: Burning Bush Press, 1958.

Anthology of statements on the genesis, development, philosophy, religious policies, and other aspects of the Conservative movement in America.

467. WEINBERGER, MOSHE. *Sefer ha-Yehudim v'ha-Yaha-dut b'New York.* New York: New Yorker Yiddishe Tsaitung, [1887].

A critical commentary in Hebrew on Jewish life and religious observance in New York City in the late nineteenth century.

468. WISCHNITZER, RACHEL. *Synagogue Architecture in the United States: History and Interpretation.* Philadelphia: Jewish Publication Society of America, 1955.

A well-documented historical survey and analysis covering the development of synagogue architectural styles from the colonial era to the mid-nineteenth century. Richly illustrated with exterior and interior photographs, as well as with architectural sketches. Selected references and glossaries of architectural and Hebrew terms.

469. ZEITLIN, JOSEPH. *Disciples of the Wise: The Religious and Social Opinions of American Rabbis.* New York: Bureau of Publications, Teachers College, Columbia University, 1945.

A study, by questionnaire, of the beliefs and pulpit statements of several hundred American-born Conservative, Reform, and Orthodox rabbis concerning theological, social, and economic issues. The author concludes that Conservative statements were distinguished from Reform by "greater detail in criticism of contemporary society and greater specificity of suggestion for social reconstruction" (pp. 195-196). Bibliography.

IX. EDUCATION

•

IX. EDUCATION

470. ADAR, ZEVI. *Ha-hinukh ha-Yehudi b'Yisrael uv-Art-zot ha-Brit.* Tel-Aviv: Gomeh, 1969.

While most of this volume deals with Jewish education in Israel, a substantial portion treats Jewish religious education in the United States.

471. ADLER, CYRUS, ed. *The Jewish Theological Seminary of America: Semi-Centennial Volume.* New York: Jewish Theological Seminary of America, 1939.

Commemorative addresses on the program and impact of the Conservative rabbinical and pedagogical institution, founded in 1886. Appended documents, lists of personnel, and illustrations.

472. ALPER, MICHAEL. *Reconstructing Jewish Education.* New York: Reconstructionist Press, 1957.

An abridgment of a Ph.D. thesis dealing with the weaknesses of traditional Jewish education in America and proposing changes in line with the principles of Reconstructionism. A Reconstructionist education would influence the American Jew to "insist on the revision of Jewish law, wherever the Jewish tradition offends against principles of democracy and social justice" (p. 149).

473. BENDERLY, S. *Aims and Activities of the Bureau of Education of the Jewish Community (Kehillah) of New York City*. New York: The Bureau, 1912.

The goals, status, and needs of Jewish schools in the early twentieth century.

474. BERKSON, ISAAC B. "Theories of Americanization: A Critical Study with Special Reference to the Jewish Group." Ph.D. dissertation, Teachers College, Columbia University, 1920.

An analysis of the nature and implications of democratic thought and practice for the adjustment of Jews in American society; a critique of parochial schools as less suitable than after-school programs of ethnic and religious education; and a detailed description of the educational work of the Central Jewish Institute in New York City. Selected references.

475. BLUMENFIELD, SHMUEL M. *Hevrah v'hinukh b'Yahadut Amerikah*. Jerusalem: Neumann, 1965.

Essays in Hebrew by an American Jewish educator on the thought and practice of Jewish education in the sociocultural context in the United States. Included are considerations of the significance of the ideas of American educators (John Dewey, William H. Kilpatrick, Robert M. Hutchins) and Jewish literary figures for Jewish education

476. BLUSHTEIN, M. *A lerer redt zich arop fun hartzn*. Atlanta, Ga.: The author, 1959.

A compilation of twenty-five essays in Yiddish on the status and problems of twentieth-century Jewish education, particularly the Yiddish-language schools, in Canada and the United States.

477. *Campus 1966: Change and Challenge.* Washington, D.C.: B'nai B'rith Hillel Foundations, 1966.

Papers and reports evaluating the work by Hillel Foundations in colleges and universities, especially in relation to intermarriage and the Jewish community.

478. *Changing patterns of Jewish Life on the Campus.* Washington, D.C.: B'nai B'rith Hillel Foundations, 1961.

Essays by rabbis and academicians on the national and international aspects of Hillel services to Jewish students in colleges and universities.

479. CHIPKIN, ISRAEL S. *Jewish Education in the United States at Mid-Century.* New York: American Association for Jewish Education, 1951.

Description and interpretation of the status, trends and problems. Reprinted from the *Jewish Education Register and Directory, 1951.*

480. CHIPKIN, ISRAEL S. *Twenty-Five Years of Jewish Education in the United States.* New York: Jewish Education Association of New York City, 1937.

An interpretation of the development of the Sunday school, the Hebrew and Yiddish afternoon schools, the day schools, and other types of Jewish education on all levels, with special attention to changes in curriculum, teacher preparation, and problems. Reprinted from the *American Jewish Year Book* (1937).

481. COHEN, JACK J. *Jewish Education in Democratic Society.* New York: Reconstructionist Press, 1964.

A critical analysis of the status, content, and issues of American Jewish education from the viewpoint of a Reconstructionist rabbi, who states that "this is a distinctly biased book; I hope it is not a prejudiced one" (p. xi).

482. *Directory of Day Schools in the United States, Canada and Mexico.* New York: Torah Umesorah, [1975].

A comprehensive listing of Jewish elementary and secondary schools, including founding dates and names of administrators.

483. DININ, SAMUEL. *Judaism in a Changing Civilization.* New York: Bureau of Publications, Teachers College, Columbia University, 1933.

A Ph.D. thesis on the implications of theories of Jewish survival for Jewish education in the United States in relation to democratic principles. The author is critical of traditional Jewish education—the separation of the secular from religious instruction in the Jewish day schools, "when it is not hypocritical, is downright childish and stupid. It makes for the worst kind of dualisms, and for serious maladjustments" (p. 192). Instead, he advocates a Jewish education based on Progressive principles and aimed at the reconstruction of American and Jewish society. References after each chapter.

484. DININ, SAMUEL. *Zionist Education in the United States: A Survey.* [New York] : Zionist Organization of America, 1944.

A report on the historical background, theoretical framework, and status of Zionist education on the adult level and in the various Jewish schools in America.

485. DUSHKIN, ALEXANDER M. *Jewish education in New York City.* New York: Bureau of Jewish Education, 1918.

A detailed study of the historical development and status, as of the early twentieth century, of the various types of Jewish schools in New York City. Documents, photographs, statistics, and bibliography. The conclusion of this unique work is that "the outlook, though problematic, is distinctly hopeful. . . . The educational system which American Jews are developing is designed to make of their children fully adjusted individuals, combining in themselves both the American and the Jewish values of life" (pp. 405-406).

486. DUSHKIN, ALEXANDER M., and URIAH Z. ENGELMAN. *Jewish Education in the United States: Report of the Commission for the Study of Jewish Education in the United States.* New York: American Association for Jewish Education, 1959.

A detailed survey presenting for the first time "a profile" of American Jewish education as it was in the 1950s. This is an analysis of the nature of the various types of Jewish schools, enrollment data, pupil and parental attitudes, communal organization for Jewish education, curriculum content, the results of instruction, and prospects for improvement. The common assumption that Jewish education in America is " 'a mile wide and an inch deep' " (p. 4) is partially contradicted by the results obtained by Jewish day school pupils on the survey's examinations in Hebrew language, Jewish history, and other knowledge.

487. EDELSTEIN, MENACHEM. *History of the Development of the Jewish Teaching Profession in America.* New York: Jewish Education Committee of New York, 1956.

A collection of articles, originally published in *Jewish Education* and *Shevilei Ha-Hinukh* (Hebrew), on the status of the Jewish teacher in East Europe and especially in the United States from 1880 to 1950.

488. ENGELMAN, URIAH Z. *Hebrew Education in America: Problems and Solutions.* New York: Jewish Teachers' Seminary and People's University Press, 1947.

A brief survey of, and recommendations for the reconstruction of, American Jewish education.

489. FELSENTHAL, BERNHARD. *Judisches Schulwesen in Amerika.* Chicago: Heunisch, 1866.

A 40-page pamphlet in German recommending the establishment of Hebrew schools all over America (including some on the advanced level) and the training of young Americans in European rabbinical institutions.

490. *Fifty Years' Work of the Hebrew Education Society of Philadelphia.* Philadelphia: The Society, 1899.

An illustrated historical review of the founding and activities of the Society founded in 1847 to provide "a thorough religious education of all Israelites . . . [through] the establishment of such schools, as will enable all Israelites of this city and county, to receive instruction in religion, the Hebrew and English languages, the usual branches of education, and all such other subjects as the circumstances of the funds and the capacity of the scholars may enable the directors to afford" (p. 9). Documents in the text, and lists of schools and teachers, as well as other information, appear in the appendix.

491. FRANZBLAU, ABRAHAM N. *Religious Belief and Character among Jewish Adolescents.* New York: Bureau of Publications, Teachers College, Columbia University, 1934.

A Ph.D. dissertation investigating the statistical relation of Jewish religious belief to character development among 701 thirteen-year-old pupils of Reform and Orthodox schools in New York City. The author found no evidence to support the principle that the "acceptance of the traditional religious dogmas is creative of superior character" (p. 78).

492. GANNES, ABRAHAM P. "Central Community Agencies for Jewish Education." Ph.D. dissertation, Dropsie College for Hebrew and Cognate Learning, 1954.

Presents the historical background, organization, activities, and achievements of bureaus of Jewish education in the United States. Bibliography and documentary appendix.

493. GELBART, GERSHON I. *Jewish Education in America: A Manual for Parents and School Board Members.* New York: Jewish Education Committee Press, 1963.

"A miniature encyclopedia of Jewish education"

which offers a concise introduction to the goals, role, structure, organization, administration, curriculum, personnel, and other aspects of American Jewish education.

494. GOLDSTEIN, ISRAEL. *Brandeis University: Chapter of Its Founding.* New York: Bloch Publishing Co., 1951.

The author's role in the actual realization of the establishment of the first Jewish-sponsored university in the United States. Documents in the text and the appendix.

495. GOODMAN, SAUL, ed. *Our First Fifty Years: The Sholem Aleichem Folk Institute; A Historical Survey.* 2 vols. New York: Sholem Aleichem Folk Institute, 1972.

Essays on the origins, aims, and activities of an institute devoted to the promotion of education and culture through the Yiddish language.

496. HERTZ, RICHARD C. *The Education of the Jewish Child: A Study of 200 Reform Jewish Religious Schools.* New York: Union of American Hebrew Congregations, 1953.

A study, based on a Ph.D. thesis, of the status of Reform Jewish education in the United States—its roots, aims, curricula, organization, teacher-training, finance, and various problems. The author concludes that "congregations are taking more seriously than ever before the role of the religious school in assuring the survival of American Judaism" (p. 155).

497. HONOR, LEO L. *Jewish Elementary Education in the United States (1901-1950).* New York: American Association for Jewish Education, [1952].

A documented essay originally published in the *Publications of the American Jewish Historical Society* in 1952.

498. [HURWITZ, HENRY, and I. LEO SHARFMAN]. *The Menorah Movement for the Study and Advancement of Jewish Culture and Ideals: History, Purposes, Activities.* Ann Arbor, Mich.: Intercollegiate Menorah Association, 1914.

Information and documents on the founding of the Harvard Menorah Society in 1906 and the development of Menorah societies on other American college campuses.

499. JANOWSKY, OSCAR I., ed. *The Education of American Jewish Teachers.* Boston: Beacon Press, 1967.

Essays by experienced Jewish educators on the backgrounds, organization, curriculum, and problems of Jewish teacher preparation and in-service education.

500. JICK, LEON A., ed. *The Teaching of Judaica in American Universities.* New York: KTAV Publishing House, 1970.

Essays by university professors of Jewish studies and others concerning the development, status, problems, and possibilities of the field.

501. JOSPE, ALFRED. *Judaism on the Campus: Essays on Jewish Education in the University Community.*

Washington, D.C. B'nai B'rith Hillel Foundations, 1963.

The aims, activities, and problems of Jewish cultural, religious, and educational work in American colleges and universities.

502. KAMINETSKY, JOSEPH, and MURRAY I. FRIED-MAN, eds. *Hebrew Day School Education: An Overview.* New York: Torah Umesorah, 1970.

A reprint of essays which appeared originally in the *Jewish Parent.* the content deals with the aims of Jewish education, the development and activity of Torah Umesorah (the National Society for Hebrew Day Schools), the school-home relationships, curriculum, and various educational issues and problems. An important source for the understanding of the objectives and functions of the Jewish day school movement in the American Jewish community as well as in society at large.

503. KATSH, ABRAHAM I. *Hebrew in American Higher Education.* New York: New York University Bookstore, 1941.

A documented study of the impact of the Hebrew Bible and language on American culture, as well as an analysis of the status (1940) of Hebrew instruction in American colleges and universities. Bibliography.

504. KATSH, ABRAHAM I. *Hebrew Language, Literature and Culture in American Institutions of Higher Learning.* New York: Payne Educational Sociology Foundation, 1950.

The historical and mid-twentieth-century status of

the teaching of Hebrew and Jewish studies in the colleges and universities in the United States.

505. KATZOFF, LOUIS. *Issues in Jewish Education: A Study of the Philosophy of the Conservative Congregational School.* New York: Bloch Publishing Co., 1949.

A Ph.D. thesis analyzing the philosophy and structure of the curricula in schools affiliated with Conservative Jewish temples in the United States. On the basis of a questionnaire to rabbis, principals, and teachers, the author concludes that the prevailing conviction of the centrality of the synagogue in American Jewish life constitutes "a separatist movement leading toward fragmentation of the Jewish community" (p. 162).

506. KLAPERMAN, GILBERT. *The Story of Yeshiva University: The First University in America.* New York: Macmillan, 1969.

A concise, documented, illustrated account of the genesis of the elementary Yeshivat Eitz Chaim (1886) and of the Rabbi Isaac Elchanan Theological Seminary (1897), the merger of both institutions (1915), and the subsequent development of what was to become known as Yeshiva University. English, Hebrew, and Yiddish sources in the bibliography and notes.

507. KONOVITZ, ISRAEL. *Beth-sifri: Heshbon ha-nefesh shel menahel Talmud Torah.* New York: Bureau of Jewish Education, 1934.

A statistical report and interpretation of the results achieved in Jewish education at the Downtown Talmud Torah, New York City. Introduction, in English, by Samson Benderly, head of the Bureau.

508. LEVINGER, LEE J., dir. *The Jewish Student in America.* Cincinnati, Ohio: B'nai B'rith, 1937.

A mimeographed statistical and analytical study by the B'nai B'rith Hillel Foundations of the social and educational situation of Jewish students in 90 percent of the colleges and universities in the United States and Canada.

509. MARGOLIS, ISIDOR. *Jewish Teacher Training Schools in the United States.* New York: National Council for Torah Education of Mizrachi-Hapoel Hamizrachi, 1964.

Documented historical and analytical accounts of Gratz College, the Teachers Institute of the Jewish Theological Seminary of America, the Teachers Institute of Yeshiva University, the Hebrew Teachers College of Boston, the Herzliah Hebrew Teachers Institute, and the College of Jewish Studies in Chicago. Classified bibliography.

510. *New Frontiers for Jewish Life on the Campus.* Washington, D.C.: N'nai B'nai Hillel Foundations, 1968.

Essays by Hillel directors and others active in the movement on the problems and challenges faced by Jewish students, mainly in American colleges and universities.

511. NEWMAN, LOUIS I. *A Jewish University in America?* New York: Bloch Publishing Co., 1923.

Two essays by Rabbi Newman on the desirability of a Jewish university "not as an answer to academic anti-Semitism, but on its own merits as a contribution by Jewish intellect and ideals to American life" (p. 16).

Editorials and letters—noncommittal, opposed to, and in favor of—and a bibliography on the Jewish question in American colleges.

512. NIGER, S. *In kampf far a neier dertsiung: Di Arbeter-Ring-Shuln, zeier opshtam, ontwiklung, vuks, un itstiker zushtand (1919-1939))* New York: Arbeter-Ring-Bildungs-Komitet, 1940.

An illustrated, documented account of the origins and development of the Yiddish schools of the Workmen's Circle movement.

513. NULMAN, LOUIS. *The Parent and the Jewish Day School.* Scranton, Pa.: Parent Study Press, 1956.

An interview study, based on a Ph.D. thesis at the University of Pittsburgh, of parental attitudes regarding the traditional Jewish education combined with secular study in the Hillel Academy in Pittsburgh. It throws light on the background of the Jewish day school movement and on the factors persuading parents to enroll their children in this type of school. Selected references and notes.

514. PASSOW, ISIDORE D., and SAMUEL T. LACHS, eds. *Gratz College Anniversary Volume: On the Occasion of the Seventy-fifth Anniversary of the Founding of the College, 1895-1970.* Philadelphia: Gratz College, 1971.

Scholarly papers in English and Hebrew on Biblical and other Jewish themes, including several on Jewish education and culture in America.

515. PHILIPSON, DAVID, *et al.*, eds.*Hebrew Union College Jubilee Volume (1875-1925).* Cincinnati, Ohio: [Hebrew Union College], 1925.

A compilation of eighteen scholarly essays dealing with the history of the Hebrew Union College, as well as historical, philosophical, and other Jewish themes. Illustrations and facsimiles.

516. PILCH, JUDAH, ed. *A History of Jewish Education in America.* New York: American Association for Jewish Education, 1969.

Concise, documented essays by historians and educators tracing the development and analyzing the current situation of American Jewish education. Documentation in English, Hebrew, and Yiddish.

517 PILCH, JUDAH, ed. *Jewish Education Register and Directory: 1965.* New York: American Association for Jewish Education, 1965.

The directory of national and local Jewish educational agencies, and of schools on various levels, is preceded by essays containing statistics, information on licensure, audiovisual and other resource materials for the teacher and administrator, and a bibliography of master's theses and doctoral dissertations in Jewish education.

518. PILCH, JUDAH, ed. *Philip W. Lown: A Jubilee Volume.* New York: Bloch Publishing Co., 1967.

Essays on the contributions by Mr. Lown to the encouragement of Jewish education, papers on American Jewish educational theory and issues, and miscellaneous studies in Jewish literature and philosophy.

519. PILCH, JUDAH, and MEIR BEN-HORIN, eds. *Judaism and the Jewish School: Selected Essays on the Direction and Purpose of Jewish Education.* New York: Bloch Publishing Co., 1966.

Essays by educational, historical, and other scholars on the backgrounds, philosophy, system, and curriculm of Jewish religious and secular education in America, with particular reference to the role of the Hebrew language.

520. POMERANTZ, I. CHAIM, YUDEL MARK, SHLOME BERCOVICH, and M. BRONSHTEIN, eds. *Shul-Pinkes.* Chicago: Sholem Aleichem Folk Institute, [1946].

A compilation of essays in Yiddish on the history of the curriculum and other aspects of Jewish education in the United States with special stress on the Yiddish-language schools. Illustrations.

521. POUPKO, BERNARD A. *Forms of Jewish Adult Religious Education in America: A Study of the History, Curriculum, and Objectives of Jewish Adult Religious Programs Conducted by the Synagogue, Temple, and Jewish Religious Organizations.* Pittsburgh, Pa.: The author, 1952. Mimeographed.

A comprehensive survey and interpretation, based mainly on publications. The appendix contains information on the curricula of Orthodox and Reform programs. Bibliography.

522. RAPPAPORT, ISRAEL B. *Education for Living as American Jews.* 3d ed. New York: American Jewish Committee, 1946.

A program for a new type of American Jewish school which will develop a wholesome, integrated Jewish personality.

523. ROTHBLATT, H. M. *Pachim ktanim: Skirot divre bekoret, bayot ha-hinuch ha-Ivri v'ha-tsibur ha-Yehudi b'Amerika.* Tel Aviv "Hamenorah," 1966.

Essays, in Hebrew, on personalities, writings, problems, and issues, chiefly on Jewish literature and education in the United States.

524. ROTHOFF, AARON. *Bernard Revel: Builder of American Jewish Orthodoxy.* Philadelphia: Jewish Publication Society of America, 1972.

A comprehensive account of Dr. Revel's life, religious educational thought, and activity as president of the Rabbi Isaac Elchanan Theological Seminary. Photographs, documentary appendix, Dr. Revel's bibliography, notes, and general bibliography.

525. SCHARFSTEIN, ZEYVI. *Toldot ha-hinukh b'israel b'dorot ha-aharonim.* 2d ed. Vol. 3. Jerusalem: Mass, 1962.

Most of this volume presents a history and analysis of Jewish education in the United States.

526. SCHARFSTEIN, ZEVI, ed. *Sefer ha-Yovel shel Agudat ha-Morim ha-Ivrim b'New York un-svivoteha: L'malot shloshim shanah l'kiyumah.* New York: Hebrew Teachers Union 1944.

A volume of Hebrew essays commemorating the thirty-year-existence of the Hebrew Teachers Union in New York City and vicinity. The subject matter comprises American Jewish educational theory, history, institutions, and reminiscences, as well as extensive bibliography in Hebrew on American Jewish education and the text of the constitution and the membership list of the Hebrew Teachers Union.

527. SCHARFSTEIN, ZEVI, ed. *Yesodot ha-hinuch ha-Yehudi ba-Amerikah.* New York: Teachers Institute, Jewish Theological Seminary, 1946.

Essays on the history, aims, curriculum, and other aspects of Jewish education in the United States.

528. SCHIFF, ALVIN I. *The Jewish Day School in America.* New York: Jewish Education Committee Press, 1966.

A survey of the growth and development of Jewish day schools since the colonial period, but with stress on the twentieth century. Footnotes, documents, chronology, and bibliography.

529. STEINBERG, STEPHEN. *The Academic Melting Pot: Catholics and Jews in American Higher Education.* New York: McGraw-Hill, 1974.

A critical, comparative examination by a sociologist of the myths of Jewish intellectualism and Catholic anti-intellectualism in historical, social, cultural, and religious contexts. The author concludes that "Jews are disproportionately represented on all levels of higher education . . . are heavily concentrated in the high-ranking institutions . . . tend to be concentrated in the more intellectual disciplines and underrepresented in the more applied fields" (pp. 167-168). Jews are "not highly represented in the academic branches" of literature, art, and music; they "entered a situation of expanding opportunities [in professional schools and the social sciences] and to some extent were carried along by the momentum of educational change. . . . Jews did have the benefit of a rich intellectual tradition and did place unusually high value on education and intellectual achievement" (pp. 168-169). Appropriate references and index.

530. UNTERMAN, ISAAC. *Jewish Youth in America.* Philadelphia: Federal Press, 1941.

Popular discussions of educational, social, spiritual, and other problems confronting American Jewish children and adolescents.

531. VORSPAN, ALBERT. *So the Kids Are Revolting . . .?* Garden City, N.Y.: Doubleday, 1970.

A satirical guide to American Jewish parents on the upbringing of their children.

532. WINTER, NATHAN H. *Jewish Education in a Pluralist Society: Samson Benderly and Jewish Education in the United States.* New York: New York University Press, 1966.

A monograph on the life, educational ideas and activities, and influence of an early twentieth century Jewish educator, with special emphasis on the development of central educational bureaus and Progressive practices. References, documentary appendix, and bibliography of titles in English, Yiddish, and Hebrew.

533. ZOHORI, MENAHEM, ARIE TARTAKOVER, and HAIM ORMIAN, eds. *Hagut ivrit ba-Amerika: Studies on Jewish Themes by Contemporary American Schol-*

ars. 3 vols. [Jerusalem] : Brit Ivrti Olamit, and Tel-Aviv: Yavneh Publishing House, 1973-1974.

Essays in Hebrew by American Jewish scholars and writers on the Ancient East, Talmud and Midrash, Hebrew literature, Jewish philosophy and history, and historical and contemporary problems and issues of Jewish education and culture in the United States.

X. POLITICAL, INTERNATIONAL, AND ECONOMIC ACTIVITY.

X. POLITICAL, INTERNATIONAL, AND ECONOMIC ACTIVITY.

534. BELSKY, JOSEPH. *I, the Union: Being Personalized Trade Union Story of the Hebrew Butcher Workers of America.* New York: Raddock, 1952.

An informal, illustrated narrative by a union official on how the union helped raise the economic level of the Jewish butcher workers.

535. BOOKBINDER, HYMAN H., *et al. To Promote the General Welfare: The Story of the Amalgamated.* New York: Amalgamated Clothing Workers of America, 1950.

An historical survey of the growth and activities of a union organized and led by American Jews.

536. BURGIN, HERTZ. *Di Geshikhte fun der Yiddisher arbeiter bewegung in Amerika, Rusland un England.* New York: Fareinigte Yiddishe Geverkshaften fun New-York, Amerika, 1915.

A detailed account of a quarter-century (1888-1913) of the Jewish labor movement in the United States, Russia, and England. A glossary rendering Yiddish Americanisms into international Yiddish.

537. CHERTOFF, MORDECAIS, ed. *The New Left and the Jews.* New York: Pitman Publishing Company, 1971.

Essays by scholars in various disciplines on Jewish participation in New Left movements and the implications for the Jewish community in America and Israel.

538. EGERT, B. P. *The Conflict between the United States and Russia.* St. Petersburg: n.p., 1912.

A Russian critique, for the consumption of English readers, of the abrogation in December, 1911, by the United States of its treaty of 1832 with Russia "exclusively to satisfy the demands of the Jews in that country" (p. 7).

539. EPSTEIN, MELECH. *Jewish Labor in U.S.A.: An Industrial, Political and Cultural History of the Jewish Labor Movement, 1882-1914.* 2 vols. New York: Trade Union Sponsoring Committee, 1950.

A comprehensive, well-documented treatment of the rise of American Jewish trade unionism. Abundant, informative notes.

540. EPSTEIN, MELECH. *The Jew and Communism: The Story of Early Communist Victories and Ultimate Defeats in the Jewish Community, U.S.A., 1919-1941.* New York: Trade Union Sponsoring Committee, [1959].

A well-documented study by a former Communist leader of the inroads by the Communist Party into some circles of the American Jewish community and its loss of support following the Stalin-Hitler pact of 1939. Biographical sketches of influential Jewish Communists. Excellent notes.

541. FEINGOLD, HENRY L. *The Politics of Rescue: The Roosevelt Administration and the Holocaust, 1938-1945.* New Brunswick, N.J.: Rutgers University Press, 1970.

A thoroughly documented monograph on the F. D. Roosevelt administration's Jewish rescue program with a focus on the "gulf between the professed good intentions . . . and the implementation of policy" (p. 296). The author concludes that "the Roosevelt Administration responded only half-heartedly to the challenge of Jewish lives" (p. 307). Bibliography.

542. FRIEDMAN, SAUL S. *No Haven for the Oppressed: United States Policy toward Jewish Refugees, 1938-1945.* Detroit, Mich.: Wayne State University Press, 1973.

An extensively documented monograph exploring the reasons why the United States did not open its doors to Jewish refugees during World War II. The author concludes that "the yoke of shame weighs heavily upon every Jew and Gentile in the United States" (p. 231).

543. FUCHS, LAWRENCE H. *The Political Behavior of American Jews.* Glencoe, Ill.: Free Press, 1956.

An analysis by a political scientist of patterns of Jewish voting behaviors during the twentieth century. The author concludes that there are "perhaps hundreds of thousands of American Jews who are not liberals" and that there are even "Jewish reactionaries, but these are the exceptions" (p. 203). Helpful bibliographical and methodological notes.

544. GOLDEN, HARRY. *Forgotten Pioneer.* Cleveland: World Publishing Co., 1963.

A concise, popular, illustrated account of the Jewish peddler with a pack on his back, mainly in America in the nineteenth and early twentieth centuries. Selected references.

545. GOLDSTEIN, ISRAEL. *American Jewry Comes of Age: Tercentenary Addresses.* New York: Bloch Publishing Co., 1955.

The second half of his book by a Conservative rabbi and leader of the World Jewish Congress consists of statements on American Jewish life, freedom, culture, and relations to Israel.

546. HERTZ, J. S. *Di Yiddishe Sotsialistishe bavegung in Amerike: 70 yor Sotsialistishe tetikeit, 30 yor Sotsialistisher Farband.* New York: Farlag "Der Vecker," 1954.

An illustrated, documented history in Yiddish of Jewish Socialist activities in the United States from the late nineteenth to the mid-twentieth century.

547. HOFFMAN, B. *Fuftsig yor Cloakmakher Yunion, 1886-1936.* New York: Cloak Operators Union Local 117, International Ladies' Garment Workers' Union, 1936.

An illustrated account of the Cloakmakers' Union, to the development of which Eastern European immigrant Jews made a great contribution.

548. HYMAN, JOSEPH C. *Twenty-Five Years of American Aid to Jews Overseas: A Record of the Joint Distribution Committee.* New York: n.p., 1939.

A review of a noted organization's relief work among Jews, particularly in Eastern Europe.

549. ISAACS, STEPHEN F. *Jews and American Politics.* Garden City, N.Y.: Doubleday, 1974.

A critical, documented analysis of the role played by Jews in political affairs in the United States. Photographs and bibliography.

550. JACOBS, PAUL. *Is Curly Jewish? A Political Self-Portrait Illuminating Three Turbulent Decades of Social Revolt, 1935-1965.* New York: Atheneum Publishers, 1965.

A "Jewish radical of a rather peculiar kind" reminisces on his thoughts and activities in left-wing politics in America. There are numerous references to Jewish life and problems in the United States and Israel.

551. KATSH, ABRAHAM I. *Hebraic Contributions to American Life.* New York: New York University Bookstore, 1941.

Documented essays on the influence of the Bible, the Hebrew language, and the Jewish tradition on American government and culture. Bibliography.

552. KATSH, ABRAHAM I. *Hebrew Foundations of American Democracy.* New York: Philisophical Library, [1951].

A detailed, documented essay on the impact of the Bible, the Hebrew language, and the Judaic spirit on colonial and early republican government in America. Reprinted from Dagobert D. Runes, ed., *The Hebrew Impact on Western Civilization,* 1951.

553. LEVINE, LOUIS. *The Women's Garment Workers: A History of the International Ladies' Garment Workers' Union.* New York: Huebsch, 1924.

A detailed, documented analysis of the development of a union in which immigrant Jews played a significant role. Illustrations, statistics, documents, and a bibliography of primary sources and monographs. Of special interest are the list of the members of the General Executive Boards of the ILGWU and the index of names, both of which reveal an abundance of Jews.

554. LIPSKY, LOUIS. *Thirty Years of American Zionism.* New York: Nesher Publishing Co., 1927.

A detailed account by a leader of the early history of Zionism in the United States.

555. MACK, JULIAN W. *Americanism and Zionism.* New York: Federation of American Zionists, 1918.

Ideological analysis by an honorary president of the Zionist Organization of America.

556. MANUEL, FRANK E. *The Realities of American-Palestine Relations.* Washington, D.C.: Public Affairs Press, 1949.

A detailed, documented history of American policy toward Palestine from the Turkish period of the nineteenth century until the recognition of the State of Israel in 1948.

557. MORSE, ARTHUR D. *While Six Million Died: A Chronicle of American Apathy.* New York: Random House, 1967.

A critique of the attitudes of American Jews and others with regard to the destruction of most of European Jewry, 1938-1945.

558. NIZER, LOUIS. *The Implosion Conspiracy.* Garden City, N.Y.: Doubleday, 1973.

A noted attorney's comprehensive analysis of the 1951 United States Federal court trial of Julius and Ethel Rosenberg.

559. SCHECHTMAN, JOSEPH B. *The United States and the Jewish State Movement; The Crucial Decade: 1939-1949.* New York: Herzl Press, Thomas Yoseloff, 1966.

A documented study of "the major aspects and phases of the United States stand in matters pertaining to Zionism and Palestine during the war years (1939-1945) and the early post-war era (1945-1949)." Bibliography.

560. SHAPIRO, YONATHAN. *Leadership of the American Zionist Organization, 1897-1930.* Urbana: University of Illinois Press, 1971.

A scholarly sociological study of the development of Zionist ideology in the United States and how it served as a force toward the survival of the American Jewish community. Bibliography in English, Hebrew, German, and Yiddish.

561. SNETSINGER, JOHN. *Truman, the Jewish Vote, and the Creation of Israel.* Stanford, Calif.: Hoover Institution Press, Stanford University, 1974.

A fully documented study of the impact on United States foreign policy by the Jews, who "represent one of the most forceful ethnic blocks in the United States today" (p. xiv). The author concludes that, "with all its contradictions and vacillations, Truman's Palestine-Israel policy offers an extraordinary example of foreign policy conducted in line with short-range political expediency rather than long-range national goals" (p. 140). Bibliography and index.

562. STOLBERG, BENJAMIN. *Tailer's Progress: The Story of a Famous Union and the Men Who Made It.* Garden City, N.Y.: Doubleday, Doran, 1944.

An illustrated, popular historical survey of the International Ladies' Garment Workers' Union, with special emphasis on the contributions of Benjamin Schlesinger, Morris Sigman, and David Dubinsky.

563. SZAJKOWSKI, ZOSA. *Jews, Wars, and Communism.* 2 vols. New York: Ktav Publishing House, 1972-1974.

A highly informative study, based on primary source materials, of American Jewish opinion with regard to World War I, the two Russian revolutions of 1917, and Communism (1914-1945); and of the impact on American Jewish life of the Red Scare of 1919-1920. Abundant illustrations, notes, and bibliographical references.

564. TCHERIKOVER, E., ed. *Geshikhte fun der Yiddisher arbeter-bavegung in die Fareinikte Shtatn.* 2 vols. New York: YIVO, 1943.

Scholarly essays on the European backgrounds of the Jewish immigrants to the United States, their socio-cultural and economic life, their labor unions, and the development of Socialist and anti-religious ideologies during the final quarters of the nineteenth century. Illustrations, facsimiles, and documents in Yiddish, English, Russian, and German.

565. TCHERIKOVER, ELIAS, ed. *The Early Jewish Labor Movement in the United States.* New York: YIVO Institute for Jewish Research, 1961.

A documented study of the Jewish workers in America against the background of Eastern Europe and the migration. An abbreviated version of a two-volume work in Yiddish. Statistical appendix.

566. WEINSTEIN, B. *Di Yiddishe yunions in Amerike: Bleter geshitkhte un erinnerungen.* New York: Farein-ikte Yiddishe Geverkshaften, 1929.

Descriptive analysis of the history of Jewish trade unions in the United States, including the actors', bakers', furriers', and women's garment workers' unions. The emphasis is on the role of the immigrant Jews from Eastern Europe.

567. WEYL, NATHANIEL. *The Jew in American Politics.* New Rochelle, N.Y.: Arlington House, 1968.

A documented survey of American Jewish political attitudes and behavior in the perspective of history.

568. WYMAN, DAVID S. *Paper Walls: America and the Re-fugee Crisis, 1938-1941.* [Amherst]: University of Massachusetts Press, 1968.

A scholarly critique of the foreign policy of the American government, influential officials of which "all too often attempted to obstruct refugee immigration" (p. vii) from Nazi Germany. Bibliographical commentary and listing of works.

569. ZAAR, ISAAC. *Reason and Liberation: America's Part in the Birth of Israel.* New York: Bloch Publishing Co., 1954.

A detailed analysis, with supporting documents, of the role of the United States policy in the formation of the State of Israel.

XI. LITERATURE

XI. LITERATURE

570. ALTER, ROBERT. *After the Tradition: Essays on Modern Jewish Writing.* New York: E. P. Dutton & Co., 1969.

Papers on Jewish history, thought, and literature in the United States, Europe, and Israel.

571. ALTMAN, SIG. *The Comic Image of the Jew: Explorations of a Pop Culture Phenomenon.* Rutherford, N.J.: Fairleigh Dickinson University Press, 1971.

An analysis of the humor about Jews in popular American culture, as shown in the mass media, the role of humor in the Jewish past, and the nature of the Jewish comedian. An annotated list of plays and a 104-item bibliography.

572. ANGOFF, CHARLES, and MEYER LEVIN, eds. *The Rise of American Jewish Literature: An Anthology of Selections from Major Novels.* New York: Simon and Schuster, 1970.

Extracts from twenty-two American Jewish novelists, preceded by an interpretative introduction.

573. APSHTEIN, AVRAHAM. *Sofrim Ivrim b'Amerikah.* 2 vols. Tel-Aviv: Dvir, 1952.

Essays on twenty-five Hebrew poets, essayists, and novelists in the United States.

574. COHEN, BERNARD. *Sociocultural Changes in American Jewish Life as Reflected in Selected Jewish Literature.* Rutherford, N.J.: Fairleigh Dickinson University Press, 1972.

Analysis of the factors and processes of change in Jewish life in the United States since the 1880s as depicted in Hebrew and English novels and short stories of Charles Angoff, Saul Bellow, Meyer Levin, and others. Bibliography.

575. COOPERMAN, JEHIEL B., and SARAH H. COOPERMAN, comps. and trans. *America in Yiddish Poetry: An Anthology.* New York: Exposition Press, 1967.

Over 500 poems by sixty-nine American Jewish poets, past and present, on various themes dealing mostly with America (e.g.,Haim Grade's *Yosemite Valley*). A unique collection.

576. EISENBERG, AZRIEL, ed. *The Golden Land: A Literary Portrait of American Jewry, 1654 to the Present.* New York: Yoseloff, 1964.

A valuable anthology of fiction and nonfiction of three centuries of the American Jewish experience.

577. GLANZ, RUDOLF. *The Jew in Early American Wit and Graphic Humor.* New York: Ktav Publishing House, 1973.

A careful analysis, with abundant quotations and pictorial illustrations, of the image of the Jew as an object of satire in American literature, mainly in the nineteenth century. The author concludes: "In American caricature the Jew is a reasoning being, laughable in his weaknesses, but formidable in what has to be—however unwillingly—recognized as his strength, rationality above all" (p. 237).

578. GLANZ, RUDOLF. *The Jew in the Old American Folklore.* New York: The author, 1961.

An appropriately documented study of the image of the Jew and his socioeconomic characteristics in American writings of the nineteenth century. Many quotations in the text.

579. GROSS, THEODORE L., ed. *The Literature of American Jews.* New York: Free Press, 1973.

An anthology of fiction, poetry, and nonfiction by native and immigrant Jews of the nineteenth and twentieth centuries. Some writings are translations from the Yiddish. Editorial introductions and comprehensive bibliography.

580. GUTTMANN, ALLEN. *The Jewish Writer in America: Assimilation and the Crisis of Identity.* New York: Oxford University Press, 1971.

Critically interpretative, documented essays on American Jewish poets, novelists, and critics, with special attention to Saul Bellow. The author concludes that "the survival in America of a significant and identifiably Jewish literature depends upon the unlikely conversion to Judaism of a stiff-necked, intractable, irreverent, attractive generation that no longer chooses to be chosen" (p. 227). Selective bibliography.

581. KABAKOFF, YAAKOV. *Halutze ha-sifrut ha-Ivrit b'Amerika.* Tel-Aviv: Yavneh; and Cleveland, Ohio: Cleveland College of Jewish Studies, 1966.

Analytical essays on five early American Jewish literary writers who published Hebrew works—Yaakov Zevi Sobel, Zevi Gershuni, Zev Shur, Gershon Rosenzweig, and Yitzchak Rabinovitz.

582. KOPELYOV, Y. *Amol in Amerike: Zichroines fun dem Yiddishn lebn in Amerike in di yorn 1883-1904.* Warsaw: Brzoza, 1928.

Reminiscences in Yiddish by a Russian-Jewish immigrant, with special stress on labor and Yiddish journalism.

583. LEWIS, JERRY D., ed. *Tales of Our People: Great Stories of the Jews in America.* [New York] : Bernard Geis, 1969.

Stories about the American Jewish experience by Jews and non-Jews.

584. LIPTZIN, SOL. *Eliakum Zunser: Poet of His People.* New York: Behrman House, 1950.

A warm account of the life of a Russian-born Yiddish poet and composer who ended his years in early twentieth-century America..

585. LIPTZIN, SOL. *The Jew in American Literature.* New York: Bloch Publishing Co., 1966.

An illuminating interpretation of the history of the image of the Jew and of the Jewish self-image in American literature. Bibliography.

586. MALIN, IRVING, ed. *Contemporary American-Jewish Literature: Critical Essays.* Bloomington: Indiana University Press, 1973.

Evaluative essays by Jewish literary critics on the writings of Philip Roth, Saul Bellow, Isaac Bashevis Singer, Karl Shapiro, Bernard Malamud, and other American Jewish writers.

587. MARMOR, KALMAN. *Der onhoib fun der Yiddisher literatur in Amerike (1870-1890).* New York: YKUF, 1944.

Essays on late nineteenth-century Yiddish literature in the United States, with particular reference to the press and to Morris Rosenfeld and David Edelstat.

588. MAYZEL, NACHMAN, ed. *Amerike in Yiddishn vort: Antologieh.* New York: Yiddisher Kultur Farband (YKUF), 1955.

An illustrated anthology of Yiddish prose and poetry reflecting Jewish life and struggles in the United States.

589. MERSAND, JOSEPH. *Traditions in American Literature: A Study of Jewish Characters and Authors.* New York: Modern Chapbooks, 1939.

Analyses of American Jewish dramatists, novelists, and poets, together with essays on the portrayal of the Jew in the history of American Jewish literature. Useful bibliographies of novels, short stories, plays, poetry, autobiographies, biographies, and works of criticism and belles-lettres pertaining to Jewish life in the United States.

590. RABINOWICZ, HARRY M. *The Jewish Literary Treasures of England and America.* New York: Yoseloff, 1962.

Most of the book describes the Judaica in American Jewish, public, and university libraries. Illustrations, glossary, and bibliography. Useful for the research worker.

591. RIBALOW, MENACHEM, ed. *Antologiah shel ha-shirah ha-ivrit b'Amerikah.* New York: Histadruth Ivrith of America, 1938.

An anthology of Hebrew poetry written in the United States, preceded by the editor's analytical introduction. Biographical sketches and portraits of the twenty-four poets.

592. RIBALOW, MENACHEM, ed. *Sefer Ha-yovel shel Hadoar.* New York: Histadruth ha-Ivrit b'Amerikah, 1927.

A volume of prose and poetry commemorating the five-years' existence of the American Hebrew-language weekly. Several essays deal with personalities and issues in American Jewish culture and education.

593. RIVKIN, B. *Grunt-tendentzn fun der Yiddisher literatur in Amerike.* New York: YKUF Farlag, 1948.

Essays on the development and characteristics of Yiddish literature in the United States and on the issues and problems of Yiddish literature in the Soviet Union.

594. SCHULMAN, ELIAHU (ELIAS). *Geshikhte fun der Yiddisher Literatur in Amerika, 1870-1900.* New York: L. W. Biderman, 1943.

A documented analysis in Yiddish of the growth and development of the Yiddish press, journalism, popular and imaginative writing, poetry, and drama in the United States. Abundant reprints of poetic examples.

595. *Sefer ha-shanah l'Yehudei Amerikah.* New York: Histadruth Ivrith of America, 1931-1949.

Eleven volumes of Hebrew poetry and prose by American Jewish writers. Edited, for the most part, by Menahem Ribalow. Some of the essays deal with developments in Jewish life, literature, society, religion, and education in the United States.

596. WALDEN, DANIEL, ed. *On Being Jewish: American Jewish Writers from Cahan to Bellow.* Greenwich, Con.: Fawcett Publications, 1974.

An anthology of prose and poetry of the twentieth century by immigrant and native men and women of letters illustrating the immigration and later periods. Interpretive introductions by the editor.
native men and women of letters illustrating the immigration and later periods. Interpretive introductions by the editor.

XII. IMMIGRATION

XII. IMMIGRATION

597. BERNHEIMER, CHARLES S., ed. *The Russian Jew in the United States*. Philadelphia: Winston, 1905.

A compilation of essays by specialists and leaders on the Russian Jewish immigrant population in New York, Philadelphia, and Chicago. Attention is given to philanthropy, economic and industrial status, religion, educational influences, social and cultural development, and other facets of life. Bibliography of studies, fiction, reports, periodical articles. This book throws light on the early decades of the Russian Jewish experience in America.

598. BRANDES, JOSEPH. *Immigrants to Freedom: Jewish Communities in Rural New Jersey since 1882*. Philadelphia: University of Pennsylvania Press, 1971.

A detailed, thoroughly documented study of the transplantation of Russian Jewish immigrants on American soil. Statistics and illustrations.

599. DAVIE, MAURICE R., *et al. Refugees in America: Report of a Committee for the Study of Recent Immigration from Europe*. New York: Harper, 1947.

A comprehensive, enlightening study dealing mainly

with the flight of German Jews during the Nazi era to the United States and their adjustment along social, economic, cultural, communal, and professional lines. The appendix includes a list of agencies aiding the refugees and names of distinguished persons in the various specialties.

600. DUGGAN, STEPHEN, and BETTY DRURY. *The Rescue of Science and Learning: The Story of the Emergency Committee in Aid of Displaced Foreign Scholars.* New York: Macmillan, 1948.

A report of the adjustment of emigre scholars from Nazi Germany, many of them Jewish but not usually identified, and their contributions to American scholarship, education, culture, science, and society. Appendix contains statistical data and lists of scholars.

601. FERMI, LAURA. *Illustrious Immigrants: The Intellectual Migration from Europe, 1930-41.* Chicago: University of Chicago Press, 1968.

A study of the European background, migration, adjustment, and achievements of Jews and non-Jews prominent in scholarship, science, and culture, including an evaluation of their contributions to America. Bibliographical notes.

602. FLEMING, DONALD, and BERNARD BAILYN, eds. *The Intellectual Migration: Europe and America, 1930-1960.* Cambridge, Mass.: Harvard University Press, 1969.

Essays on the contributions by Jewish and non-Jewish refugees from Nazi Germany to American learning, science, and culture. Illustrations and brief biographies of 300 notable emigres.

603. GLANZ, RUDOLF. *Studies in Judaica Americana*. New York: KTAV Publishing House, 1970.

Fifteen scholarly essays on the history of the immigration, adjustment, and socio-economic-cultural activities of German Jews in America during the nineteenth and early twentieth centuries. The first chapter, reprinted from the *Yivo Annual of Jewish Social Science,* Vol. VI, 1951), contains 150 documents on the history of German Jewish immigration to the United States, 1800-1880.

604. GOLD, MICHAEL. *Jews without Money*. Garden City, N.Y.: Sun Dial Press, 1946.

A reprint of a work, originally published in 1930, with the author's introduction dated 1935. Journalistic vignettes of Jewish life in the midst of poverty in the Lower East Side of New York. The author maintains that "the historic class division is true among the Jews as with any other race" [p. 10].

605. HAPGOOD, HUTCHINS. *The Spirit of the Ghetto: Studies of the Jewish Quarter of New York*. New York: Funk & Wagnalls, 1965.

This volume, originally published in 1902 by a non-Jewish writer, is a sympathetic report on scholars, rabbis, women, poets, the stage, literature, art, the press, and "odd characters," illustrated by the young Jacob Epstein's drawings from life. Interesting light on the life, education, work, and thought of the early Russian Jewish immigrants in the New World. Instructive introduction and notes by Harry Golden.

606. HIRSHLER, ERIC E., ed. *Jews from Germany in the United States*. New York: Farrar, Straus and Cudahy, 1955.

Essays by five scholars on the history of the contributions of German Jews to American life and culture, with special reference to the impact on Jewish religious life. The appendix contains four German letters, notes, and bibliographical references.

607. JAMES, EDMUND J., ed. *The Immigrant Jew in America*. New York: Buck, 1907.

Essays by non-Jewish and Jewish scholars on the adjustment of Russian Jewish immigrants in America, and on Jewish activities in philanthropy, religion, education, politics, and other aspects of life in the United States. In an appreciative preface, President James of the University of Illinois emphasized that the Russian Jewish immigrants "struggle along patiently and honestly, making gradually a more and more decent home and livelihood for themselves, and sparing no privation to secure the education and advance of their children" (p. 6). Illustrations.

608. JOSEPH, SAMUEL. *History of the Baron de Hirsch Fund: The Americanization of the Jewish Immigrant*. n.p.: Jewish Publication Society, 1935.

A documented account of a half-century of a philanthropic program aimed at "the adjustment and assimilation of the immigrant Jewish population . . . [through] relief, temporary aid, promotion of suburban industrial enterprises, removal from urban centers, land settlement, agricultural training, trade and general education" (p. viii). Illustrations and texts of documents.

609. JOSEPH, SAMUEL. *Jewish Immigration to the United States from 1881 to 1910.* New York: The author, 1914.

> A Ph.D. thesis at Columbia University analyzing the socio-economic-political context of Jewish life in Eastern Europe, the immigration, and the socio-economic-educational characteristics of the immigrants. Appended statistics and a short bibliography in English, French, and German.

610. KISCH, GUIDO. *In Search of Freedom: A History of American Jews from Czechoslovakia.* London: Edward Goldston, 1949.

> An historical account concentrating on the nineteenth and twentieth centuries. Special attention is given to the contributions by Jews of Czech origin to the Jewish religion and culture in the United States, as well as to the arts, education, medicine, industry, and other facets of American secular life. Scholarly notes, documentary texts, illustrations, and an extensive bibliography of Czech Jewish history.

611. LEROY-BEAULIEU, ANATOLE. *Les immigrants juifs et le Judaisme aux Etats-Unis.* Paris: Librairie Nouvelle, 1905.

> A concise report by a sociologist on the social, cultural, and spiritual adjustment of Jewish immigrants in the United States. The author concludes that "l'americanisation est la realite" (p. 36).

612. MANNERS, ANDE. *Poor Cousins.* New York: Crown, McCann & Geoghegan, 1972.

> A popular, interesting presentation of the nine-

teenth-century Russia abandoned by Jewish immigrants in America, the early Jewish background in the New World, and the Russian Jewish experience in the late nineteenth and the early twentieth centuries in New York City and in rural areas. Illustrations and selected bibliography. The Russian Jewish immigrants of New York City were the "Downtown Jews," the poor cousins of the "Uptown Jews"—the "deitshe Yahudim" (German Jews).

613. MCKENNA, M. J. *Our Brethren of the Tenements and the Ghetto.* New York: J. S. Ogilvie Publishing Co., 1899.

A sympathetic portrayal of the life and activities of Jewish immigrants on the Lower East Side of New York City. The author found there "Morality, Faith and Charity. Hope is not dead. . . ." (p. 99).

614. PRAIS, G. M. (GEORGE M. PRICE). *Russki Yevrei v Amerikie: Ocherki iz istorii, zhizni i byta russko-yevreiskikh emigrantov Soyedinennikh Shtatakh Sev. Ameriki s 1881 g. po 1891g.* St. Petersburg: Landau, 1893.

Survey by a Russian Jewish immigrant (1864-1942), who became a physician and a Yiddish journalist, of the historical background and life of Russian Jewish immigrants during their first decade in the United States.

615. RADKAU, JOACHIM. *Die deutsche Emigration in den USA: Ihr Einfluss auf die amerikanische Europapolitik, 1933-1945.* Dusseldorf: Bertelsmann Universitatsverlag, 1971.

An extensively documented study of the impact of

the Jewish and non-Jewish immigrants from Nazi Germany on United States foreign policy in Europe. Bibliography in German and English.

616. RIIS, JACOB A. *How the Other Half Lives: Studies among the Tenements of New York.* New York: Scribner, 1890.

Impressions, with illustrations, of the life of the various minorities in New York City. In the chapter, "Jewtown," which depicts the squalor of the Lower East Side, the author found very little that was good or attractive about the Jews: "Money is their God" (p. 107).

617. SANDERS, RONALD. *The Downtown Jews: Portrait of an Immigrant Generation.* New York: Harper & Row, 1969.

An interesting account of Jewish life, labor, and culture on the Lower East Side of New York City in the early twentieth century against the background of the Russian situation which led to the emigration to America. The focus is on the life of Abraham Cahan, Yiddish journalist and editor of the *Jewish Daily Forward (Forverts).* Photographs, glossary of Yiddish, Hebrew, and Russian terms, and brief bibliography.

618. WALD, LILLIAN D. *The House on Henry Street.* New York: Henry Holt, 1915.

An illustrated, popular account of the activities of the Henry Street Settlement on New York's Lower East Side in improving the social, educational, and other types of welfare of immigrant Jews.

619. WHITE, LYMAN C. *300,000 New Americans: The Epic of a Modern Immigrant-Aid Service.* New York: Harper, 1957.

A detailed, informative study of aid to refugees and immigrants from the European countries which had been under the control of Nazi Germany.

620. WISCHNITZER, MARK. *To Dwell in Safety: The Story of Jewish Migration since 1800.* Philadelphia: Jewish Publication Society of America, 1948.

A thoroughly documented, interesting history of the migration of Jews from Europe, particularly Eastern Europe and Germany, especially to the United States. Photographs and facsimiles. Appendix contains statistics and names of Jewish organizations active in migration and colonization work.

621. WISCHNITZER, MARK. *Visas to Freedom: The History of HIAS.* Cleveland, Ohio: World Publishing Co., 1956.

A detailed account of the development of the Hebrew Immigrant Aid Society (HIAS) from 1902 through the decade after World War II. A significant work on American Jewish aid to East European and German immigrants. Photographs and notes.

XIII. INTERGROUP RELATIONS

XIII. INTERGROUP RELATIONS

622. BARRON, MILTON L. *People Who Intermarry: Intermarriage in a New England Industrial Community.* Syracuse, N.Y.: Syracuse University Press, 1946.

A careful sociological study, based on official records, questionnaires, interviews, and correspondence of marriages involving different ethnic and religious groups in Derby, Conn., during 1929-1930 and 1940. The Jews, "one of the most endogamous religious groups," had no instance of intermarriage in 1929-1930 and only one in 1940. During 1900-1935, with few exceptions, "all rates of Jewish intermarriage were found to be low, most of them ranging from one per cent to ten per cent. Almost everywhere Jewish men intermarry more than Jewish women" (p. 341). Annotated bibliography.

623. BERMAN, LOUIS A. *Jews and Intermarriage: A Study in Personality and Culture.* New York: Thomas Yoseloff, 1968.

A detailed study by a professor of psychology of the various problems and issues of Jewish-Christian marriages in the United States in the light of researches in the behavioral sciences. The author's viewpoint is that "intermarriage *per se* is not a threat to Jewish surviv-

al, though some of the conditions that lead to intermarriage are disruptive of Jewish group life" (p. 559).
Extensive documentation, comprehensive bibliography, and glossary of Hebrew and Yiddish terms.

624. BROTZ, HOWARD. *The Black Jews of Harlem: Negro
Nationalism and the Dilemmas of Negro Leadership.*
New York: Schocken Books, 1970.

A brief account of the personalities and customs of
New York City's Black Jewish community. Most of
the book deals with the Black Jews' relations with
white Jews and Black non-Jews. Photographs and
notes.

625. FISHMAN, HERTZEL. *American Protestantism and a
Jewish State.* Detroit, Mich.: Wayne State University
Press, 1973.

A competently documented historical analysis of the
attitudes of American liberal Protestants to the Zionist movement, and to establishment and continuance
of the State of Israel. Bibliography.

626. GILBERT, ARTHUR. *Jews in Christian America.* New
York: Sheed and Ward, 1966.

Historical and contemporary perspectives by a Reform rabbi on Jewish-Christian relations, anti-Semitism, Reform Judaism, religious freedom, and related
topics.

627. GLANZ, RUDOLF. *Jew and Irish: Historic Group Relations and Immigration.* New York: The author,
1966.

A scholarly, comparative study of two immigrant

groups in America, including their social, economic, and cultural interrelationships.

628. GLANZ, RUDOLF. *Jew and Italian: Historic Group Relations and the New Immigration (1881-1924).* New York: The author, 1970.

An informative monograph on the unusual theme of interaction of two religious-ethnic-linguistic immigrant groups in New York City. Documentation in English, Italian, and Yiddish.

629. GLANZ, RUDOLF. *Jew and Mormon: Historic Group Relations and Religious Outlook.* New York: The author, 1963.

An extensively documented comparative study of two religious minorities in America and of their interrelationships. The author concludes that "Mormonism appears as the conqueror of old Christian-European inhibitions vis-a-vis Judaism and as the creator of a new relationship to the old Bible people and its religious world" (p. 332).

630. GLANZ, RUDOLF. *Jews in Relation to the Cultural Milieu of the Germans in America up to the Eighteen Eighties.* New York: The author, 1947.

A study, based mainly on German-language sources, of social, economic, cultural, and religious relations between immigrant Germans and Jews. Translated from the Yiddish essays in *Yivo Bleter.*

631. GLAZER, NATHAN, and DANIEL P. MOYNIHAN. *Beyond the Melting Pot: The Negroes, Puerto Ricans, Jews, Italians, and Irish of New York City.* 2d ed. Cambridge, Mass.: M.I.T. Press, 1970.

Minority group life and problems in a metropolis, including interminority relations. The 1970 edition contains a considerable supplement.

632. GLOCK, CHARLES Y., GERTRUDE J. SELZNICK, and JOE L. SPAETH. *The Apathetic Majority: A Study Based on Public Responses to the Eichmann Trial.* New York: Harper & Row, 1966.

A sociological study using the interview technique to determine representative public opinion in Oakland, California, regarding the trial in Israel of Adolf Eichmann, a prime perpetrator of the "Final Solution" and extermination of European Jews during World War II. The authors conclude that the trial attracted widespread interest and aroused the sympathy of "the apathetic majority," but "what has been learned about the impact of the Eichmann trial hardly provides a complete strategy for eliminating anti-Semitism" (p. 168).

633.. *Group-Life in America: A Task Force Report.* New York: Institute of Human Relations, American Jewish Committee, 1972.

A report by Jews and non-Jews, academicians and citizens, concerning the contemporary situation in the relations among religious and racial groups in the United States, with particular reference to politics, economics, education, and meritocracy vs. affirmative action.

634. HALPERN, BEN. *Jews and Blacks: The Classic American Minorities.* New York: Herder and Herder, 1971.

An examination of various implications of recent developments affecting American Jews and Blacks and their interrelationships.

635. HALPERN, BEN. *The American Jew: A Zionist Analysis.* New York: Theodor Herzl Foundation, 1956.

An American Jewish academician analyzes problems and proposed solutions associated with assimilation and relations to non-Jews in the United States.

636. HARRIS, LOUIS, and BERT E. SWANSON. *Black-Jewish Relations in New York City.* New York: Praeger Publishers, 1970.

Interviews and questionnaires involving adult Jews, Blacks, and non-Jewish whites explore recent intergroup relations in depth, as well as procedures "to reestablish a sense of accommodation so that the city will not blow apart" (p. 205). The authors see a shift in the Jewish attitude, as a consequence of Black-Jewish tensions, from liberalism to a sense of solidarity with the white community, especially the Catholic groups.

637. HERBERG, WILL. *Protestant-Catholic-Jew: An Essay in American Religious Sociology.* Garden City, N.Y.: Doubleday, 1960.

A new, fully revised edition of a comparative analysis of the three dominant denominations in the United States with reference to the historical, social, and theological contexts. The author notes that the third generation (1930s) of the East European Jewish stock "felt secure in its Americanness and no longer saw any reason for the attitude of rejection so characteristic of its predecessors. It therefore felt no reluctance about identifying itself as Jewish and affirming its

Jewishness; on the contrary, such identifications became virtually compelling since it was the only way in which the American Jew could now locate himself in the larger community" (p. 189). Abundant documentation and extensive bibliography.

638. *Intermarriage and the Future of the American Jew.* New York: Commission on Synagogue Relations, Federation of Jewish Philantrhopies of New York, 1964.

Essays and discussions by rabbis, sociologists, and social workers with different perspectives and proposals for dealing with the problem of intermarriage.

639. *Jew and Gentile: Being a Report of a Conference of Israelites Regarding Their Mutual Relations and Welfare.* New York: Revell, 1890.

Addresses and papers by three Reform rabbis (Bernard Felsenthal, Emil G. Hirsch, and Joseph Stolz) and five Protestant clergymen.

640. KATZ, SHLOMO, ed. *Negro and Jew: An Encounter in America.* New York: Macmillan, 1967.

Statements, most of them by Jewish writers, scholars, and rabbis, on the tension and conflict between Blacks and Jews in the United States.

641. LANDMAN, ISAAC, ed. *Christian and Jew.* New York: Liveright, 1929.

Jewish and non-Jewish views on better interreligious relations.

642. LASKER, BRUNO, ed. *Jewish Experiences in America:*

Suggestions for the Study of Jewish Relations with Non-Jews. New York: The Inquiry, 1930.

An anthology of writings dealing with various American Jewish developments and problems. Outline for study and discussion, reading list, suggestions for discussion leaders, and specimen attitude and opinion tests.

643. L'ESTRANGE, HAMON. *Americans No Iewes, or Improbabilities That the Americans Are of That Race.* London: Seile, 1652.

A refutation of Thomas Thorowgood's arguments in *Iewes in American* (1650) that maintain the identification of the American Indians with the Jews.

644. LIPMAN, EUGENE J., and ALBERT VORSPAN, eds. *A Tale of Ten Cities: The Triple Ghetto in American Religious Life.* New York: Union of American Hebrew Rabbis, 1962.

Frank analyses by anonymous writers of the changing Catholic-Protestant-Jewish relations in Boston, Cleveland, Los Angeles, New York City, Philadelphia, Minneapolis, St. Paul, Nashville, Muncie, and Plainview (Long Island, N.Y.). The issues under discussion include education, religion, church-state separation, politics, race, censorship, foreign affairs, and Sunday closing of business establishments.

645. MAYER, JOHN E. *Jewish-Gentile Courtships: An Exploratory Study of a Social Process.* New York: Free Press of Glencoe, 1961.

A sociological analysis, with frequent quotations of the subjects' opinions, of the processes and problems

of interfaith relationships which led to intermarriage.

646. *Negro-Jewish Relations in United States.* New York:
    Citadel Press, 1966.

    Essays and responses by Black and Jewish scholars on
    various forms of relationships involving the two
    groups. Bibliography. Originally published in *Jewish
    Social Studies,* January, 1965.

647. OLSON, BERNHARD E. *Faith and Prejudice: Inter-
    group Problems in Protestant Curricula.* New Haven,
    Conn.: Yale University Press, 1963.

    A careful study of Protestant religious school text-
    books and courses. The author observes in conclusion
    that "while some Protestant teachings can conceiv-
    ably implant or nurture certain types of anti-Judaism
    and anti-Catholicism, they also disseminate valuable
    remedies for prejudice as well" (p. 271).

648. PAWLIKOWSKI, JOHN T. *Cathechetics and Prejudice:
    How Catholic Teaching Materials View Jews, Protes-
    tants and Racial Minorities.* New York: Paulist Press,
    1973.

    A Catholic priest's summary and interpretation of
    three studies at St. Louis University of the persistence
    of prejudice toward minorities, especially Jews, in
    Catholic textbooks. In his foreword, the Rev. William
    J. Tobin, a leading Catholic religious educator, states
    that, "despite a decade of significant ecumenical and
    interreligious advances and declarations, broad-scale
    attitudinal bias may still remain" (p. 3).

649. PITT, JAMES E. *Adventures in Brotherhood.* New York: Farrar, Straus, 1955.

An account of the origin, development, and activities of the National Conference of Christians and Jews.

650. RINGER, BENJAMIN. *The Edge of Friendliness: A Study of Jewish-Gentile Relations.* New York: Basic Books, 1967.

A sociological study, based on interviews and questionnaires, of Jews in a Protestant suburban community. The conclusion is that "despite the significant contacts between Jews and Gentiles and the benign atmosphere that prevails in Lakeville, an air of uncertainty and fantasy still characterizes their relations . . . [and] an undercurrent of unresolved tension" (pp. 267-268).

651. SHERMAN, BEZALEL. *Yidn un andere etnishe grupes in di Varaynikte Shatatn.* New York: Undzer Veg, 1948.

A sociological examination of the relations of Jews to other ethnic groups in America. Bibliography in English and Yiddish.

652. SILCOX, EDWIN C., and GALEN FISHER. *Catholics, Jews and Protestants.* New York: Harper & Bros.

A careful study of interreligious relations and attitudes in the United States and Canada. Some questionable interpretations.

653. STROBER, GERALD S. *Portrait of the Elder Brother: Jews and Judaism in Protestant Teaching Materials.*

[New York] : American Jewish Committee and National Conference of Christians and Jews, 1972.

A documented analysis of what the school publications issued by U.S. Protestant churches teach about the Jewish past, religion, and recent history. Some improvement is noted, but change is very slow.

654. THOROWGOOD, THOMAS. *Iewes in America, or, Probabilities That the Americans Are of That Race: With the Removall of Some Contrary Reasonings, and Earnest Desires for Effectuall Endeavours to Make Them Christian.* London: Slater, 1650.

An identification, on the basis of similarities of words, names, customs, and other respects, of the Jews with the American Indians.

655. THOROWGOOD, THOMAS. *Jews in America: or Probabilities That Those Indians Are Judaical, Made More Probably by Some Additionals to the Former Conjectures.* London: Brome, 1660.

The second, substantially revised edition of the work which sought to encourage missionary work among the American Indians, identified by the author as Jews.

656. VOSS, CARL H. *Rabbi and Minister: The Friendship of Stephen S. Wise and John Haynes Holmes.* Cleveland: World Publishing Co., 1964.

An interesting account of the relationship between a Reform rabbi and a Protestant minister. Notes on sources, bibliography, and illustrations.

657. WEISBORD, ROBERT G., and ARTHUR STEIN. *Bit-*

tersweet Encounter: The Afro-American and the American Jew. Westport, Conn.: Negro Universities Press, 1970.

A documented study comparing and contrasting the relationships of Jews and Blacks in historical context. The authors, who are Jews, are rather more critical of their own people's attitudes than those of the blacks. Bibliography.

XIV. ANTI-SEMITISM

XIV. ANTI-SEMITISM

658. ABERNETHY, ARTHUR T. *The Jew a Negro: Being a Study of the Jewish Ancestry from an Impartial Standpoint.* Moravian Falls, N.C.: Dixie Publishing Co., 1910.

The author, a member of the faculty of Rutherford College, disclaims "an attack upon the Hebrew race" (p. 7), but denounces American Jews for disregarding the truth and engaging in shady business practices. The worst characteristics of the Jew, as perceived by the author, are correlated with those of the Negro, who is the "less cultured African brother of the Jews" (p. 105).

659. BELTH, N. C., ed. *Barriers: Patterns of Discrimination against Jews.* New York: Anti-Defamation League of B'nai B'rith, 1958.

An anthology of factual statements regarding the status of anti-Jewish discrimination in clubs, resorts, employment, education, and housing.

660. *Black Anti-Semitism and Jewish Racism.* New York: Richard W. Baron, 1969.

Outspoken essays by Black and Jewish writers, communal and religious leaders, and other leaders offering different viewpoints on the breakdown of relationship between the two groups.

661. BROUN, HEYWOOD, and GEORGE BRITT. *Christians Only*. New York: Vanguard Press, 1931.

Disclosure of specific cases of anti-Semitic practices in educational institutions, professional groups, employment, etc.

662. CARLSON, JOHN R. *Under Cover*. Philadelphia: Blakiston, 1943.

A detailed expose of the organization and activities of anti-Semitic groups in the United States.

663. COHEN, HENRY. *Justice, Justice: A Jewish View of the Black Revolution*. New York: Union of American Hebrew Congregations, 1969.

A documented, illustrated analysis by a Reform rabbi of the meaning of Jewish values in connection with racial relations, including the liberal response to Black anti-Semitism. Appendix contains a chronology, bibliography, and documents.

664. DINNERSTEIN, LEONARD. *The Leo Frank Case*. New York: Columbia University Press, 1968.

A scholarly study of "one of the most infamous outbursts of anti-Semitic feeling in the United States [which] occurred in [Atlanta,] Georgia in the years 1913, 1914, and 1915"—the conviction of Leo Frank, a Texas-born, Northern Jewish manufacturer, for the murder of the thirteen-year-old Mary Phagan. Frank was lynched by a mob. Illustrations, documents, and bibliography. 665.

665. EDITORS OF FORTUNE. *Jews in America.* New York: Random House, 1936.

A concise commentary on the participation of Jews in business, politics, and the professions in the United States. Appendix contains descriptions of main anti-Semitic organizations and a list of Jewish-owned movie companies.

666. EPSTEIN, BENJAMIN R. and ARNOLD FORSTER. *Some of My Best Friends.* . . . New York: Farrar, Straus and Cudahy, 1962.

Survey of anti-Jewish discrimination in American society, housing, higher education, and employment.

667. FINEBERG, SOLOMON A. *Overcoming Anti-Semitism.* New York: Harper & Bros., 1943.

A balanced treatment of practical procedures to combat anti-Semitism in America.

668. FORSTER, ARNOLD. *A Measure of Freedom.* Garden City, N.Y.: Doubleday, 1950.

An analysis of research findings, prepared under the auspices of the Anti-Defamation League of B'nai B'rith, of several aspects of anti-Semitism in the United States in relation to civil rights. The emphasis is on discrimination against Jews, but frequent reference is also made to other minorities. The conclusion is that the data reveal "the unwholesome racial and religious prejudices and undemocratic discriminations in the United States" (p. 211). Documentation, statistics, and appendix of anti-Semitic organizations, leaders, and publications.

669. FORSTER, ARNOLD, and BENJAMIN R. EPSTEIN. *Cross-Currents*. Garden City, N.Y.: Doubleday, 1956.

Survey of anti-Semitic attitudes and activities in the United States, Germany, and the Middle East.

670. FORSTER, ARNOLD, and BENJAMIN R. EPSTEIN. *The New Anti-Semitism*. New York: McGraw-Hill, 1974.

A meticulously documented analysis of the sources, types, and prevalence of anti-Jewish attitudes and behavior in the United States and abroad in the 1960s and 1970s. Special attention is given to Blacks, education, the clergy, the mass media, the arts, and the Radical Left and Right. The authors conclude that there exists in the United States "a large measure of indifference to the most profound apprehensions of the Jewish people; a blandness and apathy in dealing with anti-Jewish behavior; a widespread incapacity or unwillingness to comprehend the necessity of the existence of Israel to Jewish safety and survival throughout the world. This is the heart of the new anti-Semitism" (p. 324).

671. FORSTER, ARNOLD, and BENJAMIN R. EPSTEIN. *The Trouble-Makers: An Anti-Defamation League Report*. Garden City, N.Y.: Doubleday. 1952.

A detailed examination of the activities of the practitioners of anti-Jewish and other forms of prejudice, during the late 1940s and early 1950s in the United States.

672. GELTMAN, MAX. *The Confrontation: Black Power, Anti-Semitism, and the Myth of Integration*. Englewood Cliffs, N.J.: Prentice-Hall, 1970.

A detailed, disillusioned, frank analysis of the recent relations between Jews and Blacks in the United States. The author, who writes for the *National Review* and edits the *Mediterranean Survey,* concludes that "for his own soul, for his own future, for his own peace of mind, the Jew must separate himself at every level from participation in Negro affairs and must persist only on terms of individual friendship wherever possible" (p. 239).

673. GLOCK, CHARLES Y., and RODNEY STARK. *Christian Beliefs and Anti-Semitism.* New York: Harper & Row, 1966.

A questionnaire study exploring the relation between Christian techniques and attitudes toward Jews in America. The authors express "a sense of shock and dismay that a faith which proclaims the brotherhood of man can be so perverted into a *raison d'etre* for bigotry" (p. 207), and conclude that "until the process by which religion fosters anti-Semitism has been abolished, the Christian conscience must bear the guilt of biogotry" (p. 212).

674. GOLDEN, HARRY. *A Little Girl Is Dead.* Cleveland, Ohio: World Publishing Co., 1965.

A detailed, popular account, based on documentary materials, of the case of Leo Frank, who was lynched for the alleged murder of a fourteen-year-old girl in Atlanta. According to the author, this case "paralleled the agony of Alfred Dreyfus in France" (p. xiv). Illustrations, documents, and selected references.

675. GRAEBER, ISACQUE, and STEUART H. BRITT, eds. *Jews in a Gentile World.* New York: Macmillan, 1942.

Essays by sixteen Jewish and non-Jewish scholars on the history, psychology, sociology, and other aspects of anti-Semitism. Bibliographies.

676. HANDLIN, OSCAR and MARY. *Danger in Discord.* New York: Anti-Defamation League of B'nai B'rith, 1954.

A concise account of the historical context of anti-Semitism in the United States.

677. HECHT, BEN. *A Guide for the Bedevilled.* New York: Charles Scribner's Sons, 1944.

A Jewish writer's critical analysis of the various types of anti-Semitism.

678. HIGHAM, JOHN. *Anti-Semitism in the Gilded Age: A Reinterpretation.* New York: Anti-Defamation League of B'nai B'rith, 1958.

A brief report on anti-Semitic sentiment and action in the United States, 1870-1900.

679. HIGHAM, JOHN. *Social Discrimination against Jews in America, 1830-1930.* New York: Anti-Defamation League of B'nai B'rith, 1958.

A brief historical analysis of factors and trends in the social treatment of Jews by the non-Jewish population in the United States.

680. HIGHAM, JOHN. *Strangers in the Land: Patterns of American Nativism, 1860-1925.* New Brunswick, N.J.: Rutgers University Press, 1955.

A scholarly analysis of prejudiced attitudes and activities against religious and ethnic minorities in the United States. The author points out that after the Civil War the Jews "lost in reputation as they gained in social and economic status" (p. 26), that "beginning with the late eighties, the first serious anti-Semitic demonstrations in American history began in the lower South where Jewish supply merchants were common" (p. 92), and that until the post-World War I period "anti-Jewish sentiment, though unique in kind, did not exceed in degree the general level of feeling against other European nationalities" (pp. 277-278). Bibliographical note.

681. HOLMES, JOHN H. *Through Gentile Eyes.* New York: Jewish Opinion Publishing Co., 1939.

An influential Protestant minister's essays on the roots of anti-Semitism and on the need for understanding and goodwill toward Jews.

682. KNORTZ, KARL. *Das amerikanische Judentum.* Leipzig: Engel, 1914.

A bitter, pre-Nazi, anti-Jewish attack published in Germany by Professor Karl Knortz of North Tarrytown, N.Y.

683. LEVINGER, LEE J. *Anti-Semitism in the United States: Its History and Causes.* New York: Bloch Publishing Co., 1925.

A sociological approach to the problems and possible solutions, e.g., assimilation, Zionism, group adaptation, in historical perspective.

684. LEVINGER, LEE J. *Anti-Semitism: Yesterday and Tomorrow.* New York: Macmillan, 1936.

A survey of the history of anti-Semitism from ancient times to the twentieth century. Analysis of causes and treatment from the standpoint of an American Jew. Selected references.

685. LIVINGSTON, SIGMUND. *Must Men Hate?* New York: Harper & Bros., 1944.

A critical treatment of the different aspects of anti-Semitism. Appendix of Jewish contributions to culture and of Jewish heroes of World War II. Bibliography.

686. MCWILLIAMS, CAREY. *A Mask for Privilege: Anti-Semitism in America.* Boston: Little, Brown and Company, 1948.

A documented, well-written analysis of the roots and pattern of American anti-Semitism. The author concludes: "Anti-Semitism is one of the greatest barriers to self-knowledge and social understanding of our times because it masks a reality—the reality of social, economic, and political injustice" (p. 269).

687. MYERS, GUSTAVUS. *History of Bigotry in the United States.* New York: Capricorn Books, 1960.

Originally published in 1943, this revised edition, edited by Henry M. Christman, presents in detail the development of religious, ethnic, and racial prejudice in America from colonial times to the mid-twentieth century. Several chapters deal with the history of anti-Semitism in the United States. Footnotes, but no bibliography.

688. ROY, RALPH L. *Apostles of Discord: A Study of Organized Bigotry and Disruption on the Fringes of Protestantism.* Boston: Beacon Press, 1953.

An analysis of the prejudiced views and activities of some Protestant groups, with particular reference to anti-Semitism.

689.. SELZNICK, GERTRUDE J., and STEPHEN STEIN-BERG. *The Tenacity of Prejudice: Anti-Semitism in Contemporary America.* New York: Harper & Row, 1969.

A portion of the Five-Year Study of Anti-Semitism, sponsored by the Anti-Defamation League and directed by the Survey Research Center, University of California (Berkeley). This interview study analyzed the prevalence and extent of anti-Semitic beliefs and stereotypes in relation to the "support of discriminatory practices" and "susceptibility to political anti-Semitism." The basic conclusions indicate that "anti-Semitism continues at significant levels, and lack of education is the primary factor in its acceptance. . . . Anti-Semitism is widespread and pervasive, but not in a dangerous form" (p. 184).

690. SOKOLSKY, GEORGE E. *We Jews.* Garden City, N.Y.: Doubleday, Doran, 1935.

A Jewish writer's vigorous and subjective statement on anti-Semitism, as well as a plea for the return to religious tradition.

691. SPARGO, JOHN. *The Jew and American Ideals.* New York: Harper & Bros., 1921.

A defense of American values against anti-Semitism, particularly in criticism of the reprint by Henry Ford's *Dearborn Independent* of the notorious forgery, *Protocols of the Elders of Zion.*

692. SPIVAK, JOHN L. *Plotting America's Pogroms.* New York: New Masses, 1934.

A Marxist interpretation of organized anti-Semitism in the United States in the light of the class struggle.

693. STARK, RODNEY, and STEPHEN STEINBERG. *It Did Happen Here: An Investigation of Political Anti-Semitism, Wayne, New Jersey, 1967.* New York: Anti-Defamation League of B'nai B'rith, 1967.

A concise case study of a school board election in which anti-Semitic agitation played an important part in the campaign.

694. STEMBER, CHARLES H. *et al. Jews in the Mind of America.* New York: Basic Books, 1966.

Studies by sociologists, social psychologists, and historians of the backgrounds, status, and prospects of Christian-Jewish relations and of anti-Semitism in the United States on the basis of public opinion polls and the analysis of pertinent literature. Of special interest is Thomas F. Pettigrew's comparison of anti-Semitic and anti-Negro attitudes. In his conclusion of the study of public attitudes, Dr. Stember states: "Anti-Jewish prejudice obviously is not yet a thing of the past, any more than anti-Jewish discrimination is, but both are unmistakably in a state of decline . . . the current trend toward more and more complete acceptance of the Jew—both individually and in the abstract—appears unlikely to be reversed by anything short of a catastrophic crisis in American society" (p. 217).

695. STOCK, ERNEST, *et al. Ha-tzibur ha-Yehudi nochah ha-Antishemiut ha-Kushit b'Artzot Ha-Brit.* Jeru-

salem: Institute for Contemporary Jewry, Hebrew University, 1970.

Comments by American and Israeli scholars on the response by American Jews to Black anti-Semitism.

696. STRONG, DONALD S. *Organized Anti-Semitism in America.* Washington, D.C.: American Council on Public Affairs, 1941.

A meticulous examination of the organization and anti-Semitic activities of Nazi and similar groups in the United States, 1930-1940. Bibliography. A valuable resource for the period. 697.

697. *The International Jew: The World's Foremost Problem.* 4 vols. Dearborn, Mich.: Dearborn Publishing Co., 1920-1922.

Reprint of a series of eighty anti-Semitic articles in the *Dearborn Independent,* 1920-1922, and later translated into several languages and circulated abroad widely. Volume 2 is entitled "Jewish Activities in the United States"; volume 3, "Jewish Influences in American Life," including one article on "Jewish Degradation of American Baseball"; volume 4, "Aspects of Jewish Power in the United States."

698. *To Bigotry No Sanction: A Documented Analysis of Anti-Semitic Propaganda.* Rev. ed. New York: American Jewish Committee, 1944.

Refutation of anti-Jewish propaganda during World War II and an account of positive Jewish contributions to America. Bibliographies.

699. WEINTRAUB, RUTH G. *How Secure These Rights?*

Anti-Semitism in the United States in 1948: An Anti-Defamation League Survey. Garden City, N.Y.: Doubleday, 1949.

A comprehensive analysis of the status of anti-Semitic attitudes and actions during a single year.

XV. PERIODICALS, YEARBOOKS, AND ENCYCLOPEDIAS

XV. PERIODICALS, YEARBOOKS, AND ENCYCLOPEDIAS

700. *Algemeiner Zhurnal.* New York, 1972- .

   A Yiddish-language weekly (*General Journal*), successor to the *Tog-Morgan Zhurnal,* reflecting an Orthodox viewpoint on Jewish affairs and developments.

701. *American Hebrew and Jewish Tribune.* New York, 1879-?

   This publication presented articles on various subjects of Jewish interest.

702. *American Israelite.* Cincinnati, Ohio, 1854- .

   Earlier known as the *Israelite,* this weekly was founded and edited, until 1900, by Rabbi Isaac Mayer Wise, the key figure in American Reform Judaism.

703. *American Jewish Archives.* Cincinnati, Ohio: Hebrew Union College, 1948- .

   A semiannual periodical containing scholarly studies and other essays, annotated bibliographies and book listings, and other information of value to the study of American Jewish history. Illustrations and indexes.

704. *American Jewish Historical Quarterly.* New York and
     Waltham, Mass.: American Jewish Historical Society,
     1961- .

     A continuation of the *Publications of the American
     Jewish Historical Society* (vols. 1-50). Studies, critical
     book reviews, illustrations, and indexes.

705. *American Jewish Year Book.* Philadelphai: Jewish Pub-
     lication Society of America, 1899- .

     An invaluable source of data and studies on the status
     and development of Jewish communal, cultural, phil-
     anthropic, and religious life, activities, and problems
     of American Jews during the twentieth century. Also
     included are analyses of Jewish life and problems all
     over the world. Statistics, necrology, organizational
     directory, miscellaneous data, indexes. The index to
     volumes 1-50 (1899-1949) was prepared by Elfrida C.
     Solis-Cohen in 1967.

706. *American Zionist.* New York: Zionist Organization of
     America, 1910- .

     A monthly featuring articles on Israel and on rela-
     tions between the United States and Israel.

707. *The Asmonean.* New York, 1849-1858.

     An important periodical for the history of American
     Jewry.

708. *Bitzaron.* New York, 1939- .

     A scholarly and literary monthly (*Stronghold*) in the
     Hebrew language.

709. *B'nai B'rith Messenger.* Los Angeles, 1897- .

    A weekly of Jewish community news.

710. *California Jewish Voice.* Los Angeles, 1922- .

    A weekly devoted to the Jewish community in Los Angeles and elsewhere.

711. *CCAR Journal.* New York: Central Conference of American Rabbis, 1953- .

    A quarterly with a stress on religious thought and issues.

712. *Commentary: A Jewish Review.* New York: American Jewish Committee, 1945- .

    A monthly periodical containing, although not specializing in, interpretive and critical articles on American Jewish life and culture. Successor to *Contemporary Jewish Record,* 1939-1945.

713. *Congress Bi-Weekly.* New York: American Jewish Congress, 1933- .

    Formerly known as *Congress Weekly.* Articles on the developments and problems of the American Jewish community.

714. *Conservative Judaism.* New York: Rabbinical Assembly of America, 1955- .

    A quarterly with articles on religion, education, the community, and related areas.

715. *Der Amerikaner.* New York: 1901- .

A Yiddish-language weekly magazine for family reading.

716. *Der Aufbau.* New York, 1934- .

A German-language periodical (*Reconstruction*) published by Jewish refugees from Nazi Germany.

717. *Der Groiser Kundes.* New York, 1908-1927.

A humorous weekly (*The Big Prankster*) in Yiddish.

718. *Der Jude.* New York, 1887-1917?

A German-language weekly (*The Jew*) with Jewish news and literary articles.

719. *Der Tog.* New York, 1914-1953.

A humorous weekly (*The Meddler*) in Yiddish.

720. *Derr Tog.* New York, 1914-1953.

A daily Yiddish newspaper (*The Day*) with a liberal political viewpoint.

721. *Der Yiddisher Puck.* New York, 1894-1896.

A humorous weekly in Yiddish borrowing the title of the British *Puck*.

722. *Di Varheit.* New York, 1905-1919.

A daily Yiddish newspaper (*The Truth*) with nationalistic leanings.

723. *Di Yiddishe Heim.* Brooklyn, N.Y.: Agudas Neshei U'Bnos Chabad, 1958- .

A quarterly (*The Jewish Home*) with articles in Yiddish and English reflecting the philosophy of the Lubavitcher Hasidic movement.

724. *Zukunft*. 1892- .

A Yiddish-language monthly (*The Future*) containing articles on social, labor, educational, and literary themes.

725. *Die Deborah*. Cincinnati, Ohio, 1855-1903.

A German-language supplement to the *American Israelite*.

726. *Dimensions in American Judaism*. New York: Union of American Hebrew Congregations, 1966 to 1972.

Articles on religious, social, cultural, and related themes, chiefly in connection with the American Jewish community.

727. *Dos Yiddishe Vort*. New York: Agudath Israel of America, 1952- .

A Yiddish-language monthly (*The Jewish Word*) with articles on religious and communal issues, plus news of the Orthodox Jewish community.

728. *Echo des Judenthums*. New York, 1892-1917?

A German-language weekly (*Echo of Judaism*) with Jewish fraternal news.

729. *Eglyeit Elet*. New York, 1922-?

A Jewish periodical (*Social Life*) in Hungarian.

730. *El Kirbatch Americano.* New York, 1917-?

A humorous periodical (*The American Whip*) in Ladino (Judeo-Spanish).

731. *Encyclopaedia Judaica.* 16 vols. Jerusalem: Keter Publishing House, and New York: Macmillan, 1971-1972.

This recently completed reference work includes long articles on American Jewish history, society, culture, education, religion, and other fields.

732. *Forverts (Jewish Daily Forward).* New York, 1897- .

A Yiddish-language newspaper that has reflected the Socialist point of view on Jewish and general events.

733. *Freie Arbeiter Shtimme.* New York, 1899- .

A Yiddish weekly (*Free Worker's Voice*) with an anarchist viewpoint.

734. *Freiheit.* New York, 1922- .

A daily Yiddish-language newspaper (*Freedom*), propounding the views of the Communist Party.

735. *Hadassah Magazine.* New York: Hadassah, Women's Zionist Organization of America, 1921- .

Formerly the *Hadassah Newsletter,* this monthly features articles on the organizational activities in behalf of Israel public health and related matters.

736. *Hadoar.* New York, 1921- .

A weekly magazine (*The Post*) in Hebrew on Jewish

thought and activity in the United States and a-
broad.

737. *Ha-Ivri.* New York 1892-1902.

A Hebrew-language weekly (*The Hebrew*) with news
and literary articles.

738. *Hapardes.* Chicago, 1927- .

A Hebrew-language monthly (*The Orchard*), mainly
written for and read by Orthodox rabbis, dealing with
religious questions.

739. *Harofe Haivri.* New York 1926- .

A semiannual publication (*The Hebrew Physician*) in
Hebrew on medical subjects.

740. *Ha-Toren.* New York, 1916-1925.

A Hewbrew weekly (*The Mast*), later monthly, reflecting Zionist ideas.

741. *Ha-Tzofeh b'Eretz ha-Hadashah.* New York, 1870-1876.

The first Hebrew-language periodical (*The Observer in
the New Land*) in the United States (a weekly).

742. *Historia Judaica.* New York,1938- .

A semiannual scholarly publication devoted to specialized studies in Jewish history.

743. *Horeb.* New York: Yeshiva University, 1934- .

A scholarly semiannual publication in Hebrew on themes of Jewish content and interest.

744. *Ideas: A Journal of Contemporary Jewish Thought.* Long Island City, N.Y., 1972- .

A quarterly with articles on American and foreign Jewish thought, culture, and communal issues.

745. *Igazsag.* New York, 1939-?

A Hungarian and English monthly (*Justice*), containing Jewish news.

746. *Intermountain Jewish News.* Denver, 1913- .

A weekly publication of Jewish communal and other developments in the Rocky Mountain region.

747. *The Jew.* New York, 1823-1825.

The first Jewish periodical in the English language, this monthly journal was concerned with defense against the widespread activities of Christian missionaries in New York City.

748. *Jewish Advocate.* Boston, 1902- .

A weekly with local, national, and international news concerning Jews.

749. *Jewish Book Annual.* New York: Jewish Book Council of America, 1943- .

Although international in scope, this yearbook contains articles and bibliographies in English, Hebrew, and Yiddish which are helpful to the bibliographer and historian of the Jews of the United States.

750. *Jewish Chronicle.* New York, 1844-1855.

A Christian missionary publication.

751. *The Jewish Community Voice.* Cherry Hill, N.J.: Jewish Federation of Camden and Burlington Counties, 1941- .

A semi-monthly newspaper with Jewish news of local and wider interest.

752. *Jewish Education.* New York, 1928- .

A quarterly which deals with the history, aims, methods, content, and problems of Jewish education in the United States, Israel, and other countries.

753. *Jewish Encyclopedia.* 12 vols. New York, 1901-1906.

An older, but still useful reference work with articles on subjects pertinent to the history of Jewish experience in the United States.

754. *Jewish Evangelist.* Brooklyn, N.Y., 1902-1917.

A periodical aiming at the conversion of Jews to Christianity.

755. *Jewish Exponent.* Philadelphia, 1887- .

A weekly emphasizing Jewish community news, but also including international developments.

756. *Jewish Frontier.* New York: Labor Zionist Letters, 1934- .

A montly concentrating on a Socialist approach to the American Jewish and Israeli scenes.

757. *Jewish Heritage.* Washington, D.C.: Department of Adult Jewish Education, B'nai B'rith, 1957- .

A quarterly journal emphasizing ideas and news of Israel and the United States from the viewpoint of Mizrachi-Hapoel Hamizrachi.

758. *Jewish Horizon.* New York: Religious Zionists of America, 1937- .

A quarterly journal emphasizing and news of Israel and the United States from the viewpoint of Mizrachi-Hapoel Hamizrachi.

759. *Jewish Leader.* Pittsburgh, 1889- .

A monthly periodical with Jewish articles and news of local and wider interest.

760. *Jewish Life.* New York: Union of Orthodox Jewish Congregations of America, 1933- .

A bimonthly periodical dealing with Jewish thought, developments, and problems in the United States and in other countries.

761. *Jewish Observer.* New York: Agudath Israel of America, 1962- .

A monthly with commentaries on the American Jewish community from an Orthodox point of view.

762. *Jewish Parent.* New York: National Association of Hebrew Day School P.T.A.'s, Torah Umesorah, 1948- .

A quarterly containing articles and news concerning the aims, content, and problems of the Orthodox Jewish day school movement in the United States.

763. *Jewish Post and Opinion.* New York, 1933- .

A weekly newspaper with a variety of Jewish information and articles of local, national, and international scope.

764. *Jewish Press.* Brooklyn, N.Y., 1950- .

A weekly newspaper with local, national, and international Jewish news, presented with an Orthodox interpretation.

765. *Jewish Quarterly Review.* Philadelphia: Dropsie University for Hebrew and Cognate Learning, 1910- .

An internationally known periodical with scholarly articles on Jewish history, literature, religion, and related subjects.

766. *Jewish Social Studies.* New York: Conference on Jewish Relations, 1939- .

A quarterly presenting scholarly articles and book reviews on Jewish social, economic, and political developments, in the past and present, in the United States and other countries.

767. *Jewish Spectator.* New York, 1935- .

A monthly journal with articles reflecting a traditional attitude toward Jewish communal, religious, and educational issues.

768. *Jewish Telegraphic Agency Community News Reporter.* New York, 1962- .

A weekly with news of local Jewish communities.

769. *Jewish Telegraphic Agency Daily News Bulletin.* New York, 1917- .

A valuable daily compendium of national and international Jewish news.

770. *Jewish Telegraphic Agency Weekly News Digest.* New York, 1933- .

A convenient weekly compilation of national and international Jewish developments.

771. *Jewish Veteran.* Washington: Jewish War Veterans of the U.S.A., 1896- .

A monthly of primary interest to Jewish ex-service personnel.

772. *Journal of Jewish Communal Service.* New York: National Conference of Jewish Communal Service, 1924- .

Known until 1956 as the *Jewish Social Service Quarterly,* this publication deals with professional issues and problems relating to social work within the American Jewish community.

773. *Judaism.* New York: American Jewish Congress, 1952- .

A quarterly stressing theological, intellectual, and communal concerns.

774. *The J.W.B. Circle.* New York: National Jewish Welfare Board, 1945- .

A periodical with communal news and reviews of new books and music of Jewish interest.

775. *Kultur un Dertziung.* New York: Education Department, Workmen's Circle, 1930- .

A bimonthly in Yiddish (*Culture and Education*) featuring articles on Jewish literary, cultural, and educational subjects.

776. *La America.* New York, 1910-1923.

A Jewish news weekly in the Ladino language (Judeo-Spanish in Hebrew letters).

777. *La Bos del Pueblo.* New York, 1915-1920.

A Ladino-language weekly (*The Voice of the People*) with a Socialist viewpoint on Jewish and other news.

778. *La Vara.* New York, 1922-1949.

A Ladino-language weekly published for the Sephardi Jewish community.

779. *Menorah Journal.* New York, 1915-1962.

An intellectual quarterly with articles by Jews and non-Jews on literature, education, and other subjects of interest to American Jewish intellectuals.

780. Detroit: Jewish Hospital Society of Michigan, 1960- .

A semiannual periodical containing essays, information, documents, facsimiles, and illustrations concerning the history of the Jews of Michigan, especially in Detroit, during the nineteenth and twentieth
centuries. The June, 1970 issue includes a ten-year
index.

781. *Midstream.* New York: Theodore Herzl Foundation,
1955- .

A monthly with articles on political, social, intellectual, and other areas of Jewish concern.

782. *Morgen Zhurnal.* New York, 1901-1972.

A daily Yiddish newspaper with an Orthodox approach to news and developments.

783. *Nasza Trybuna.* New York, 1940-?

A Polish-language periodical (*Our Tribune*) published
for Polish Jewish immigrants.

784. *National Jewish Monthly.* Washington, D.C.: B'nai
B'rith, 1886- .

Articles and information on various aspects of the
American Jewish people and their community.

785. *The Occident and American Jewish Advocate.* Philadelphia, 1843-1868.

Edited by Rabbi Isaac Leeser, proponent of traditional Judaism, this journal contains considerable

material of significance to the historian of the Jewish community in nineteenth-century America.

786. *Ordens Echo.* New York: Independent Order of True Sisters, 1884-1917.

A German-language monthly (*Echo of the Order*) with Jewish news.

787. *Pedagogic Reporter.* New York: American Association for Jewish Education, 1949- .

An educational publication appearing three times a year and intended for teachers and administrators in American Jewish religious and cultural schools.

788. *Present Tense.* New York: American Jewish Committee, 1972- .

A "magazine of world Jewish affairs," including developments in the U.S.

789. *Proceedings.* New York: American Academy for Jewish Research, 1928- .

An annual volume containing scholarly essays in English and Hebrew on literary, religious, historical, cultural, and related themes in world Jewish history.

790. *Proceedings of the Rabbinical Assembly of America.* New York, 1937- .

Views and information on the American Jewish community and religious life from the Conservative standpoint.

791. *Publications of the American Jewish Historical Society.*
New York: The Society, 1893-1961.

An indispensable source of monographic studies for
the study of all aspects of American Jewish history.
In addition to the articles and longer studies, there
are biographical summaries of deceased American
Jewish historians. Occasional book reviews. Documents and indexes. The "Index to the Publications of
the American Jewish Historical Society: Numbers 1
to 20" was published by the Society in 1914.

792. *Rabbinical Council Record.* New York: Rabbinical
Council of America, 1954- .

A bimonthly periodical of news and comment on
Jewish affairs from an Orthodox viewpoint.

793. *Reconstructionist.* New York, 1934- .

A periodical analyzing religious, communal, and educational issues from the viewpoint of the ideology of
Reconstructionism.

794. *The Record.* Washington, D.C.: Jewish Historical Society of Greater Washington, 1966- .

Illustrated, documented essays on Jewish life and personalities in the District of Columbia in the nineteenth and twentieth centuries. Documents and facsimiles.

795. *Response: A Contemporary Jewish Review.* Waltham,
Mass.: Brandeis University, 1967- 7- .

Essays, fiction, and poetry on literary, political, religious, and other topics of Jewish concern.

796. *Rhode Island Jewish Historical Notes.* Providence: Rhode Island Jewish Historical Association, 1954- .

Studies, facsimiles, and information pertaining to the history of the Jews in Rhode Island. Illustrations and indexes.

797. RIBALOW, MENACHEM, and ZEVI SCHARFSTEIN, eds. *Sefer Hashanah l'Yehudei Amerikah.* New York: Histadrut Ha-Ivrit b'Amerikah, 1931.

The first volume of a Hebrew-language series of yearbooks dedicated to literary, historical, educational themes, relating both to Jewish life in the United States and elsewhere.

798. ROTH, CECIL, ed. -in-chief. *The Standard Jewish Encyclopedia.* Garden City, N.Y.: Doubleday, 1959.

A one-volume reference work which includes concise articles on American Jewish history, culture, personalities, and related themes. A second edition appeared in 1970.

799. *Sentinel.* Chicago, 1911- .

A weekly with Jewish communal news, as well as national and international content.

800. *Sheviley Hahinuch.* New York, 1936- .

A Hebrew-language quarterly (*Paths of Education*) on developments, trends, and problems in Jewish education in the United States and elsewhere.

801. *Sh'ma.* New York, 1970- .

A fortnightly periodical dealing with religious, social, and intellectual issues and concerns of American Jewry.

802. *Southern Israelite.* Atlanta, Ga., 1925- .

A monthly with emphasis on regional Jewish news.

803. *Sura.* New York: Yeshiva University, 1954- .

An annual publication containing scholarly articles on topics in the area of Hebraica and Judaica.

804. *Talpioth.* New York: Yeshiva University, 1943- .

A Hebrew-language semiannual publication with scholarly articles on religious, literary, and historical subjects.

805. *Tradition.* New York: Rabbinical Council of America, 1958- .

A quarterly with philosophical and scholarly articles and book reviews dealing with religious, educational, and communal issues emphasizing Orthodox values.

806. *United Synagogue Review.* New York: United Synagogue of America, 1943- .

A quarterly covering ideas and practices pertaining to the Conservative movement in America.

807. *Universal Jewish Encyclopedia.* 10 vols. New York, 1939-1943.

Includes many long articles on historical and contemporary aspects of Jewish life and experience in the United States.

808. *Western States Jewish Historical Quarterly*. Santa Monica: Southern California Historical Society, 1968- .

Documented essays on Jewish history, mainly in California. Documents, illustrations, book reviews, and indexes.

809. *Yearbook of the Central Conference of American Rabbis*. Cincanniti, Ohio, 1890- .

An official publication of the Reform Jewish leadership. The proceedings of the annual conferences and various articles and studies are useful for those concerned with American Jewish history, religion, and community.

810. *Yedies fun YIVO (News of the YIVO)*. New York: Yiddish Scientific Institute—YIVO, 1943- .

A quarterly newsletter in English and Yiddish on recent news and documentary acquisitions, many of them of interest to the American Jewish historian.

811. *Yiddishe Kultur*. New York: Yiddisher Kultur Farband—YKUF, 1938- .

A Yiddish-language monthly with articles on various themes in areas of Jewish culture.

812. *Yiddishe Zeitung*. Brooklyn, N.Y., 1971- . A Yiddish-language daily newspaper published by and for the Hasidic community in the Williamsburg section of Brooklyn.

813. *Yiddisher Kemfer.* New York: Labor Zionist Letters, 1906- .

A Yiddish-language weekly covering, from a Socialist standpoint, developments and problems of American and Israeli Jewry.

814. *Yiddishes Tageblatt.* New York, 1885-1928.

A daily Yiddish-language newspaper which reflected traditional Jewish values.

815. *Yiddishe Sprakh.* New York: YIVO Institute for Jewish Research, 1941- .

Issued three times a year, this journal is devoted to the analysis and promotion of the Yiddish language.

816. *YIVO Annual Jewish Social Science.* New York: Yiddish Scientific Institute-YIVO, 1946- .

These volumes contain scholarly articles in English on various aspects of American Jewish history and community.

817. *YIVO Bleter.* New York: YIVO Institute for Jewish Research, 1931- .

An irregularly published periodical with scholarly articles in Yiddish on historical, sociological, and other themes pertinent to the Jewish communities of the United States and other countries.

818. *Young Israel Viewpoint.* New York: National Council of Young Israel, 1912- .

A periodical offering commentaries on American Jewish life and issues from an Orthodox standpoint.

XVI. BIBLIOGRAPHIES

XVI. BIBLIOGRAPHIES

819. BLOCH, JOSHUA. *Of Making Many Books: An Annotated List of the Books Issued by the Jewish Publication Society of America, 1890-1952.* Philadelphia: Jewish Publication Society of America, 1953.

A useful listing, in chronological order, of works on various subjects of Jewish interest, including many dealing with Jewish life in the United States. Indexes of authors, editors, titles, and serial publications. Dr. Bloch presents an interpretative and evaluative introduction.

820. BLOCH, JOSHUA, comp. *The People and the Book: The Background of Three Hundred Years of Jewish Life in America.* New York: New York Public Library, 1954.

An annotated bibliography of 111 illuminated manuscripts, rare books, documents, and other materials throwing light on the history of Jewish religion and thought, including the earliest works published in America. Many facsimiles. Interpretive introduction by Dr. Bloch.

821. COLEMAN, EDWARD D. *The Jew in English Drama: An Annotated Bibliography.* New York: New York Public Library and KTAV Publishing House, 1970.

A reprint of a valuable reference work, originally published in 1943, on the treatment of the Jew in English and American dramatic works. Informative essays by Mr. Coleman on the Jew in English drama and by Edgar Rosenberg on the Jew in Western drama. Addenda to the Coleman bibliography and a checklist on the Jew in Western drama by D. Rosenberg. Thoroughly indexed.

822. DEINARD, EPHRAIM. *Koheleth America.* St. Louis, Mo.: Moinester, [1926].

Essays in Hebrew on literature and an annotated bibliography of the Hebrew books published in America, 1735-1926.

823. DUKER, ABRAHAM G. "An Evaluation of Achievement in American Jewish Local Historical Writing," *Publications of the American Jewish Historical Society* 69 (June 1960), pp. 215-253.

A critical, informative appraisal of selected monographs and other writings dealing with Jewish history in the various states, with suggestions for improvements and needed studies. See also comments by Selig Adler and Hyman Berman, *ibid.*, pp. 254-264.

824. Educational Research Council of America of Cleveland, Ohio, and the American Association for Jewish Education of New York. *The American Jewish Experience: A Graded, Annotated Bibliography for Grades 7-12.* [Cleveland, Ohio] : Educational Research Council of America, 1972.

Concise annotations of selected works on Jewish history, religion, sociology, intergroup relations, biography, literature, and fiction in the United States. An appropriate resource for teachers in public secondary schools.

825. GLANZ, RUDOLF. *The German Jew in America: An Annotated Bibliography Including Books, Pamphlets and Articles of Special Interest.* Cincinnati, Ohio: Hebrew Union College Press, and New York: Ktav Publishing House, 1969.

A significant compilation of 2527 titles, mainly in German and English, on history, bibliography, culture, economy, communal life, religion, scholarship, biography, literature, and other categories of the German Jewish experience in the United States. The emphasis is on the main period of the immigration of German Jews, 1820-1880. Very brief, infrequent annotations. Thoroughly indexed.

826. INGLEHART, BABETTE F., and ANTHONY R. MANGIONE. *The Image of Pluralism in American Literature: An Annotated Bibliography on the American Experience of European Ethnic Groups.* New York: Institute on Pluralism and Group Identity, American Jewish Committee, 1974.

The section, "Literature Dealing with the Jewish-American Experience" (pp. 32-45) contains concise, apt annotations of ninety works of literature—novels, short stories, anthologies reflecting the adjustment of Jews to American life.

827. JACOBS, JOSEPH. *Directory of the Jewish Press in America.* New York: Joseph Jacobs Organization, 1970.

Specific details about national, regional, and local

publications in the United States and Canada. Additional historical information and a glossary.

828. LEVINE, ALLAN E. *An American Jewish Bibliography: A List of Books and Pamphlets by Jews or Relating to Them Printed in the United States from 1851 to 1875, Which Are in the Possession of the Hebrew Union College-Jewish Institute of Religion Library in Cincinnati.* Cincinnati, Ohio: American Jewish Archives, 1959.

A comprehensive compilation which is valuable for research on nineteenth-century American Jewish history.

829. LINZER, NORMAN, ed. *Jewish Communal Services in the United States, 1960-1970: A Selected Bibliography.* New York: Commission on Synagogue Relations, Federation of Jewish Philanthropies of New York, 1972.

A comprehensive, well-classified listing of books, articles, and other references on service to the aged, religious education, the family, the synagogue, youth, intergroup relations, communal service, relations with Israel, and other topics on the American Jewish experience. Editorial introductions to each topic.

830. *Manuscript Catalog of the American Jewish Archives, Cincinnati.* 4 vols. Boston: G.K. Hall, 1971.

A lsiting of the "documents, letters, memoirs, genealogies, and organizational records" of Jewish life in the Western Hemisphere, mainly in the United States, from the seventeenth century through the mid-twentieth century. These materials are located on the Cincinnati campus of the Hebrew Union College-Jewish Institute of Religion.

831. *Manuscript Collections in the American Jewish Historical Society: Cataloged Jan. 1968-Jun. 1969.* Waltham, Mass.: American Jewish Historical Society, [1969].

An excellent annotated listing of manuscript holdings pertaining to American Jewish history and available in the Society's library.

832. MARCUS, JACOB R. *A Selected Bibliography of American Jewish History.* New York: American Jewish Historical Society, 1962.

An unclassified, briefly annotated listing of 287 works covering the history and life of American Jewry. Reprinted from the *American Jewish Historical Quarterly* (December 1961).

833. MARCUS, JACOB R., comp. *An Index to Americana in Foreign-Jewish Periodicals (1806-1938).* 3 vols. Cincinnati, Ohio: Hebrew Union College, [1939].

A duplicated reference work which lists articles on American Jewish life published in French, German, Italian, and Hebrew-language journals. A helpful research tool. Copy in the New York Public Library.

834. MARCUS, JACOB R., ed. *An Index to Scientific Articles on American Jewish History.* Cincinnati, Ohio: American Jewish Archives, and New York: Ktav Publishing House, 1971.

A valuable guide to the essays in thirteen scholarly and other American Jewish periodicals, 1884-1968. Arrangement is by author, subject, and title.

835. [MARCUS, JACOB R., ed.] *Jewish Americana.* Cincinnati, Ohio: American Jewish Archives, 1954.

A 115-page supplement to A. S. W. Rosenbach's *An American Jewish Bibliography* (1926). Preface by Jacob R. Marcus.

836. MEYER, ISIDORE S. *American-Jewish Biography: An Introductory List.* New York: American Jewish Historical Society and National Jewish Welfare Board, 1949.

Brief annotations of biographical works concerning leading American Jewish personalities in culture, education, labor, scholarship, business, politics, religion, and other fields.

837. MEYER, ISIDORE S., ed. *The American Jew in the Civil War: Catalog of the Exhibit of the Civil War Centennial Jewish Historical Commission.* New York: American Jewish Historical Society, 1961.

A collection of source materials, facsimiles, photography, other illustrations, and bibliographical references in English, Hebrew, and Yiddish on the American Jewish community during 1861-1865, Jewish attitudes toward slavery and the Civil War, the Chaplain controversy, Jewish military and civic participation in the Civil War on both sides, and Abraham Lincoln's relations to the Jews. A valuable, indexed work of reference. Reprinted from *Publications of the American Jewish Historical Society,* 50 (June 1961), pp. 261-424.

838. RISCHIN, MOSES. *An Inventory of American Jewish History.* Cambridge, Mass.: Harvard University Press, 1954.

A bibliographical commentary on a large number of general and specialized works, source materials, reference books, and other pertinent works. An excellent, unique guide for the student and specialist that is deserving of updating and expansion.

839. ROSENBACH, A. S. W. *An American Jewish Bibliography.* [New York] : American Jewish Historical Society, 1926.

A valuable resource for the books and pamphlets published during 1640-1850 in the United States by or concerning Jews. Many facsimile title pages and documents. Index.

840. ROSENTHAL, FRANK, ed. *Abstracts of Doctoral and Masters' Dissertations in Jewish Education and Related Areas.* [Los Angeles, Calif.] : University of Judaism, 1964.

A well-classified and fully indexed compilation of these, most of them annotated and on the historical and other aspects of Jewish education in the United States.

841. SILBER, MENDEL. *America in Hebrew Literature.* New Orleans, La.: The author, 1928.

A collection of references in Hebrew writings, from the sixteenth through the nineteenth centuries, concerning the New World and the United States. A somewhat longer version of the author's work in Hebrew.

842. SILBER, MENDEL. *Amerika b'sifrat Yisrael.* New Orleans, La.: The author, 1920.

An annotated bibliography of writings in Hebrew (and one in German-Yiddish) containing information on America, including Jewish developments, from the sixteenth through the nineteenth centuries.

843. SOLIS-COHEN, ELFRIDA C., ed. *American Jewish Year Book Index to Volumes 1-50, 1899-1949 (5660-5709)*. New York: KTAV Publishing House, 1967.

A subject and name index constituting a useful guide to materials related to a half-century of the development of Jewish life and activity in the U.S. and in other countries.

844. STERN, NORTON B., ed. *California Jewish History: A Descriptive Bibliography*. Glendale, Calif.: Arthur H. Clark Co., 1967.

A well-annotated bibliography of 475 publsihed and unpublished works dealing with the history of Jewish life in California from the mid-nineteenth to the mid-twentieth century. List of California's Anglo-Jewish newspapers.

845. TUMIN, MELVIN M. *An Inventory and Appraisal of Research on American Anti-Semitism*. New York: Freedom Books, 1961.

This volume presents "a series of digests of researches, theories, and hypotheses about anti-Semitism in America" and statements on "the major issues at stake" and their implications (p. 1). The thoughtful analyses and detailed digests make this work a valuable resource for research on the American Jewish experience.

846. WOLF, EDWIN, 2d. "Some Unrecorded American Judaica Printed before 1851," in Jacob R. Marcus,

ed., *Essays in American Jewish History to Commemorate the Tenth Anniversary of the Founding of the American Jewish Archives.* Cincinnati, Ohio: American Jewish Archives, 1958, pp. 187-245.

A list of 245 items supplementing the bibliographies of A. S. W. Rosenbach's *An American Jewish Bibliography* (1926) and Jacob R. Marcus' *Judaica Americana* (1954).

847. ZAFREN, HERBERT C., comp. "The Writings of Jacob Rader Marcus," in Jacob R. Marcus, ed., *Essays in American Jewish History to Commemorate the Tenth Anniversary of the Founding of the American Jewish Archives.* Cincinnati, Ohio: American Jewish Archives, 1958, pp. 493-512.

A bibliography of 163 titles, many of them dealing with American Jewish history.

APPENDIX

LETTER FROM THE DIRECTORS IN HOLLAND TO STUYVESANT: JEWS: TAXES AND THE REFUSAL OF THE PEOPLE TO BE TAXED WITHOUT THEIR CONSENT: REVENUES: FORT ON LONG ISLAND: BOUNDARIES.*

26th of April 1655.

Honorable, Prudent, Pious, Dear, Faithful.

Our last letters to you were sent by the ships *"Swarte Arent"* and *"Grote Christoffel"* on the 16th resp. 23d of November 1654, in which we give you full details: since that time the ships *"Schel"* and *"Bear"* arrived here on the 15th of December by which we received your letter and packages of the 22d and 25th of Sept 1654 and later by way of *England* your letter of the 27th of October, same year, all of which will be answered now as far as required, while we shall add, what we consider necessary.

We would have liked to agree to your wishes and request, that the new territories should not be further invaded by people of the Jewish race, for we foresee from such immigration the same difficulties, which you fear, but after having further weighed and considered this matter, we observe, that it would be unreasonable and unfair, especially because of the considerable loss, sustained by the Jews in the taking of *Brasil* and also because of the large amount of capital, which they have invested in shares of this Company. After many consultations we have decided and resolved upon a certain petition made by said *Portuguese* Jews, that they

*B. Fernow, ed., *Documents Relating to the History of the Early Colonial Settlements Principally on Long Island.* (Albany, N. Y.: Weed, Parsons, 1883), pp. 315, 318.

shall have permission to sail to and trade in *New Netherland* and to live and remain there, provided the poor among them shall not become a burden to the Company or to the community, but be supported by their own nation. You will govern yourself accordingly.

Herewith etc.
Amsterdam,
26th of April 1655.   The Directors of the W. I. Co.
                                                       Dept. of *Amsterdam*
                                                       J. Bontemantel.
                                                       Edward Man.
To Director *Stuyvesant* and Council in *New Netherland.*

LETTER FROM THE DIRECTORS TO STUYVESANT: TRADE BETWEEN VIRGINIA AND NEW NETHERLAND PROHIBITED; JEWS; LUTHERANS; PUBLIC RECORD.*

The 14th of June 1656

Honorable, Vigorous, Pious, Dear, Faithful,

Our last letter to you, dated the 13th of March last past, was sent by the *"Bontekoe;"* we have since received by the ship *"Nieuw Amsterdam," Pieter Dircksen Waterhont,* skipper, your letter of the 21st of the same month, to which we shall briefly reply, as several points have been answered by ours of the 13th of March, that we are well satisfied with the expedition, which agreeably to our former orders you have caused to be led so discreetly and without difficulty or bloodshed against the *English* on *Long Island,* who encroached there upon the Company's territory. We approve of what has been done there and recommend you to act henceforth in the same way in regard to encroachments or usurpations by the *English;* but be as cautious as possible, that no acts of open hostility occur, which must be avoided and harmony maintained.

We have seen and heard with displeasure, that against our orders of the 15th of February 1655, issued at the request of the *Jewish* or *Portuguese* nation, you have forbidden them to trade to *Fort Orange* and the South river, also the purchase of real estate, which

*B. Fernow, ed. *Documents Relating to the History of the Early Colonial Settlements Principally on Long Island.* (Albany, N. Y.: Weed, Parson, 1883) pp. 350-351, 353.

is granted to them without difficulty here in this country, and we wish it had not been done and that you had obeyed out orders, which you must always execute punctually and with more respect: *Jews* or *Portuguese* people however shall not be employed in any public service, (to which they are neither admitted in this city), nor allowed to have open retail shops, but they may quietly and peacefully carry on their business as before said and exercise in all quietness their religion within their houses, for which end they must without doubt endeavor to build their houses close together in a convenient place on one or the other side of *New Amsterdam,* —at their own choice—as they have done here.

We would also have been pleased, if you had not published the placat against the Lutherans, a copy of which you sent us, and committed them to prison, for it has always been our intention, to treat them quietly and leniently. Hereafter you will therefore not publish such or similar placats without our knowledge, but you must pass it over quietly and let them have free religious exercises in their houses.

Herewith etc etc
Amsterdam
the 14th of June 1656.   Your good friends
                                    The Directors of the W. I. Company,
                                                    Dept. of *Amsterdam.*
                                                            Edward Mann.

EXTRACTS FROM THE MINUTES OF THE SHEARITH ISRAEL CONGREGATION CONCERNING ITS RELIGIOUS SCHOOL

1731: "On the 21st of Nisan, the 7th day of Pesach, the day of completing the first year of the opening of the synagogue, there was made codez [consecrated] the Yeshibat called Minhat Areb, in the name of the following gentlemen, Mosseh son of Sarah and Jahacob, of Abraham, and of Mosseh Mendez de Costa, for the use of this Congregation Sheerit Israel and as a Beth Hamidras for the pupils, in conformity with the direction to that effect given by Jahacob Mendez da Costa Signior, residing in London, to Messrs, Mordechay and David Gomez of New York. And may God bestow His blessing upon us. Amen."

JANUARY 30, 1737: David Mendes Machado, was elected "to act as hazan or reader to this our K. K. de Seherit Yiserael. The said Mr. Machado promising and obliges himself to keep a publick school in due form for teaching the Hebrew language, either the whole morning or afternoon as he shall think most proper, and any poor that shall be thought unable to pay for their children's learning they shall be taught gratis."

1744: Joshua Isaacs bequeathed "£50 to our congregation of Jews in New York, the income to be for the support of a Hebrew School to teach poor children the Hebrew tongue."

APRIL 15, 1747: It was agreed that the Hazan "David Mendez Machado shall attend at the Hebra to Teach Children the Hebrew, from Nine to Twelve Each morning and from Two till Five Thurs-

*Alexander M. Dushkin, *Jewish Education in New York City*. (New York: Bureau of Jewish Education, 1918), p. 449.

day afternoons, to receive Eight Shillings pr quarter from Each child that comes to said School and one Load wood Yearly from Each child. Also that the parnass or one of the adjuntos shall visit the said school weekly. Also that said Mr. Machado shall Teach such children Gratis that Cant afford Payment."

DECEMBER 7, 1755: It was decided at a Meeting of the Parnasim and Elders of the Congregation "that Twenty Pounds pr annum be added to the Salary of the Hazan on condition that he opens a School at his own house every day in the weed (Fryday afternoon, Holy Days and Fast Days Excepted) & teaches such poor children Gratis that shall have an order from the Parnas Presidents, the Hebrew, Spanish, English, writting & Arithmetick. In the Summer from 9 to 12 in the forenoon & from 2 to 5 in the afternoon & that the children may be strictly kept to their learning, the Parnasim and the Elders according to their Seniority to visit sd school monthly to examine the children and judge if the Scholars under the Hazans care advance in their learning; the above additional Salary to commence from last Rosh a Shanah & to continue whilst the Hazan discharges the duty above expressed."

A LETTER OF JONAS PHILLIPS TO THE FEDERAL CONVENTION.*

BY HERBERT FRIEDENWALD, Ph. D., *Philadelphia.*

The subjoined letter of Jonas Phillips was brought to my attention through the kindness of Mr. S. M. Hamilton of the Department of State, who found it among the papers of the Federal Convention while examining them preparatory to publication. All of these invaluable documents are kept in a small box known to the Department of State as "the little red trunk"; and tradition has it, that the box was once the property of Thomas Jefferson, who left it when he retired from the office of Secretary of State.

Pasted on the inside of the cover of the box is a piece of paper on which the following, in the handwriting of Daniel Brent, Chief Clerk of the Department of State, 1817-1833, is written:

"This trunk contains the Journal of the Federal Convention of 1787, which framed the Constitution of the United States, together with Copies, distinct, of the various questions submitted to and decided by that Convention, and separate sheets of the Yeas and Nays of the Several States upon those questions—as also Copies of the Reports of Com-

Publications of the American Jewish Historical Society, Vol. 2, 1894, pp. 108-111.

mittees and projects of a Constitution. It also contains a transcript, made at the Department of State, by direction of M.ʳ Secretary Adams, of those Proceedings &c. &c. for publication, under a Resolution of Congress.

The Original Books and Papers were deposited in the Department of State in 1796, by President Washington, he having been President of the Convention, to be there preserved.   D. B.

Mem.   Some of the Originals were communicated by Gov.ʳ Bloomfield, the Exer [of] Mr. Brearley, who had been a member of the Convention."

This letter of Mr. Phillips was sent to the Federal Convention ten days before it rose, and bears evidence of a curious condition of mind concerning the object of the Convention. Three weeks before it was written, that clause of the Constitution, as finally adopted, providing that " no religious test shall ever be required as a qualification to any office or public trust under the United States," had been considered and, after scarcely any debate, unanimously adopted.   Beyond what Mr. Phillips himself states, nothing, I believe, is known as to the reason why he, a prominent citizen of Philadelphia, should have written such a letter.   It reads:

" Sires
With leave and submission I address myself To those in whom there is wisdom understanding and knowledge, they are the honourable personages appointed and Made overseers of a part of the terrestrial globe of the Earth, Namely the 13 united states of america in Convention Assembled, the Lord preserve them amen—
I the subscriber being one of the people called Jews of the

City of Philadelphia, a people scattered & dispersed among all nations do behold with Concern that among the laws in the Constitution of Pennsylvania, there is a Clause Sect 10 to viz—I do believe in one God the Creatur and governor of the universe and Rewarder of the good & the punisher of the wicked—and I do acknowledge the Scriptures of the old & New testiment to be given by divine inspiration—to swear & believe that the new testiment was given by divine inspiration is absolutely against the Religious principle of a Jew, and is against his Conscience to take any such oath—By the above law a Jew is deprived of holding any publick office or place of Government which is a Contridictory to the bill of Right Sect 2 viz

That all men have a natural & unalienable Right to worship almighty God according to the dictates of their own Conscience and understanding & that no man ought or of Right can be Compelled to attend any Religious Worship or Creed or support any place of worship or Maintain any minister contrary to or against his own free will and Consent, nor can any man who acknowledges the being of a God be Justly deprived or abridged of any Civil Right as a Citizen on account of his Religious sentiments or peculiar mode of Religious Worship, and that no authority can or ought to be vested in or assumed by any power whatever that shall in any case interfere or in any manner Controul the Right of Conscience in the free Exercise of Religious Worship.—

It is well known among all the Citizens of the 13 united states that the Jews have been true and faithful whigs, & during the late Contest with England they have been foremost in aiding and assisting the states with their lifes & fortunes, they have supported the cause, have bravely fought and bled for liberty which they can not Enjoy.—

Therefore if the honourable Convention shall in their Wisdom think fit and alter the said oath & leave out the words to viz—and I do acknowledge the scripture of the new testiment to be given by divine inspiration, then the Israelites will think themself happy to live under a government where all Religious societys are on an Equal footing—I solicit this favour for myself my children & posterity, & for the benefit of all the Israelites through the 13 united states of America.

My prayers is unto the Lord. May the people of this states Rise up as a great & young lion, May they prevail against their Enemies, may the degrees of honour of his Excellency the president of the Convention George Washington, be Exhalted & Raise up. May Everyone speak of his glorious Exploits.

May God prolong his days among us in this land of Liberty—May he lead the armies against his Enemys as he has done hereuntofore. May God Extend peace unto the united states—May they get up to the highest Prosperitys—May God Extend peace to them & their seed after them so long as the sun & moon Endureth—and May the almighty God of our father Abraham Isaac & Jacob indue this Noble Assembly with wisdom Judgment & unanimity in their Counsells & may they have the satisfaction to see that their present toil & labour for the wellfair of the united states may be approved of Through all the world & particular by the united states of america, is the ardent prayer of Sires

Your Most devoted obed. Servant

JONAS PHILLIPS

PHILADELPHIA 24th Ellul 5547 or Sepr 7th 1787."

It is addressed " To His Excellency the president and the

Honourable Members of the Convention assembled," and is endorsed in the hand of Timothy Pickering, a member of the Convention, as follows.

"No. 8.

"Letter from Jonas Phillips a Jew, dated Sept 7. 1787. to the President and Members of the Convention."

CORRESPONDENCE BETWEEN WASHINGTON AND JEWISH CITIZENS.

By Lewis Abraham, *Washington, D. C.*

The number of Israelites in this country prior to the Declaration of Independence was not large, but there is undoubted evidence that they were staunch supporters of the Colonies in their efforts to secure severance from foreign yoke.

When Washington had concluded his labors in the field of war and had attained deserved civic honors, and laurels from all quarters were being showered upon him, the Hebrews joined their fellow-citizens in felicitating the hero and statesman.

The following correspondence is gathered from the *United States Gazette* of 1790; a partial file of this paper can be found in the Congressional Library. It is strange that the letters are not all to be found in books in which the Washington correspondence is compiled.

The original letter addressed to the "Beth Elohim" congregation of Charleston, South Carolina, was carefully preserved among the many other valuable records of that city, but was destroyed by the great fire of 1838. His Honor the Mayor endeavored to obtain a copy from the department of the general government, but after a thorough examination of the records no such document could be found, and

Publications of the American Jewish Historical Society, Vol. 3, pp. 87-96.

after a prolonged search the undersigned was written to and supplied the missing letter.*

* See *Year Book of the City of Charleston* for 1884, p. 280.

THE ADDRESS FROM THE HEBREW CONGREGATION OF THE CITY OF SAVANNAH, GEORGIA, WHICH WAS PRESENTED TO WASHINGTON, THE FIRST PRESIDENT OF THE UNITED STATES, BY MR. JACKSON, ONE OF THE REPRESENTATIVES FROM GEORGIA.

" *Sir:*—We have long been anxious of congratulating you on your appointment, by unanimous approbation, to the presidential dignity of this country, and of testifying our unbounded confidence in your integrity and unblemished virtue. Yet however exalted the station you now fill, it is still not equal to the merit of your heroic services through an arduous and dangerous conflict, which has embosomed you in the hearts of her citizens.

Our eccentric situation, added to a diffidence founded on the most profound respect, has thus long prevented our address, yet the delay has realized anticipation, given us an opportunity of presenting our grateful acknowledgments for the benediction of heaven through the magnanimity of federal influence and the equity of your administration.

Your unexampled liberality and extensive philanthropy have dispelled that cloud of bigotry and superstition which has long as a vail shaded religion—unrivetted the fetters of enthusiasm—enfranchised us with all the privileges and immunities of free citizens, and initiated us into the grand mass of legislative mechanism. By example you have taught us to endure the ravages of war with manly fortitude, and to enjoy the blessings of peace with reverence to the Deity and benignity and love to our fellow-creatures.

May the Great Author of the world grant you all happiness—an uninterrupted series of health—addition of years to the number of your days, and a continuance of guardianship to that freedom which under auspices of heaven your magnanimity and wisdom have given these States.

LEVI SHEFTAL, *President.*
In behalf of the Hebrew Congregations."

To which the President was pleased to return the following:

ANSWER.—TO THE HEBREW CONGREGATIONS OF THE CITY OF SAVANNAH, GEORGIA.*

" *Gentlemen :*—I thank you with great sincerity for your congratulations on my appointment to the office which I have the honor to hold by the unanimous choice of my fellow-citizens, and especially the expressions you are pleased to use in testifying the confidence that is reposed in me by your congregations.

As the delay which has naturally intervened between my election and your address has afforded me an opportunity for appreciating the merits of the Federal Government and for communicating your sentiments of its administration, I have rather to express my satisfaction rather than regret at a circumstance which demonstrates (upon experiment) your attachment to the former as well as approbation of the latter.

I rejoice that a spirit of liberality and philanthropy is much more prevalent than it formerly was among the enlightened nations of the earth, and that your brethren will benefit thereby in proportion as it shall become still more extensive ; happily the people of the United States have in many instances exhibited examples worthy of imitation, the salutary influence of

*This reply is printed in Jared Sparks' Collection, vol. XII, p. 185.

which will doubtless extend much farther if gratefully enjoying those blessings of peace which (under the favor of heaven) have been attained by fortitude in war, they shall conduct themselves with reverence to the Deity and charity toward their fellow-creatures.

May the same wonder-working Deity, who long since delivered the Hebrews from their Egyptian oppressors, planted them in a promised land, *whose providential agency has lately been conspicuous in establishing these United States as an independent nation*, still continue to water them with the dews of heaven and make the inhabitants of every denomination participate in the temporal and spiritual blessings of that people whose God is Jehovah. G. WASHINGTON."

ADDRESS OF THE NEWPORT CONGREGATION TO THE PRESIDENT OF THE UNITED STATES OF AMERICA.

"*Sir:*—Permit the children of the stock of Abraham to approach you with the most cordial affection and esteem for your person and merit, and to join with our fellow-citizens in welcoming you to Newport.

With pleasure we reflect on those days of difficulty and danger when the God of Israel, who delivered David from the peril of the sword, shielded your head in the day of battle; and we rejoice to think that the same spirit which rested in the bosom of the greatly beloved Daniel, enabling him to preside over the provinces of the Babylonian Empire, rests and ever will rest upon you, enabling you to discharge the arduous duties of the Chief Magistrate of these States.

Deprived as we hitherto have been of the invaluable rights of free citizens, we now—with a deep sense of gratitude to the Almighty Disposer of all events—behold a government erected by the majesty of the people—a government which to bigotry gives no sanction, to persecution no assistance, but generously affording to all liberty of conscience and immunities of citizenship, deeming every one of whatever nation, tongue or language, equal parts of the great governmental machine.

This so ample and extensive Federal Union, whose base is philanthropy, mutual confidence and public virtue, we cannot but acknowledge to be the work of the great God who rules in the armies of the heavens and among the inhabitants of the earth, doing whatever seemeth to Him good.

For all the blessings of civil and religious liberty which we enjoy under an equal and benign administration, we desire to send up our thanks to the Ancient of days, the great Preserver of men, beseeching Him that the angels who conducted our forefathers through the wilderness into the promised land may graciously conduct you through all the difficulties and dangers of this mortal life; and when, like Joshua, full of days and full of honors, you are gathered to your fathers, may you be admitted into the heavenly paradise to partake of the water of life and the tree of immortality.

Done and signed by order of the Hebrew Congregation in Newport, Rhode Island.   Moses Seixas, *Warden.*

Newport, *August* 17, 1790."

Washington's Reply to the Hebrew Congregation in Newport, Rhode Island.

"*Gentlemen:*—While I received with much satisfaction your address replete with expressions of esteem, I rejoice in the opportunity of assuring you that I shall always retain grateful remembrance of the cordial welcome I experienced on my visit to Newport from all classes of citizens.

The reflection on the days of difficulty and danger which are past is rendered the more sweet from a consciousness that they are succeeded by days of uncommon prosperity and security.

If we have wisdom to make the best use of the advantages with which we are now favored, we cannot fail, under the just administration of a good government, to become a great and happy people.

The citizens of the United States of America have a right to applaud themselves for having given to mankind examples of an enlarged and liberal policy—a policy worthy of imitation.   All possess alike liberty of conscience and immunities of citizenship.

It is now no more that toleration is spoken of as if it were the indulgence of one class of people that another enjoyed the exercise of their inherent natural rights, for, happily, the Government of the United States, which gives to bigotry no factions, to persecution no assistance, requires only that they who live under its protection should demean themselves as good citizens in giving it on all occasions their effectual support.

It would be inconsistent with the frankness of my character not to avow that I am pleased with your favorable opinion of my administration and fervent wishes for my felicity.

May the children of the stock of Abraham who dwell in this land continue to merit and enjoy the good will of the other inhabitants—while every one shall sit in safety under his own vine and fig tree and there shall be none to make him afraid.

May the father of all mercies scatter light, and not darkness, upon our paths, and make us all in our several vocations useful here, and in His own due time and way everlastingly happy.   G. WASHINGTON."

THE ADDRESS OF THE HEBREW CONGREGATIONS IN THE CITIES OF PHILADELPHIA, NEW YORK, RICHMOND AND CHARLESTON TO THE PRESIDENT OF THE UNITED STATES.

"*Sir :*—It is reserved for you to unite in affection for your character and person every political and religious denomination of men; and in this will the Hebrew congregations aforesaid yield to no class of their fellow-citizens.

We have hitherto been prevented by various circumstances peculiar to our situation from adding our congratulations to those which the rest of America have offered on your elevation to the chair of the Federal Government. Deign, then, illustrious sir, to accept this our homage.

The wonders which the Lord of Hosts had worked in the days of our forefathers have been taught us to observe the greatness of His wisdom and His might throughout the events of the late glorious revolution ; and while we humble ourselves at His footstool in thanksgiving and praise for the blessing of His deliverance, we acknowledge you, the leader of American armies, as His chosen and beloved servant. But not to your sword alone is present happiness to be ascribed ; that, indeed, opened the way to the reign of freedom ; but never was perfectly secure until your hand gave birth to the Federal Constitution and you renounced the joys of retirement to seal by your administration in peace what you had achieved in war.

To the eternal God, who is thy refuge, we commit in our prayers the care of thy precious life ; and when, full of years, thou shalt be gathered unto thy people, thy righteousness shall go before thee, and we shall remember, amidst our regret, 'that the Lord hath set apart the godly for himself,' whilst thy name and thy virtues will remain an indelible memorial on our minds. MANUEL JOSEPHSON,
For and in behalf and under the authority of the several congregations aforesaid."

To which the President was pleased to return the following:

ANSWER. — TO THE HEBREW CONGREGATIONS IN THE CITIES OF PHILADELPHIA, NEW YORK, CHARLESTON AND RICHMOND.

"*Gentlemen:*—The liberality of sentiment toward each other, which marks every political and religious denomination of men in this country, stands unparalleled in the history of nations.

The affection of such a people is a treasure beyond the reach of calculation, and the repeated proofs which my fellow-citizens have given of their attachment to me and approbation of my doings form the purest source of my temporal felicity.

The affectionate expressions of your address again excite my gratitude and receive my warmest acknowledgment.

The power and goodness of the Almighty, so strongly manifested in the events of our late glorious revolution, and His kind interposition in our behalf, have been no less visible in the establishment of our present equal government. In war He directed the sword, and in peace He has ruled in our councils. My agency in both has been guided by the best intentions and a sense of duty I owe to my country.

And as my exertions have hitherto been amply rewarded by the approbation of my fellow-citizens, I shall endeavor to deserve a continuance of it by my future conduct.

May the same temporal and eternal blessings which you implore for me, rest upon your congregations.

G. WASHINGTON."

Appropriate in view of the foregoing expressions of the father of his country to his Hebrew fellow-citizens is the following correspondence of patriots of the early days of the United States.

In 1818 the Mill Street Synagogue was consecrated. Mordecai M. Noah delivered an eloquent address on the occasion, and sent copies thereof to distinguished statesmen. Among the replies received were the following, which are worthy of preservation:

COPY OF A LETTER FROM THOMAS JEFFERSON.*

"MONTICELLO, *May* 28, 1818.

Sir:—I thank you for the discourse on the consecration of the Synagogue in your city, with which you have been pleased to favor me. I have read it with pleasure and instruction, having learnt from it some valuable facts in Jewish history which I did not know before. Your sect by its sufferings has furnished a remarkable proof of the universal spirit of religious intolerance inherent in every sect, disclaimed by all while feeble, and practiced by all when in power. Our laws have applied the only antidote to this vice, protecting our religious, as they do our civil rights, by putting all on an equal footing. But more remains to be done, for although we are free by the law, we are not so in practice; public opinion erects itself into an Inquisition, and exercises its office with as much fanaticism as fans the flames of an *Auto-de-fe.*

The prejudice still scowling on your section of our religion, although the elder one, cannot be unfelt by yourselves; it is to be hoped that individual dispositions will at length mould themselves to the model of the law, and consider the moral

Travels in England, France, Spain and the Barbary States in the Years 1813-14 *and* 15. By Mordecai M. Noah; New York and London, 1819. Appendix, pp. xxv and xxvi.

basis, on which all our religions rest, as the rallying point which unites them in a common interest; while the peculiar dogmas branching from it are the exclusive concern of the respective sects embracing them, and no rightful subject of notice to any other; public opinion needs reformation on that point, which would have the further happy effect of doing away the hypocritical maxim of '*intus et lubet, foris ut moris.*' Nothing, I think, would be so likely to effect this, as to your sect particularly, as the more careful attention to education, which you recommend, and which, placing its members on the equal and commanding benches of science, will exhibit them as equal objects of respect and favor.   I salute you with great respect and esteem.

(Signed)   THOMAS JEFFERSON.

M. M. NOAH, Esq."

COPY OF A LETTER FROM JAMES MADISON, ESQ., ON THE SAME SUBJECT.

" MONTPELIER, *May* 15, 1818.

Sir:—I have received your letter of the 6th, with the eloquent discourse delivered at the consecration of the Synagogue.   Having ever regarded the freedom of religious opinions and worship as equally belonging to every sect, and the secure enjoyment of it as the best human provision for bringing all, either into the same way of thinking, or into that mutual charity which is the only proper substitute, I observe with pleasure the view you give of the spirit in which your sect partake of the common blessings afforded by our Government and laws.

As your foreign mission took place whilst I was in the administration, it cannot but be agreeable to me to learn that your accounts have been closed in a manner so favorable to you.

(Signed)   JAMES MADISON."

COPY OF A LETTER FROM JOHN ADAMS, ESQ.

"QUINCY, *July* 31, 1818.

Sir:—Accept my best thanks for your polite and obliging favour of the 24th, and especially for the discourse inclosed. I know not when I have read a more liberal or more elegant composition.

You have not extended your ideas of the right of private judgment and the liberty of conscience, both in religion and philosophy, farther than I do.   Mine are limited only by morals and propriety.

I have had occasion to be acquainted with several gentlemen of your nation, and to transact business with some of them, whom I found to be men of as liberal minds, as much honor, probity, generosity and good breeding, as any I have known in any sect of religion or philosophy.

I wish your nation may be admitted to all privileges of citizens in every country of the world.   This country has done much.   I wish it may do more; and annul every narrow idea in religion, government, and commerce.   Let the wits joke; the philosophers sneer!   What then?   It has pleased the Providence of the 'first cause,' the universal cause, that Abraham should give religion, not only to Hebrews, but to Christians and Mahometans, the greatest part of the modern civilized world.

(Signed)   JOHN ADAMS."

A POLITICAL DOCUMENT OF THE YEAR 1800.*
By DR. CYRUS ADLER.

To the Printer of the Gazette of the United States.
  Sir,
  I HOPE, if you take the liberty of inserting calumnies against individuals, for the amusement of your readers, you will have so much regard to justice, as to permit the injured through the same channel that conveyed the slander, to appeal to the public in self defence. I expect of you therefore, to insert this reply to your ironical reporter of the proceedings at the meeting of the republican citizens of Philadelphia, contained in your gazette of the fifth instant; so far as I am concerned in that statement. I am no enemy Mr. Wayne to wit; nor do I think the political parties have much right to complain, if they enable the public to laugh at each others expence, provided it be managed with the same degree of ingenuity, and some attention to truth and candor. But your reporter of the proceedings at that meeting is as destitute of truth and candor, as he is of ingenuity, and I think, I can shew, that the want of prudence of this Mr. Marplot, in his slander upon me, is equally glaring with his want of wit, his want of veracity, his want of decency, and his want of humanity.
  I am accused of being a *Jew,* of being a *Republican,* and of being *Poor.*
  I *am* a *Jew.* I glory in belonging to that persuasion, which even its opponents, whether Christian, or Mahomedan, allow to be of

Publications of the American Jewish Historical Society, No. 1, 1892. 2d ed. Philadelphia: The Society, 1905, pp. 111-115.

divine origin—of that persuasion of which christianity itself was originally founded, and must ultimately rest—which has preserved its faith secure and undefiled, for near three thousand years, whose votaries have never murdered each other in religious wars, or cherished the theological hatred so general, so unextinguishable among those who revile them. A persuasion, whose patient followers have endured for ages the pious cruelties of Pagans, and of Christians, and persevered in the unoffending practice of their rites and ceremonies, amidst poverties and privations; amidst pains, penalties, confiscations, banishments, tortures and deaths, beyond the example of any other sect, which the page of history has hitherto recorded.

To be of such a persuasion, is to me no disgrace; though I well understand the inhuman language of bigotted contempt, in which your reporter by attempting to make me ridiculous, as a Jew, has made himself detestable, whatever religious persuasion may be dishonored by his adherence.

But I am a Jew. I am so; and so were Abraham, and Isaac, and Moses and the prohets, and so too were Christ and his apostles; and I feel no disgrace in ranking with such society, however, it may be subject to the illiberal buffoonery of such men as your correspondents.

I am a *Republican!* Thank God I have not been so heedless and so ignorant of what has passed, and is now passing in the political world. I have not been so proud or so prejudiced as to renounce the cause for which I have *fought,* as an American, throughout the whole of the revolutionary war, in the militia of Charleston, and in Polafkey's legion, I fought in almost every action which took place in Carolina, and in the disastrous affair of Savannah, shared the hardships of that sanguinary day, and for three and twenty years I felt no disposition to change my political any more than my religious principles. And which in spite of the witing scribblers of aristocracy, I shall hold sacred until death, as not to feel the ardour of republicanism. Your correspondent, Mr. Wayne, cannot have known what it is to serve his country from principle in time of danger and difficulties, at the expence of his health and his peace, of his pocket and his person, as I have done. As I do not suspect you Mr. Wayne of being the author of the attack on me, I shall not enquire what share you or your relations had in establishing the liberties of your country. On religious grounds I am a republican. Kingly government was first conceded to the foolish complaints of the Jewish people as a punishment and a curse; and so it was to them until their dispersion, and so it has been to every nation who have been as foolishly tempted to submit to it. Great Britain has a king and her enemys need not wish her the sword, the pestilence, and the famine.

In the history of the Jews, are contained the earliest warnings against kingly government, as any one may know who has read the fable of Abimelick, or the exhortations of Samuel. But I do not recommend them to your reporter, Mr. Wayne; to him the language of truth and soberness would be unintelligible.

I am a Jew, and if for no other reason, for that reason am I a republican. Among the pious priesthood of church establishments, we are compassionately ranked with Turks, Infidels and Heretics. In the *monarchies* of Europe we are hunted from society, stigmatized as unworthy of common civility, thrust out as it were from the converse of men; objects of mockery and insult to froward children, the buts of vulgar wit and low buffoonery, such as your correspondent, Mr. Wayne, is not ashamed to set us an example of. Among the nations of Europe we are inhabitants every where; but citizens no where *unless in republics.* Here, in France, and in the Batavian republic alone, we are treated as men and as brethern. In republics we have *rights,* in monarchies we live but to experience *wrongs.* And why? because we and our forefathers have *not* sacrificed our principles to our interest, or earned an exemption from pain and poverty, by the direliction of our religious duties, no wonder we are objects of derision to those, who have *no* principles, moral or religious, to guide their conduct.

How then can a Jew but be a Republican? in America particularly. Unfeeling and ungrateful would he be if he were callous to the glorious and benevolent cause of the difference between his situation in this land of freedom and among the proud and privileged law-givers of Europe.

But I am *poor;* I am so, my family also is large, but soberly and decently brought up. They have not been taught to revile a christian because his religion is not *so old* as theirs. They have not been taught to mock even at the errors of good intentions, and conscientious belief. I trust they will always leave this to men as unlike themselves, as I hope I am to your scurrilous correspondent.

I know that to purse proud aristocracy proverty is a crime, but it may sometimes be accompanied with honesty even in a Jew: I was bankrupt some years ago; I obtained my certificate and was discharged from my debts. Having been more successful afterwards, I called my creditors together, and eight years afterwards, unsolicited, I discharged all my old debts. I offered interest which was refused by my creditors, and they gave from under their hands without any solicitations of mine, as a testimonial of the fact, (to use their own language) "as a tribute due to my honor and honesty." This testimonial was signed by Messrs. J. Ball, W. Wister, George Meade, J. Philips, C. G. Paleske, J. Bispham, J. Cohen, Robert Smith, J. H. Leuffer, A. Kuhn, John Stille, S. Pleasants, M. Woodhouse, Thomas Harrison, M. Boraef, E. Laskey, and Thomas Allibone, &c.

I was discharged by the insolvent act; true, because having the amount of my debts owing to me from the French republic, the differences between France and America have prevented the recovery of what was due to me, in time to discharge what was due to my creditors. Hitherto it has been the fault of the political situation of the two countries that my creditors are not paid. When peace shall enable me to receive what I am entitled to, it will be my fault if they are not fully paid.

This is a long defence Mr. Wayne, but you have called it forth, and therefore, I hope you at least will not object to it. The public will now judge who is the proper object of ridicule and contempt, your facetious reporter, or

Your humble servant,
BENJAMIN NONES.

PHILADELPHIA, August 11, 1800.

The original copy of the above document was secured from Mr.

John M. Noah, of the U. S. National Museum, grandson of Mordecai M. Noah. It was evidently written in the heat of a political
campaign and is at once dignified and spirited.

Benjamin Nones was of French birth. Some years since I made a
copy of his naturalization certificate, dated October 9th, 1784. In
that instrument he was described as a "merchant." Some account
of his military career may be found in Markens' "The Hebrews in
America." p. 126.

THE DAMASCUS AFFAIR OF 1840 AND THE JEWS OF AMERICA.[*]

By Joseph Jacobs, Esq., *New York City.*

In a measure, modern Jewish history may be said to date from the Damascus affair of 1840, when a monk named Father Thomas, with his attendant, mysteriously disappeared, and thirteen Jews of that ancient city were seized and examined under torture on the charge of having put him to death in order to use his blood for ritual purposes.

The sole basis for such a charge was an alleged confession extorted by torture from a Jewish barber named Negrim, who told a quite improbable tale, implicating the richest Jews of Damascus. Notwithstanding the fact that the majority of them, when cast into prison, withstood every attempt to make them "confess," the Moslem governor of Damascus expressed his belief in their guilt, and reported to Mehemet Ali that they were worthy of capital punishment.[1]

---

[*]*Publications of the American Jewish Historical Society,* Vol. 8, 1900, p. 145-154.

[1] Jost's account in *Geschichte der Israeliten*, X, 345–381, is very full and clear. J. G. Lowenstein's *Damascia* and two pamphlets, *Persecutions contre les Juifs de Damas*, and David Salomons' *An Account of the Recent Persecution of the Jews at Damascus*, give contemporary accounts.

It happened that at that moment the eyes of all Europe were directed towards Syria, which had fallen into the power of Mehemet Ali, the ambitious Viceroy of Egypt, through his successful war against his Suzerain, Sultan Mahmud II, in the preceding year. The mysterious disappearance of Father Thomas and the accusations thereupon brought against the Jews of Damascus became the subject of universal comment throughout the European press, and sides were taken, dictated partly by the anti-semitism largely latent in mid-Europe, and partly by the political tendencies of the writers.

The Jews of Western Europe felt themselves arraigned at the bar of history equally with their unfortunate brethren of Damascus, who had immediately appealed to the Rothschilds at Paris and London, to Amsterdam Jewish notabilities and to the heads of the Constantinople community. The blood-accusation assailed their honor as Jews, and it was felt that every means should be taken both to repel the charge and to rescue the unfortunate victims of it. The important thing to notice is that concerted action was taken by Jews of different nationalities. For the first time in Jewish history since the Fall of Jerusalem Israelites of different nations took counsel and action together for general defence against a common peril. The latent national consciousness sprang into overt existence and the New Israel of modern times was born. That most recent outcome of this consciousness, known as Zionism, can in large measure be traced back to it; before 1840 what corresponded to Zionism was mainly religious and only unconsciously national.

There was one circumstance which should be specially mentioned, as it was the direct cause of this international action on the part of the Jews. The chief promoter of the persecution of the Jews at Damascus was the French consul there, the notorious Count (if he was a count) Ratti-Menton. Now it was the policy of France at the moment to support the claims of Mehemet Ali to the possession of Syria while England was engaged in consolidating the Quadruple Alliance with Austria, Russia and Prussia, which before the end of the year 1840 was to wrest Syria from Mehemet Ali's hands and restore it to those of his Suzerain, the Sultan of Turkey. Here I would remark in passing that, but for this action of England, Syria would still be conjoined to Egypt and would be, at the present moment, administered by English officials.

The political situation at the beginning of 1840 rendered the policy of the Western Jews in their action on behalf of their Damascus brethren rather complicated. It would not be desirable for the English Jews, as represented by Sir Moses Montefiore, to act alone since England was pursuign a policy directly opposed to the ambitions of Mehemet Ali. Again it would be doubtful policy for the French Jews, as represented by M. Cremieux, to drive the furrow alone, as it would be difficult for the French Government to bring any pressure on their ally, the Egyptian Pasha, or to repudiate the action of their accredited agent, Ratti-Menton. After several *pourparlers*—which consumed more than three months—a meeting was held at London by the Board of Deputies of British Jews on June 15, which was attended by M. Cremieux from Paris, and at which it was decided that both he and Sir Moses Montefiore should go to Egypt to demand the release of the Damascus Jews from the Viceroy. It was a characteristic point that the disunion of the Christian powers should have led to the concerted action of the Jews. When at last Montefiore and Cremieux started on July 21 on their eventful and ultimately successful journey, there was scarcely a synagogue in the whole of Europe in which prayers were not offered up for the success of their mission.

Meanwhile news of the dire events at Damascus had reached the shores of America, and the Jews of this country prepared to join in, for the first time in their history, with the exertions of their European brothers, on a matter affecting the honour of all Jewry. It is somewhat difficult to account for the lateness of their action. So far as I can ascertain, it took about 30 days for the European mails to reach America,[1] yet it was not till Aug. 17, more than two months after the Board of Deputies meeting in London, that a meeting was held in New York with J. B. Kursheet as Chairman and Theodore J. Seixas as Secretary[1] which passed resolutions expressing their horror at the treatment of the Damascus Jews and calling upon the President of the United States to intervene on their behalf. Five days later—time went more leisurely in those days—this resolution was sent to Washington, whence almost by return on Aug. 26th Mr. John Forsyth, the Secretary of State, replied informing the New York Jews that already on the 14th inst. a letter had been sent to Mr. Gliddon, the U. S. consul at Alexandria, ordering him to do all in his power to help redress the wrongs of the Damascus Jews. Mr. Forsyth, possibly for reasons of diplomatic etiquette, since the communication had not yet been received by the person addressed, forbore to mention that an even more pressing missive had been sent on the 17th to Mr. David Porter, U. S. Minister at the Sublime Porte. In this letter, communicated by Mr. Max

---

[1] Bryce, *Studies in History and Jurisprudence*, p. 330.

[1] See *Pub. Am. Jew. Hist Soc.*, No. 8, pp. 141-4.

J. Kohler to the last volume of the *Publications* (No. 9, p. 153) occurs the remarkable statement that an intervention to a Mahommedan power on behalf of Jews might most appropriately come "from a friendly power whose institutions, " political and civil, places upon the same footing the wor- "shippers of God of any form or faith, acknowledging no "distinction between the Mahommedan, the Jew and the " Christian."

On Thursday evening, Aug· 27th, the Jews of Philadelphia held in the vestry of the Mikve Israel Synagogue a memorable meeting at which were present not alone the chief Jews of the city but several representative Christian clergymen, Dr. Ducachet, Rector of St. Stephens, Dr. Ramsay, a Presbyterian minister, and the Rev. Mr. Kennedy, all of whom ultimately spoke. The meeting appears to have been summoned by Hyman Gratz, but the most important figure at it and the orator of the evening was undoubtedly Isaac Leeser, then in the height of his powers. He took the bold course of repudiating the blood-accusation by the simple argument that as both Christianity and Islam were derived from Judaism, if the last advocated ritual murder, the daughter-religions would equally be guilty of the same practice. He contrasted the position of the Eastern Jews with that of the Israelites of this happy land and declared in no uncertain tones, that while the Jews of every land felt themselves true citizens of the lands in which they dwelt, they still retained full sympathy with their brethren in faith throughout the world, especially when charges were brought against them which affected the honor and good fame of their religion. In a moving peroration Leeser expressed the hope that the sufferings of the Damascenes might not be in vain if they helped to move the mighty of the earth to recognize the injustice of their ways towards the Jews and thus aid the coming of the Kingdom of Peace and brotherly love. A series of resolutions was carried expressing horror at the atrocities, hope for the success of the two envoys and calling upon the U. S. Government for help in ensuring it, and on the 31st, again after four days' delay, these resolutions were sent to Washington, whence on the next day Mr. Forsyth replied in similar terms to those he had used to New York and enclosing once more his letter to Mr. Gliddon at Alexandria.

Isaac Leeser's address and the resolutions adopted by the meeting were printed in pamphlet form.[1] This publication is so rare—only one copy being known to me and that, appropriately enough, being preserved in the Leeser Library —that a transcript of the address has been made for preservation in the archives of this Society. The resolutions and the correspondence with the Secretary of State, so far as it is not already given in the publications of this Society, are presented as an appendix to the present paper.

At the Philadelphia meeting reference was made to action that had been taken both at New York and Richmond, Va., and it would appear that still another meeting was held at the latter place on September 4, with the Rev. A. H. Cohen as chairman, Messrs. G. A. Myers, Samuel Marx and Samuel H. Myers as members of committee, and Mr. Jacob Ezekiel, father of the well-known sculptor, as secretary, in which a resolution of thanks to the President for the action he had taken was passed and forwarded to Washington. Fifty-nine years later, Mr. Jacob Ezekiel, still living and a member of the American Jewish Historical Society, con-

[1] "Persecution of the Jews in the East, containing the proceedings of a Meeting held at the Synagogue Mikve Israel, Philadelphia, on Thursday evening, the 28th of Ab, 5600 (27th Aug., 1840)." Philadelphia, 1840. 8vo. pp. 30.

tributed to the eighth volume of its *Publications* the correspondence which passed on this occasion (p. 144).

As is well known, the action taken by the American Jews proved to be unnecessary. Cremieux and Montefiore had landed at Alexandria on Aug. 4th, interviewed Mehemet Ali the next day, and, after much intriguing, had extorted from him on the 28th a promise to set the prisoners free, which took place on Sept. 6, at least as regards nine of them, four having succumbed to the horrors of imprisonment and torture. The very news of the action of America, whether by President Van Buren, or by the Jews of New York, Richmond and Philadelphia, could not by that time have reached Europe, where it nevertheless created great interest and was duly recorded at length by Jost in his very full account of the affair in the admirable tenth volume of his *Geschichte*, still in many ways unsurpassed for fullness and sobriety of treatment of the external annals of Israel in modern times. Characteristically enough Graetz, in his treatment of the affair, entirely omits all reference to the action in America, though it is tolerably clear that he had before him Jost's account.

But though the action of the American Jews had no immediate effect, it was not for naught that they had taken a worthy share in the universal protest of Israel against the blood-accusation which affected the honor of all Jews. When the next occasion arose for united action in the Mortara case, even distant California took part in the universal protest of all Jewry, and in the Russian and Roumanian atrocities of the past 20 years the Jews of America have been expected to take their share in any diplomacy or action that was needed, and have nobly fulfilled that expectation. Their part in the Damascus affair was thus the beginning of the diplomatic or international phase in the history of the American Jews, and in this sense, I venture to think, deserves somewhat fuller attention than has hitherto been given to it.

APPENDIX.

A.

Preamble.

The Israelites residing in Philadelphia, in common with those in other places, have heard with the deepest sorrow, that in this enlightened age the absurd charge of their requiring human blood at the celebration of their Passover has been revived, and that an accusation of this nature having been brought against their brethren at Damascus, and the Isle of Rhodes, has been the cause of a most cruel persecution being waged against them by order of the Mussulman authorities, instigated, as it is feared, by one or more of the European residents.

They have learned also with unfeigned horror, that several prominent men at Damascus have been seized by their ruthless persecutors, and tortured until some confessed themselves guilty of a crime which they never committed; and others died under the most exquisite barbarities, which ignorant bigotry, urged by the love of plunder and the hatred of the Jewish name, could invent.

Although the Israelites of Philadelphia, living in a land where, under the blessing of Providence, equality of civil and religious rights so eminently prevails, are not in any danger of persecution for opinion's sake; still they cannot rest while so foul a blot is cast upon their ancient and sacred faith, a faith on which both the Christian and the Mahomedan religions are founded, and which is essentially a law of justice, of mercy, and benevolence; and they would deem themselves traitors to brotherly love and the rights of outraged humanity, were they to withhold their expression of sympathy for their suffering brethren, who writhe under unmerited tortures, and languish in loathsome dungeons, and to offer their aid, if practicable, to have impartial justice administered to them under the present and any future occasion. The Israelites of Philadelphia have therefore met in public meeting and

Resolved, That they experience the deepest emotions of sympathy for the sufferings endured by their fellows in faith at Damascus and

Rhodes, under the tortures and injuries inflicted on them by merci-less and savage persecutors; and that, while they mourn for those upon whom such cruel enormities have been heaped, they cannot but admire the fortitude evinced by many of the sufferers who pre-ferred enduring every torture rather than subscribing to the false-hoods dictated by their vindictive enemies.

Resolved, That the crime charged upon the Israelites at Damascus, of using Christian blood for their festival of redemption from Egypt, is utterly at variance with the express injunction of the Decalogue and other parts of the Pentateuch, and incompatible with the principles inculcated by the religion they profess, which enjoins them "to love their neighbour as themselves," and "to do justice, love mercy, and walk humbly before God."

Resolved, That they will co-operate with their brethren elsewhere in affording pecuniary aid, if required, to relieve the victims of this unholy persecution, and to unite in such other measures as may be devised to mitigate their sufferings.

Resolved, That the thanks of this meeting be accorded to the con-suls of those European powers, who made efforts to stay the arm of persecution, and who by this deed deserve well of the cause of suffering humanity.

Resolved, That this meeting highly appreciates the prompt and energetic measures adopted by our brethren in Europe, and else-where, for the promotion of the object of this meeting, and the noble undertaking of Monsieur Cremieux and Sir Moses Montefiore, in coming forward not only as the champions of the oppressed, but also as the defenders of the Jewish nation; and this meeting expresses the hope that the God of Israel will shield and protect them, and restore them to their families in the enjoyment of unim-paired health.

The foregoing preamble and resolutions having been read, were unanimously adopted.

B.

Copy of a Letter Addressed to the President of the United States, by the Committee of Correspondence, Appointed at the Meeting of Israelites in Philadelphia, August 27th, 1840.

Philadelphia, 31st August, 1840.

To His Excellency the President of the United States,

Sir.—The subscribers were appointed a committee of correspond-ence, on behalf of the Jewish inhabitants of Philadelphia, at a meeting convened for the purpose of taking into consideration the persecution of the Jews in the East, on the evening of the 27th instant. In furtherance of this appointment, it has become their duty to address to your Excellency the following resolution adopted at the said meeting:

Resolved, That in conjunction with our brethren of other cities, a letter be addressed to the President of the United States, respectfully requesting him to instruct the representative of the United States at Constantinople, and the United States Consul in the dominions of the Pacha of Egypt, to co-operate with the Ambassadors and Consuls of other powers, to procure for our accused brethren at Damascus and elsewhere an impartial trial; and to urge upon the Emperor of Turkey and the Pacha of Egypt to prohibit the use of torture in their judicial proceedings; and further, that he be requested to instruct the representatives of this country to urge the governments to which they are accredited, to exert their influence for the same purpose.

In adopting this resolution, the idea was entertained, that the moral influence of the Chief Magistrate of the United States would be, under Heaven, the best aid we could invoke for the protection of our persecuted brethren under the Mohammedan dominion, and we hasten, therefore, to seize the first possible moment after our appointment, to present the above to your consideration, not doubting that your own sense of humanity will impel you to comply with our requests.

With sentiments of regard, and cordial wishes for your health and happiness, we subscribe ourselves,

Your Excellency's most humble and obedient servants,

JOHN MOSS, *Chairman.*

DAVID SAMUEL,
ISAAC LEESER,
J. L. MOSS,
L. J. LEVY,
} *Committee of Correspondence.*

DEPARTMENT OF STATE,
WASHINGTON, 2d SEPTEMBER, 1840.

JOHN MOSS, *Chairman.*
DAVID SAMUEL,
ISAAC LEESER,
LYON JOSEPH LEVY,
JOSEPH L. MOSS,
} *Committee.*

GENTLEMEN.—The President having referred to this Department your communication of the 31st ultimo, containing a resolution adopted at a meeting of the Jewish inhabitants of Philadelphia, requesting him to instruct the representatives of the United States, to co-operate with those of other powers in behalf of their accused brethren at Damascus, and elsewhere, &c., I have the honour to refer you to the accompanying correspondence with a Committee of the Israelites of New York.   I deem it proper to add in reference to that portion of the resolution which you have communicated, relating to the use of torture, that particular instructions were given to our Minister at Constantinople, to direct his efforts against the employment of such barbarous means to extort the confession of imputed guilt.   I have the honour to be,

Gentlemen, very respectfully, your obedient servant,

JOHN FORSYTH.

PERSECUTION OF THE JEWS IN 1840. [**]

By Jacob Ezekiel, *Cincinnati.*

From my scrap-book I am enabled to present these important documents relative to the persecution of the Jews at Damascus, being the correspondence on that subject by the Israelites at New York, and Richmond, Va. Although upward of half a century has elapsed it may be perused with much interest, and will serve to show that at that time, the President of the United States gave precipitate and unsolicited expression of sentiment to the Ottoman Government, which would have been well worthy of imitation during the recent crisis of the persecution of our brethren in Russia.[*]

CORRESPONDENCE.

New York, *August* 24, 1840.

To His Excellency Martin Van Buren, *President of the United States.*

Sir:—At a meeting of Israelites of the City of New York, held on the 19th inst., for the purpose of uniting in

---

[**]*Publications of the American Jewish Historical Society*, Vol. 8, 1900, pp. 141-144.

[*] Cincinnati, Nov. 28th, 1897.

an expression of sympathy for their brethren at Damascus, and of taking such steps as may be necessary to procure for them equal and impartial justice, the following resolution was unanimously adopted:

Resolved, That a letter be addressed to his Excellency, the President of the United States, respectfully requesting that he will direct the Consuls of the United States, in the Dominions of the Pacha of Egypt, to co-operate with the Consuls or other agents accredited to the Pacha, to obtain a fair and impartial trial for our brethren at Damascus.

In transmitting the same to your Excellency, we beg leave to express what we are persuaded is the unanimous opinion of the Israelites throughout the Union, that you will cheerfully use every possible effort to induce the Pacha of Egypt to manifest more liberal treatment toward his Jewish subjects, not only from the dictates of humanity, but from the obvious policy and justice by which such a course is recommended by the intolerant spirit of the age in which we live. The liberal and enlightened views in relation to matters of faith, which have distinguished our Government from its very inception to the present time, have secured the sincere gratitude and kind regard of the members of all religious denominations, and we trust the efforts of your Excellency in this behalf will only serve to render more grateful and to impress more fully on the minds of the citizens of the United States, the kindness and liberality of that Government under which we live.

With the best wishes of those in whose behalf we address you—for your health and happiness, and for the glory and honor of our Common Country, we have the honor to be,

Your Excellency's obedient servants,

J. B. KURSHEEDT, *Chairman.*
THEODORE J. SEIXAS, *Secretary.*

COPY OF REPLY FROM THE HONORABLE THE SECRETARY
OF STATE.

WASHINGTON, *August* 26, 1840.

MESSRS. J. B. KURSHEEDT, *Chairman,* AND THEODORE J.
SEIXAS, *Secretary.*

Gentlemen:—The President has referred to this Department your letter of the 24th inst., communicating a resolution unanimously adopted at a meeting of t! Israelites in
the City of New York, held for the purpose of uniting in an
expression of sentiment on the subject of the persecution of
their brethren in Damascus.   By his direction I have the
honor to inform you that the heart-rending scenes which took
place at Damascus had previously been brought to the
notice of the President by a communication from our Consul
at that place, in consequence thereof, a letter of instructions
was immediately written to our Consul at Alexandria, a
copy of which is herewith transmitted for your satisfaction.

About the same time our Charge d'Affairs at Constantinople, was instructed to interpose his good offices in behalf
of the oppressed and persecuted race of the Jews in the
Ottoman Dominions, among whose kindred are found some
of the most worthy and patriotic of our own citizens, and
the whole subject, which appeals so strongly to the universal
sentiment of justice and humanity, was earnestly recommended to his zeal and discretion.   I have the honor to be,
gentlemen,

Very respectfully,
Your obedient servant,
JOHN FORSYTH.

————————

COPY OF A LETTER FROM THE SAME TO JOHN GLIDDON, ESQ.,
UNITED STATES CONSUL AT ALEXANDRIA.

WASHINGTON, *August* 14, 1840.

JOHN GLIDDON, ESQ., *United States Consul at Alexandria, Egypt.*

Sir:—In common with all civilized nations, the people of the United States have learned with horror, the atrocious crimes imputed to the Jews of Damascus, and the cruelties of which they have been the victims. The President fully participates in the public feeling, and he cannot refrain from expressing equal surprise and pain, that in this advanced age, such unnatural practices should be ascribed to any portion of the religious world, and such barbarous measures be resorted to, in order to compel the confession of imputed guilt; the offences with which these unfortunate people are charged, resemble too much those which, in less enlightened times, were made the pretexts of fanatical persecution or mercenary extortion, to permit a doubt that they are equally unfounded.

The President has witnessed, with the most lively satisfaction, the effort of several of the Christian Governments of Europe, to suppress or mitigate these horrors, and he has learned with no common gratification, their partial success. He is moreover anxious that the active sympathy and generous interposition of the Government of the United States should not be withheld from so benevolent an object, and he has accordingly directed me to instruct you to employ, should the occasion arise, all those good offices and efforts which are compatible with discretion and your official character, to the end that justice and humanity may be extended to these persecuted people, whose cry of distress has reached our shores. I am, sir,

Your obedient servant,
(Signed) JOHN FORSYTH.

MEETING AT RICHMOND, VA.

RICHMOND, VA., *September* 4, 1840.

At a meeting of the Executive and Corresponding Committee of the Israelites of Virginia, a communication was read from our worthy and much esteemed brethren, J. B. Kursheedt and Theodore Seixas, Chairman and Secretary of the Executive Committee of the Israelites of New York, relative to a correspondence between them and the Hon. John Forsyth, Secretary of State, on the subject of our persecuted brethren in the East, whereupon the following resolution was adopted :

Resolved, That a letter be addressed to the President of the United States, expressing the acknowledgments of the Israelites of Virginia in common with their brethren throughout the United States and elsewhere, for the prompt and handsome manner in which he has acted in reference to the persecutions practised upon our brethren of Damascus.

And the Rev. A. H. Cohen, G. A. Myers, Samuel Marx, and Samuel H. Myers were appointed a sub-committee to carry the said resolution into effect.

A. H. COHEN, *Chairman,*
JACOB EZEKIEL, *Secretary.*

RICHMOND, *September* 4, 1840.

HIS EXCELLENCY, MARTIN VAN BUREN, *President of the United States.*

Sir :—In performing the duty assigned them under the annexed Resolution, it may well be supposed that it is with sentiments of the highest gratification, that the undersigned, in common with their brethren here and elsewhere, have recognized, in the voluntary act of the Chief Magistrate of this Great Republic, in behalf of the persecuted Jews of the

East, an act alike honorable to him as an individual and as a high public functionary, and which assures to us his sympathy in whatever may hereafter be attempted or done toward extending to the ancient race of Israel, wherever dispersed, the civil and religious privileges secured to us by the Constitution of this favored land.

Accept, Sir, from us and through us from the Israelites here, our heartfelt thanks for what you have done—thanks, which we are sensible can add but little to, but certainly will not subtract from, the feelings which your own approving conscience will suggest.   We have the honor to be, Sir,

With great respect, Yours,

A. H. COHEN,   G. A. MYERS,
SAMUEL MARX,   SAMUEL H. MYERS,
Committee.

HEBREW INSTITUTE. *

The readers of the Occident will surely recollect a plan of Judge Noah, published in the September number of last year, for the establishment of a Hebrew College. But it seems that up to this moment it has not proceeded beyond the plan, and its realization is reserved for a future period.

Now we cannot persuade ourselves that the reason of the abandonment, or delay only, of so holy and desirable an enterprise is to be sought for in an entire indifference, or absolute carelessness towards our holy religion on the part of our fellow-Israelites; for though we evidently see that they do not live as strictly according to the Mosaic laws as they did formerly: the Israelite still remains an Israelite, and the desire to retain his children in the profession of his own religion, still burns strongly in the breast of every parent.

Nor are we inclined to believe that the reason of the failure of the above project is to be found in the fact, that Israelites do not recognise or mistake the meritorious object of the projector; for besides that the Judge is known amongst us as a very excellent and deserving personage, the enterprise speaks loudly for itself, and is evidently such a one as is the holiest to, and most to be desired by every one who calls himself a *Jew,* or who deserves this honourable distinction in the smallest degree. It cannot be doubted that most parents desire to have their children educated in the sciences, as

The Occident, and American Jewish Advocate, Vol. II, August, 1844, pp. 249-252.

far as their talents will permit them. This desire should however be especially dwelling in the bosom of our fellow-Israelites in America, where the paths of honour are open to the Jew no less than to the other citizens, and where each parent has a right to hope to see his son one day filling the highest offices in the gift of the people.

And still we find in this free country few Jewish youth in the public institutions, in proportion to the immense number of students of our persuasion in Europe, who frequent the high schools with the most distinguished success; and it is not to be denied, that many fathers in this country try to repress the well-founded expectations of their children by denying them a liberal education, whilst the European Jews endeavour to bring forward their offspring on the road to preferment, deceiving themselves with vain hopes of more liberality towards our religion, whilst the prospect becomes in truth darker with every day.

Is this to be accounted for on the supposition that precisely in America Israelites have no taste for sciences? or are they afraid of them or fly from them as from some deadly monster? or have they no ambition, which would instigate them to send their children to colleges and universities?

No! an aversion to sciences can surely not exist among Israelites, not exist among a nation from the midst of which sprung a Maimonides, an Abarbanel, a Nachmanides, and many other lights of the world; a nation, the youth of which, according to the testimony of all the faculties where Jewish students are, endeavour to excel their fellows; such a nation, I say, can never lose all taste and incentive for the pursuit of the sciences.

We are therefore obliged to seek the reason of the just mentioned neglect in this country, in the fear entertained by many, that our youth may lose their attachment to the paternal faith by frequenting Christian institutions, which alone they can under present circumstances resort to, and be persuaded there, through the influence of teachers and associates, to abjure their religion for another. this fear is not without its reason; for from what source can we expect them to be armed with a strong affection for their paternal religion? whence is to spring a firm attachment for our faith? Where are in this country such schools as will enable the

And in good truth, this fear is not without its reason; for from what source can we expect them to be armed with a strong affection for their paternal religion? whence is to spring a firm attachment for our faith? Where are in this country such schools as will enable the Jewish child to become acquainted with the principles of our heavenly religion? Where are the teachers who make the youth acquainted with the absolute superiority of the Mosaic law and its holiness, so as to implant in their yet uncorrupted hearts that love and esteem for the same which are requisite for the formation of a religious life? Or is it supposed that the instruction imparted in the Sunday schools, given only once a week, and this for about one or two hours, can be sufficient to give a child a satisfactory knowledge of the whole law? Can we in truth imagine that this small amount of instruction will be sufficient to fortify the heart against the allurements and charms of sin, and excite such a conviction in our faith, that all the efforts of the proselyte-makers must recoil without effect?

This can never be effected by such means. Simple as the law of Moses is, excellent as its doctrines are in comparison with those of other creeds: it is evidently not without good cause that we are commanded to meditate day and night on the subject of our faith, and to teach it diligently to our children; and it cannot have been in vain, that in former days the men of Israel spent the greater portion of their life in the study of the law. All this is evidently a proof, that it is the chief obligation of the Jew to acquire a profound knowledge of the law; since the more he becomes familiar with it, the stronger will be his conviction of its divine origin; and the more his love and esteem for it increases, the more will he become strengthened in believing, and the closer will he cleave to it with body and soul all the days of his life.

Thus it was in ancient times, when the study of the law was pursued by our brethren with a passionate fondness; in those times no sacrifice was too great which the Jew would not have willingly brought for his religion; and life, property, country, every thing dear to man, was yielded, only to retain his hold on his faith.

And so it will always be, so it must be, as soon as we have a profound knowledge of our religion, as soon as our children are deeply instructed in its tenets.

But alas! we must confess it to our shame, that this holy pursuit even has been too much neglected in this country; so that we find neither schools nor teachers of religion, and that out of ten children hardly one knows what religion is, not to mention what doctrines it comprises.

And if we consider this fact well, we cannot blame our fellow-Israelites for not sending their children to Christian institutions; yes, we would praise them were this the reason why they obstruct them in the pursuit of an elevated standing, and renounce voluntarily their future advancement.

The realization of Judge Noah's plan would have remedied this evil, and nothing would be more desirable than to see such an institution flourishing among us, in which Jewish children could obtain a classical education without paying therefor at the cost of their religion.

Other causes may have, doubtlessly, operated to prevent Judge Noah's project being carried into effect; but we trust that American Israelites are at length convinced that we are greatly in need of such institutions, wherein our children may acquire a classical and religious education; and they can be easily established in all the larger cities were the Jewish inhabitants are numerous.

The object of the undersigned is, therefore, to establish in this city an institution of this kind; and as he has acquired a good classical and theological education in several German universities, and has made these studies his sole occupation, he does not hesitate to promise that nothing shall be wanting on his part to farther the success of the institution if it be once established.

It is proposed to teach in this school, Hebrew grammar, translating the daily prayers and the Scriptures into English, Catechism, Latin, Greek, English Grammar, Mathematics, Geography, History, German, and French.

In order to be able to put the charges at the lowest possible rate, he intends himself to give instruction in most of the above branches, and to engage competent teachers for the other departments.

Children of poor parents shall receive their education gratuitously

The time of commencing the school cannot be determined until about twenty pupils shall be offered, when a convenient schoolroom and the necessary furniture will be at once procured.

The subscriber farther requests that those who may be willing to entrust him with their children, to call on him in person, as soon as convenient, in order to enable him to commence at the earliest possible day.

H. FELSENHELD,
South Second Street, 2d door below Federal.

JUDAH TOURO, MERCHANT AND PHILANTHROPIST.*

By Max J. Kohler, A. M., LL. B.

It is a strange circumstance that no paper devoted to Judah Touro has thus far been presented at any of our meetings, nor has any sketch of his distinguished career, worthy of the name, been thus far published, certainly not any emanating from a Jewish pen. The result is that little definite information concerning Touro is conveniently accessible, and, in consequence, we find the four enormous tomes of Fortier's History of New Orleans, just published, absolutely ignoring the very name of one who would probably by common consent be singled out as the most prominent American Jew of the first half of the nineteenth century. One familiar with the relations between the investigations of local historical societies and more general historical writings, can readily account for the general historian's neglect of an individual's career, ignored even by his own near ones. It is, accordingly, to such specialized investigations as our own, that the general historian is likely to turn before including or excluding an individual in his general histories, particularly if the man in question did not figure prominently in the political or military history of his time.

A couple of biographical sketches of Judah Touro, written

*Publications of the American Jewish Historical Society, Vol. 13, 1905, pp. 158-176.

within a few years after his death, and strangely enough, by non-Jewish writers, are still our most detailed and satisfactory authorities on his career and tend to show in what high regard his contemporaries held him.   Judge Alexander Walker's biography [1] and the Rev. Theodore Clapp's personal reminiscences in his "Autobiographical Sketches and Recollections During a Thirty-five Years' Residence in New Orleans" (1858) are still our chief sources of information; though few persons seeking light on Touro's career would be likely to look for it in such little-known works.   The biography of him which Isaac Leeser called for in his obituary sketch [2] still remains unwritten, though to-day the personal reminiscences and documentary material of half a century ago are for the most part no longer, it is to be feared, extant. Judah Touro, merchant prince and philanthropist, was known in his day from Newport and Boston, the cities of his infancy and early youth, to far distant New Orleans, the city of his maturity, as "An Israelite indeed, in whom there was no guile," as typical of what is best in the Jewish character, and more than any other resident co-religionist, inspired respect and admiration among Jew and Gentile alike for the Jewish name in America.   And beyond that, his generous, well-nigh unprecedentedly large-scaled and diversified philanthropic gifts made it possible for the various American Jewish communities to undertake institutional charitable work theretofore impossible, in view of the small and humble means at their disposal, so that, throughout the land he pre-eminently laid the foundations for those noble Jewish charities which have ever since been the pride and the boast of American Jewry.

Judah Touro was born at Newport, Rhode Island, on June

---

[1] In the second volume of Hunt's "Lives of American Merchants," published in 1856.

[2] *The Occident*, Vol. XI, p. 594, March, 1854.

16, 1775, and in his maturity he often rejoiced at the circumstance that his individual career thus began with that of his beloved country. His father was the Rev. Isaac Touro, minister of the Newport Jewish Congregation, whose assumption of activities at its helm was marked soon after, in 1763, by the dedication of its first synagogue building, its first cemetery being more than a century older, and concerning whose career our society has already published various items.[3] Isaac Touro married Reyna Hays, the sister of Moses Michael Hays, in 1773, and they had three children—Abraham, Judah, and Rebecca; the latter became the wife of Joshua Lopez, and died in New York in 1833. The large majority of the members of the Jewish community of Newport having left the city during the Revolution, Rev. Isaac Touro and his family departed for Kingston, Jamaica, where he died on December 8, 1783. His widow and children returned to this country, and became members of the household of Moses Michael Hays, brother of Mrs. Touro, who was at this time one of the leading merchants of Boston; there Mrs. Touro died on September 18, 1787. In the home and office of Moses M. Hays, Abraham and Judah Touro had inculcated in them not merely those principles of rectitude and business acumen which stood them in such good stead throughout their lives, but they were also brought into close contact and personal intimacy with eminent non-Jews, and acquired respect for the opinions and views

[3] See Max J. Kohler on "The Jews in Newport," *American Jewish Historical Society Publications*, Vol. VI; Prof. Morris Jastrow, "References to Jews in the Diary of Ezra Stiles," *Ibid.*, No. 10; Rev. W. Willner, "Ezra Stiles and the Jews," *Ibid.*, No. 8; N. Taylor Phillips, "The Levy and Seixas Families of Newport and New York," *Ibid.*, No. 4; George E. Mason's "Reminiscences of Newport," Rev. A. P. Mendes, "The Jewish Cemetery at Newport," *Rhode Island Historical Magazine*, Vol. VI, pp. 81-105; Rev. Geo. A. Kohut, "Ezra Stiles and the Jews."

of those of different faith and mental equipment, and the accompanying increased breadth of view. Michael Moses Hays was an intimate friend of Harrison Gray Otis, a son of the patriot James Otis, and himself United States Senator and Mayor of Boston, and of Thomas H. Perkins, projector of the first American railroad and a distinguished philanthropist, while such younger men as Rev. Samuel J. May, the abolitionist leader, made the Hays' household a second home. To these early associations can probably be traced the sentiments which induced Judah Touro, in his New Orleans home, to purchase slaves with a view to restoring them to liberty. Abraham and Judah Touro acquired a practical knowledge of affairs and commercial procedure in their uncle's counting-room, and in 1798 Judah was sent along as supercargo in connection with a valuable shipment made by his uncle to the Mediterranean. The voyage was marked by a desperate conflict between their vessel and a French privateer, in spite of which it was a commercial success. His Boston associates and connections advised him, soon after, to migrate to New Orleans, then still a French possession, where he arrived in February, 1802, after a voyage lasting from October. His numerous Yankee friends knew that they could absolutely rely on his integrity and judgment to handle, with the best results, the consignments they made to him, and he soon built up a flourishing business in New Orleans, which made him one of this country's " merchant princes." A copy of Mason's " Reminiscences of Newport," expanded by the insertion of portraits and manuscripts into six volumes, which was acquired by the Lenox Library from the collections of the distinguished historian, George Bancroft, contains an autograph business letter from Judah Touro to one of his New England correspondents, C. G. Champlain, United States Senator from Rhode Island, which throws light on the scope of his business dealings.

Tradition has it that he formed a romantic attachment for his cousin, Catherine Hays, in these early days, but that their near relationship precluded their marrying, so that each remained single. She subsequently removed to Richmond, Va., and died the very month Judah Touro himself died, January, 1834. She was remembered in his will, executed that very month in ignorance of her death.

Abraham Touro, Judah's brother, died, unmarried, in Boston, October 18, 1822, at the age of 48, in consequence of an accident to the carriage in which he was driving; at his especial request he was buried in the Jewish Cemetery at Newport, though the Jewish community of that town had been scattered long before. Two years previously he had caused a substantial brick wall to be erected around the cemetery, for which he made further provision by his will, which contained a number of larger charitable bequests, principally to Boston institutions, though the Jewish synagogues of New York and Newport were liberally remembered. It is due particularly to the overshadowing fame of his brother that posterity recognizes the philanthropic gifts of Abraham Touro so slightly.

Returning to Judah Touro's career, we note that he patriotically recognized the claims of his country upon him during the War of 1812, and thrust aside his large business interests, in order to enlist in the ranks during the siege of New Orleans. After having served as a common soldier, he volunteered his services to aid in carrying shot and shell to one of the American batteries during a British cannonade, and while in the performance of this duty he was struck by a twelve-pound shot on January 1, 1813, and so seriously injured that he was left for dead. Here an intimate friend, Rezin D. Shepherd, found him and saved his life after the physicians had abandoned all hope. Their intimacy till Touro's death was great to the point of romance, and nearly forty years later

Judah Touro, in his last will, refers to the circumstance of Shepherd's preservation of his life "under Divine Providence," and appointed him his residuary legatee. As Shepherd had independent means of his own, he treated this large bequest as a trust to be administered for charitable purposes, so that Touro's bequests even exceeded the amounts so described in the will itself.

Judge Walker, in the biographical sketch already referred to, summarizes his commercial career as follows: " He began a brisk and profitable trade in soap, candles, codfish, and other exports of New England, making prompt returns to his friends in Boston. His fidelity, integrity, and good management soon secured him a large New England trade, every vessel from that section bringing him large consignments, and many ships being placed at his disposal, as agent, to obtain cargoes and collect freight. His business was prosperous, his funds accumulated. He invested his surplus judiciously in ships and in real estate, which rapidly advanced in value. His career as a merchant was one of honest, methodical labor and stern fidelity to the principles of legitimate trade, never embarking in any hazardous ventures or speculations, never turning aside from his line of business, and adhering rigidly to the cash system. Such a career presents but few incidents of interest." He was as methodical and regular as a clock. His neighbors were in the habit of judging the time of day by his movements. In his business he rarely employed more than one clerk, and he was generally a lad. It was his custom to open his store himself at sunrise and close it at sunset. He attended to all his affairs himself, and had them so well arranged that there was no possibility of any misunderstanding.

It is the circumstance that Judah Touro's whole life was devoted to personal charitable service, knowing no limits of

age, creed, or race, and so intelligently administered as to
work the maximum of good in every instance, that has made
his name immortal, as are the names of few other philanthropists.   Other men during his liftime also amassed large fortunes and gave liberally spasmodically or by their last wills,
yet unlike Judah Touro they are forgotten.   The public, notwithstanding his modesty and retiring disposition, knew that
his whole life was consistently devoted to intelligent philanthropic action.   Judge Walker, who was a resident of New
Orleans at the time of his death and for many years previously, well says of him: "It was the death of a man who
had won a renown nobler, higher, and more enduring than
that which the most successful merchant, the most daring
warrior, or the most gifted author ever earned.   Who that saw
him in life would have anticipated such fervent demonstrations of popular affection and grief at his death?   How little
of the hero or great man was there in the simple, humble
aspect of that timid, shrinking old man, who was wont to
glide so silently and diffidently through the streets, with his
hands behind him, his eyes fixed on the pavement, and his
homely old face, wrinkled with age but replete with the expression of genial kindness and benevolence.   He was, too,
a man of no great deeds, or public services, or brilliant qualities.   And yet, when the tidings of his decease go forth a
whole people, a reckless, frivolous and cynical people, turn
aside from their various pursuits of pleasure or ambition, to
bewail with heartfelt sorrow his departure.   And he died a
millionaire.   The people do not usually sorrow over the death
of the rich man. . . . It is rare, indeed, that the man who
does his duty by his fellow-men in life, accumulates large
wealth. . . . Wealth seemed to flow into his coffers as the
reward of a boundless and incessant benevolence and benefi-
cence—an ever-active philanthropy.   His career was a

splendid illustration of the Divine injunction and promise 'Cast thy bread on the waters, and after many days it shall return to thee.' Avarice, the love of money for its own sake, were as foreign to his nature as dishonesty and falsehood. He deprived himself of all other luxuries in order to enjoy and gratify with keener relish and greater intensity his single passion and appetite—to do good to his fellow-men. He was a miser only in the exercise of his charity and benevolence, from which he jealously excluded others. His only art and stealth were displayed in the concealment of his benefactions, and his chief vexation and trouble were to avoid the ostentation and display which are too often the main incentive to liberal and benevolent deeds."

Turning from Judge Walker's panegyric, we must confess that Judah Touro's shrinking, retiring nature permitted the public to know of but a small fraction of his many benefactions, and familiarity with but a fraction, numerous as they are, has been handed down to us. The time was one when large gifts to charitable and other public ends were not as common as they are now. When he donated $10,000 towards the erection of the Bunker Hill Monument in 1840, those interested in raising the necessary funds had almost given up their project in despair. Though the cornerstone was laid already in 1826, on the fiftieth anniversary of the battle, Amos Laurence's generous offers of aid met with no material response, even when aided by the eloquent appeals of Edward Everett and Daniel Webster, until Judah Touro privately offered to contribute $10,000, duplicating a similar offer of Amos Laurence made in 1839, provided the remaining necessary $30,000 would be raised. It is said that he was so indignant at the publication of his name, notwithstanding his injunctions of secrecy in connection with the offer, that he seriously thought of withdrawing his offer for a time. Probably this generous benefaction to New England from a Jewish resident of distant New Orleans, more than any other single gift, made Touro's benefactions familiar to the world, and well might it be, when, on the occasion of the dedication of the monument in 1843, in the presence of the President of the United States and Daniel Webster as orator, his generosity was commemorated by the presiding officer who read these lines, since become famous:

> Amos and Judah—venerated names!
> Patriarch and prophet press their equal claims,
> Like generous coursers, running neck and neck,
> Each aids the work by giving it a check.
> Christian and Jew, they carry out a plan—
> For though of different faith, each is in heart a man.

Judah Touro's private benefactions were munificent throughout his lifetime, and the recipients thereof were often astonished at the degree of his generosity. An illustration in point is set forth by the Rev. Theodore Clapp.[4] A Christian church in New Orleans, of which Mr. Clapp was the minister, found itself in serious financial difficulties with $45,-000 of indebtedness. Twenty-five thousand dollars was raised by private efforts, whereupon Mr. Touro purchased the building itself for $20,000 and permitted the congregation to occupy the building rent-free until it was destroyed, after many years, by fire, when he furnished its most generous contribution for a new building. To a friend who had suggested that he could profitably erect business buildings on the site, he promptly remarked on purchasing the church edifice: " I am a friend to religion and I will not pull down the church to increase my means! " Mr. Clapp, moreover, received from him no less than $20,000 during his lifetime. When his sister

---

[4] " Autobiographical Sketches and Recollections," p. 24, *et seq.*

died, leaving an estate of approximately $60,000 to him, he declined to accept the money, requesting instead that it be distributed among deserving charities. The Touro Infirmary at New Orleans was established during his lifetime. He became interested in reports concerning the " Old Stone Mill " of Newport, supposed to be a relic of the early Northmen's settlements in America, and bequeathed $10,000 for the acquisition of the site by that municipality. For many years he was practically the only Jewish resident of New Orleans; subsequently, as the Jewish population increased, he erected a synagogue building and donated it for such uses at an expense of approximately $40,000. Thereafter he was a regular and devoted worshiper at its services. By his will, signed January 6, 1854, less than two weeks before his death, he distributed upwards of half a million of dollars to charitable purposes, two-thirds of the sum to non-Jewish purposes. Mr. Clapp, in commenting on this circumstance says: " I have never heard of but one religionist in the United States who can be compared with Mr. Touro, as regards the liberality of his benefactions to his own church; and he bestowed nothing on other denominations. But Mr. Touro gave more to strangers than to his brethren. With a generous profusion, he scattered his favors broadcast over the wide field of humanity. He knew well that many of the recipients of his bounty hated the Hebrews, and would, if possible, sweep them into annihilation."

One cannot read the will of Judah Touro without being surprised at the accurate knowledge and familiarity acquired by him at this early date concerning the many Jewish communities of the country near and far, their congregations, and their charitable institutions, many of which owed their continued existence to his generous bounty.[5] Had it not been for his

---

[5] The will is appended as an appendix hereto chiefly because it is the best contemporary enumeration I know to be extant of

wise philanthropy, many of our boasted communal institutions in most distant sections of the country, would have found their efforts stifled for many years, at least, by want of necessary support. Rev. Isaac Leeser, at his funeral, ably summarized his will, containing upwards of 65 distinct bequests, as follows:

He thought of the widow and orphan in his own city and where he had dwelt in his youth, and devoted a portion of his means to their relief; and those to whom he has confided this trust are not of his own faith and kindred, and probably no Israelite will ever claim any benefit from the funds. He thought of the poor in his own city, and endowed a home of refuge to receive them in the day of their distress. He thought of those of his own persuasion who suffer from the heavy hand of disease, and supplied the means to afford them relief, in several cities. He thought of the new and weak congregations in various towns, and afforded them the means to carry on their holy mission in dispensing the blessings which our faith is so well calculated to bestow. He thought of the necessity of diffusing religious education to the children of Israel; and with wise discrimination selected those institutions best calculated to farther this end, to make Jewish religion and Jewish literature accessible to the greatest number. He thought of those heavenly societies, whose mission it is to glide gently into the abodes of the poor, to leave the traces of benevolence, to cheer spirits which, without this, would droop into despair and gloom. He thought of the afflicted in the land of Israel, to provide for them assistance in their distress, and protection against the arm of violence; he, the merchant in the far West, who had lived for years separated from his people, almost a solitary worshiper of one God, amidst those who acknowledged Him not alone, forgot not those who still linger on the soil consecrated by so many wonderful events which marked our early history, to cheer them on in the deprivations to which they are subjected.

the various Jewish communities of the United States and their institutions. Judah Touro obviously sought the best information obtainable concerning Jewish communities throughout the country, and came to their assistance in a will which seems to have omitted no deserving Jewish community.

One reading the will cannot regard it as accidental that he should have expressed his "earnest wish to co-operate with Sir Moses Montefiore of London, Great Britain, in endeavoring to ameliorate the condition of our unfortunate Jewish brethren," and to make a comparison between these two Jewish philanthropists of the nineteenth century is an obvious temptation.

At the funeral exercises at New Orleans, Jew and Gentile vied with each other in their expressions of grief and respect, and these were even more marked at the obsequies at Newport, Rhode Island, on June 6, of the same year, 1854, which were attended by delegations from the numerous organizations he had so generously remembered, coming from all over the land. By official resolution of the public authorities of Newport, which had benefited so largely by his philanthropy, his executors and all these delegations became the guests of the municipality. During the funeral procession, the bells of the various churches were tolled, and all places of business were closed. Among those who officiated at Newport were Rev. J. K. Gutheim of New Orleans, Isaac Leeser of Philadelphia, and Rev. M. J. Raphall and Rev. S. M. Isaacs of New York. A project to erect a monument to his memory was bitterly assailed, a few years later, as an alleged violation of Jewish law. Streets in both Newport and New Orleans were named after him in order to commemorate his generous philanthropy.

His tomb-stone, in the Newport Cemetery, bears the following appropriate inscription:

> By righteousness and integrity he collected his wealth;
> In charity and for salvation he dispensed it.
> The last of his name, he inscribed it in the book of philanthropy
> To be remembered forever.

WILL OF THE LATE JUDAH TOURO.

UNITED STATES OF AMERICA,

STATE OF LOUISIANA, CITY OF NEW ORLEANS.

Be it known that on this sixth day of January, in the year of our Lord eighteen hundred and fifty-four, and of the independence of the United States of America the seventy-eighth, at a quarter before 10 o'clock a. m.,

Before me, Thomas Layton, a Notary Public, in and for the city of New Orleans aforesaid, duly commissioned and sworn, and in presence of Messrs. Jonathan Montgomery, Henry Shepherd, Jr., and George Washington Lee, competent witnesses, residing in said city, and hereto expressly required—

Personally appeared Mr. Judah Touro, of this city, merchant, whom I, the said Notary, and said witnesses, found sitting in a room, at his residence, No. 128 Canal Street, sick of body, but sound in mind, memory, and judgment, as did appear to me, the said Notary, and to said witnesses. And the said Mr. Judah Touro requested me, the Notary, to receive his last will or testament, which he dictated to me, Notary, as follows, to wit, and in presence of said witnesses:

1. I declare that I have no forced heirs.

2. I desire that my mortal remains be buried in the Jewish Cemetery in Newport, Rhode Island, as soon as practicable after my decease.

3. I nominate and appoint my trusty and esteemed friends Rezin Davis Shepherd of Virginia, Aaron Keppell Josephs of New Orleans, Gershom Kursheedt of New Orleans, and Pierre Andre Destrac Cazenave of New Orleans, my testamentary executors, and the detainers of my estate, making, however, the following distinction between my said executors, to wit: To the said Aaron Keppell Josephs, Gershom Kursheedt, and Pierre Andre

Destrac Cazenave, I give and bequeath to each one separately, the sum of ten thousand dollars, which legacies I intend respectively, not only as tokens of remembrance of those esteemed friends, but also as in consideration of all services they may have hitherto, rendered me, and in lieu of the commissions to which they would be entitled hereafter in the capacity of Testamentary Executors as aforesaid. And as regards my other designated executor, say my dear, old and devoted friend, Rezin Davis Shepherd, to whom, under Divine Providence, I was greatly indebted for the preservation of my life when I was wounded on the 1st of January, 1815, I hereby appoint and institute him, the said Rezin Davis Shepherd, after the payment of my particular legacies and the debts of my succession, the universal legatee of the rest and residue of my estate, movable and immovable.

In case of the death, absence or inability to act of one or more of my said Executors, I hereby empower the remaining Executor or Executors to act in carrying out the provisions of this my last will; and in the event of the death or default, of any one or more of my said Executors before my own demise; then and in that case, it is my intention that the heirs or legal representatives of those who may depart this life before my own death, shall inherit in their stead the legacies herein above respectively made to them.

4. I desire that all leases of my property and which may be in force at the time of my demise, shall be faithfully executed until the same shall have expired.

5. I desire that all the estate, real, personal and mixed, of which I may die possessed, shall be disposed of in the manner directed by this my last will or testament.

6. I give and bequeath to the Hebrew Congregation the " Dispersed of Judah " of the City of New Orleans, all that certain property situated in Bourbon Street, immediately adjoining their Synagogue, being the present schoolhouse, and the residence of the said Mr. Gershom Kursheedt, the same purchased by me from the bank of Louisiana; and also to the said Hebrew Congregation, the two adjoining brick houses purchased from the heirs of David Urquhart, the revenue of said property to be applied to the founding and support of the Hebrew school connected with said Congregation, as well as to the defraying of the salary of their Reader or Minister, said property to be conveyed accordingly by

my said executors to said Congregation with all necessary restrictions.

7. I give and bequeath to found the Hebrew Hospital of New Orleans the entire property purchased for me, at the succession sale of the late C. Paulding, upon which property the building now known as the " Touro Infirmary " is situated; the said contemplated Hospital to be organized according to law, as a charitable institution for the relief of the indigent sick, by my executors and such other persons as they may associate with them conformably with the laws of Louisiana.

8. I give and bequeath to the Hebrew Benevolent Association of New Orleans five thousand dollars.

9. I give and bequeath to the Hebrew Congregation " Shangarai Chassed " of New Orleans five thousand dollars.

10. I give and bequeath to the Ladies' Benevolent Society of New Orleans, the sum of five thousand dollars.

11. I give and bequeath to the Hebrew Foreign Mission Society of New Orleans, five thousand dollars.

12. I give and bequeath to the Orphans' Home Asylum of New Orleans, the sum of five thousand dollars.

13. I give and bequeath to the Society for the relief of Destitute Orphan Boys in the Fourth District, five thousand dollars.

14. I give and bequeath to the St. Armas Asylum for the relief of destitute females and children, the sum of five thousand dollars.

15. I give and bequeath to the New Orleans Female Orphan Asylum, at the corner of Camp and Prytania streets, five thousand dollars.

16. I give and bequeath to the St. Mary's Catholic Boys' Asylum, of which my old and esteemed friend Mr. Anthony Rasch is chairman of its Executive Committee, the sum of five thousand dollars.

17. I give and bequeath to the Milne Asylum of New Orleans, five thousand dollars.

18. I give and bequeath to the " Firemen's Charitable Association " of New Orleans, five thousand dollars.

19. I give and bequeath to the " Seamen's Home," in the First District of New Orleans, five thousand dollars.

20. I give and bequeath, for the purpose of establishing an " Alms House " in the City of New Orleans, and with a view of

contributing, as far as possible, to the prevention of mendicity in said city, the sum of eighty thousand dollars, (say $80,000) and I desire that the " Alms House " thus contemplated shall be organized according to law; and further, it is my desire that after my executors shall have legally organized and established said contemplated Alms House, and appointed proper persons to administer and control the direction of its affairs, then such persons legally so appointed and their successors, in office, conjointly with the Mayor of the City of New Orleans, and his successors in office, shall have the perpetual direction and control thereof.

21. I give and bequeath to the City of Newport, in the State of Rhode Island, the sum of ten thousand dollars, on condition that the said sum be expended in the purchase and improvement of the property in said city, known as the " Old Stone Mill," to be kept as a public park or prom enade ground.

22. I give and bequeath to the " Redwood Library " of Newport aforesaid, for books and repairs, three thousand dollars.

23. I give and bequeath to the Hebrew Congregation " Ohabay Shalome " of Boston, Massachusetts, five thousand dollars.

24. I give and bequeath to the Hebrew Congregation of Hartford, Connecticut, five thousand dollars.

25. I give and bequeath to the Hebrew Congregation of New Haven, Connecticut, five thousand dollars.

26. I give and bequeath to the North American Relief Society, for the Indigent Jews of Jerusalem, Palestine, of the City and State of New York (Sir Moses Montefiore of London, their agent), ten thousand dollars.

27. It being my earnest wish to co-operate with the said Sir Moses Montefiore of London, Great Britain, in endeavoring to ameliorate the condition of our unfortunate Jewish Brethren, in the Holy Land, and to secure to them the inestimable privilege of worshipping the Almighty according to our religion, without molestation, I therefore give and bequeath the sum of fifty thousand dollars, to be paid by my Executors for said object, through the said Sir Moses Montefiore, in such manner as he may advise, as best calculated to promote the aforesaid objects; and in case of any legal or other difficulty or impediment in the way of carrying said bequest into effect, according to my intentions, then and in that case, I desire that the said sum of fifty thousand dollars be invested by my Executors in the foundation of a Society in the

City of New Orleans, similar in its objects to the "North American Relief Society for the Indigent Jews of Jerusalem, Palestine, of the City of New York," to which I have before referred in this my last will.

28. It is my wish and desire that the Institutions to which I have already alluded in making this will, as well as those to which in the further course of making this will, I shall refer, shall not be disqualified from inheriting my legacies to them respectively made, for reason of not being incorporated, and thereby not qualified to inherit by law; but on the contrary, I desire that the parties interested in such institutions and my executors shall facilitate their organization as soon after my decease as possible, and thus render them duly qualified by law to inherit in the premises according to my wishes.

29. I give and bequeath to the Jews' Hospital Society of the City and State of New York twenty thousand dollars.

30. I give and bequeath to the Hebrew Benevolent Society "Meshibat Nafesh" of New York, five thousand dollars.

31. I give and bequeath to the Hebrew Benevolent Society "Gemilut Chased" of New York, five thousand dollars.

32. I give and bequeath to the "Talmud Torah" School Fund attached to the Hebrew Congregation "Shearith Israel," of the City of New York, and to said Congregation, thirteen thousand dollars.

33. I give and bequeath to the Educational Institute of the Hebrew Congregation "B'nai Jeshurun" of the City of New York, the sum of three thousand dollars.

34. I give and bequeath to the Hebrew Congregation "Shangarai Tefila," of New York, three thousand dollars.

35. I give and bequeath to the Ladies' Benevolent Society of the City of New York, the same of which Mrs. Richey Levy was a directress at the time of her death, and of which Mrs. I. B. Kursheedt was first directress in 1850, three thousand dollars.

36. I give and bequeath to the Female Hebrew Benevolent Society of Philadelphia (Miss Gratz, Secretary), three thousand dollars.

37. I give and bequeath to the Hebrew Education Society of Philadelphia, Pennsylvania, twenty thousand dollars.

38. I give to the United Hebrew Benevolent Society of Philadelphia, aforesaid, three thousand dollars.

39. I give and bequeath to the Hebrew Congregation "Ahabat

Israel," of Fell's Point, Baltimore, three thousand dollars.

40. I give and bequeath to the Hebrew Congregation " Beth Shalome," of Richmond, Virginia, five thousand dollars.

41. I give and bequeath to the Hebrew Congregation " Shearith Israel," of Charleston, South Carolina, the sum of five thousand dollars.

42. I give and bequeath to the Hebrew Congregation " Shangarai Shamoyim," of Mobile, Alabama, two thousand dollars.

43. I give and bequeath to the Hebrew Congregation " Mikve Israel," of Savannah, Georgia, five thousand dollars.

44. I give and bequeath to the Hebrew Congregation of Montgomery, Alabama, two thousand dollars.

45. I give and bequeath to the Hebrew Congregation of Memphis, Tennessee, two thousand dollars.

46. I give and bequeath to the Hebrew Congregation " Adas Israel," of Louisville, Kentucky, three thousand dollars.

47. I give and bequeath to the Hebrew Congregation " Bnai Israel," of Cincinnati, Ohio, three thousand dollars.

48. I give and bequeath to the Hebrew School, " Talmud Yelodim," of Cincinnati, Ohio, five thousand dollars.

49. I give and bequeath to the Jews' Hospital, of Cincinnati, Ohio, five thousand dollars.

50. I give and bequeath to the Hebrew Congregation, " Tifereth Israel," of Cleveland, Ohio, three thousand dollars.

51. I give and bequeath to the Hebrew Congregation, " Bnai El," of St. Louis, Missouri, three thousand dollars.

52. I give and bequeath to the Hebrew Congregation, " Beth El," of Buffalo, New York, three thousand dollars.

53. I give and bequeath to the Hebrew Congregation of " Beth El," of Albany, New York, three thousand dollars.

54. I give and bequeath to the three following Institutions, named in the will of my greatly beloved brother, the late Abraham Touro, of Boston, the following sums:

First, to the Asylum of Orphan Boys, in Boston, Massachusetts, five thousand dollars.

Second. To the Female Orphan Asylum of Boston aforesaid, five thousand dollars.

Third. And to the Massachusetts Female Hospital, ten thousand dollars.

55. I give and bequeath ten thousand dollars for the purpose of

paying the salary of a Reader or Minister to officiate in the Jewish Synagogue of Newport, Rhode Island, and to endow the Ministry of the same, as well as to keep in repair and embellish the Jewish Cemetery in Newport aforesaid; the said amount to be appropriated and paid, or invested for that purpose in such manner as my executors may determine concurrently with the corporation of Newport aforesaid, if necessary. And it is my wish and desire, that David Gould and Nathan H. Gould, sons of my esteemed friend the late Isaac Gould, Esq., of Newport aforesaid, should continue to oversee the improvements in said Cemetery and direct the same; and as a testimony of my regard and in consideration of services rendered by their said father, I give and bequeath the sum of two thousand dollars to be equally divided between them, the said David and said Nathan H. Gould.

56. I give and bequeath five thousand dollars to Miss Catharine Hays, now of Richmond, Virginia, as an expression of the kind remembrance in which that esteemed friend is held by me.

57. I give and bequeath to the Misses Catharine, Harriet and Julia Myers, the three daughters of Mr. Moses M. Myers, of Richmond, Virginia, the sum of seven thousand dollars, to be equally divided between them.

58. I give and bequeath the sum of seven thousand dollars to the surviving children of the late Samuel Myers, of Richmond, Virginia, to be equally divided between them, in token of my remembrance.

59. I give and bequeath to my friend Mr. Supply Clapp Twing, of Boston, Mass., the sum of five thousand dollars, as a token of my esteem and kind remembrance.

60. I give and bequeath the sum of three thousand dollars to my respected friend the Rev. Isaac Leeser, of Philadelphia, as a token of my regard.

61. I give and bequeath the sum of three thousand dollars to my friends the Rev. Moses N. Nathan, now of London, and his wife, to be equally divided between them.

62. I give and bequeath the sum of three thousand dollars to my friend the Rev. Theodore Clapp, of New Orleans, in token of my remembrance.

63. To Mistress Ellen Brooks, wife of Gorham Brooks, Esquire, of Boston, Massachusetts, and daughter of my friend and executor Rezin Davis Shepherd, I give the sum of five thousand dol-

lars, the same to be employed by my executors, in the purchase of a suitable memorial to her as an earnest of my very kind regard.

64. I give and bequeath the sum of twenty-five hundred dollars, to be employed by my executors in the purchase of a suitable memorial of my esteem, to be presented to Mrs. M. D. Josephs, wife of my friend, Aaron K. Josephs, Esq., of this city.

65. I give and bequeath the sum of twenty-five hundred dollars to be employed by my executors in the purchase of a suitable memorial of my esteem for Mistress Rebecca Kursheedt, wife of Mr. Benjamin Florance, of New Orleans.

66. I revoke all other wills or testaments, which I may have made previously to these presents.

Thus, it was, that this testament or last will was dictated to me, the notary, by the said testator, in presence of the witnesses herein above named, and undersigned, and I have written the same, such as it was dictated to me, by the testator, in my own proper hand, in presence of said witnesses; and having read this testament in a loud and audible voice to the said testator, in presence of said witnesses, he, the said testator, declared in the same presence, that he well understood the same and persisted therein.

All of which was done at one time without interruption or turning aside to other acts.

Thus done and passed at the said City of New Orleans, at the said residence of the said Mr. Judah Touro, the day, month and year first before written in the presence of Messrs Jonathan Montgomery, Henry Shepherd, Jr., and George Washington Lee, all three being the witnesses as aforesaid, who, with the said testator, and me, the said notary. have hereunto signed their names.   (Signed.)

> J. Touro,
>
> J. Montgomery,
>
> H. Shepherd, Jr.,
>
> Geo. W. Lee,
>
> Thos. Layton, *Notary Public.*

GENERAL ORDER NO. 11 *

PADUCAH, K.Y., Dec. 29, 1862.

Hon. Abraham Lincoln, President of the United States.

General Order No. 11 issued by General Grant at Oxford, Miss., December the 17th, commands all post commanders to expel all Jews without distinction within twenty-four hours from his entire Department. The undersigned good and loyal citizens of the United States and residents of this town, for many years engaged in legitimate business as merchants, feel greatly insulted and outraged by this inhuman order; the carrying out of which would be the grossest violation of the Constitution and our rights as good citizens under it, and would place us, besides a large number of other Jewish families of this town, as outlaws before the world. We respectfully ask your immediate attention to this enormous outrage on all law and humanity and pray for your effectual and immediate interposition. We would especially refer you to the post commander and post adjutant as to our loyalty, and to all respectable citizens of this community as to our standing as citizens and merchants. We respectfully ask for immediate instructions to be sent to the Commander of this Post.

D. WOLFF & BROS.
C. J. KASKEL.
J. W. KASKEL.

*Markens, Issac. *Abraham Lincoln and the Jews.* New York: The Author, 1909, p. 11.

BARON DE HIRSCH FUND *

45 Broadway, New York City.

Deed of trust executed in March, 1890, by Baron Maurice de Hirsch for the benefit of Russian and Roumanian Jewish immigrants.

Capital, $2,500,000.

Annual Income, $100,000.

Trustees: President, M. S. Isaacs, New York; Vice-President, Jacob H. Schiff, New York; Treasurer, Emanuel Lehman, New York; Henry Rice, New York; James H. Hoffman, New York; Abraham Abraham, Brooklyn; William B. Hackenburg, Philadelphia; Mayer Sulzberger, Philadelphia; General Agent, A. S. Solomons; Agricultural Agent, Arthur Reichow; Superintendent Agricultural School, H. L. Sabsovich.

Chairman of the Philadelphia Committee, William B. Hackenburg; Chairman of the Baltimore Committee, Dr. Aaron Friedenwald; Chairman of the St. Louis Committee, Elias Michael; Chairman of the Boston Committee, Jacob H. Hecht.

Co-operates in other cities with existing societies when circumstances warrant.

SYNOPSIS OF THE WORK

The work of the Baron de Hirsch Fund of America may be treated of under the following headings:

*Cyrus Adler, ed., "The American Jewish Year Book 5660: September 5, 1899 to September 23, 1900" (Philadelphia: Jewish Publication Society of America, 1899), pp. 42-49.

I. Reception of immigrants.
II. English education.
III. Mechanical education.
IV. Productive work of the Baron de Hirsch Fund in its agricultural and industrial department, with its leading educational feature, the Woodbine Agricultural and Industrial School.

In the last two departments, the Jewish Colonization Association has latterly enabled the Baron de Hirsch Fund to carry out its programme effectively, as appears from the last report of the Colonization Association, presented by its President, M. Nareisse Leven, at the statutory meeting of shareholders in Paris, May 21, 1899, from which the account given below is quoted.

I. RECEPTION OF IMMIGRANTS.—Upon the arrival of immigrants at United States ports an agent sees to it that they reach their destinations, provided they have determined to leave the city; if not, as many as possible are sent out of town to places where employment has previously been found for them. The policy is to scatter them throughout the country, so that they will not congest in large cities. Whenever necessary, their expenses to their new homes are paid, and they are supported *en route*. Those who remain in New York, and need advice and assistance, are directed to the Labor Bureau of the United Hebrew Charities, supported in part by the fund, and employment is found for them when possible. If absolutely necessary, support is given to immigrants for a short time, until they are able to earn a living. Occasionally they are established in trades, and in extreme cases temporary relief is afforded to families. Not more than five per cent. of the number thus assisted has made application for addition help.

II. ENGLISH EDUCATION.—Immediately upon arrival the immigrant children are taught English in large, well-ventilated classrooms, by college graduates, who prepare them to enter the public schools. As they are taught according to the method employed in the public schools, and are noted for their rapid advance and exact attainments, they are welcomed with eagerness by the principals. There are now about 400 children in the day classes.

There are also evening classes, composed of 400 workingmen

and women, most of whom come to their classes direct from the workshop.

In some cases of students of Russian or Roumanian birth who have entered colleges, and have made creditable progress, loans are advanced to enable them to complete their studies and be graduated.

III. MECHANICAL EDUCATION.—In 1890 the Baron de Hirsch Trade School was established in a building rented for the purpose at 225-227 East Ninth Street, in New York, wherein two classes have been graduated each year since.

On January 1, 1899, rhtough the munificence of the late Baroness de Hirsch-Gereuth, a new building, constructed upon the most modern principles, was opened. A class of fifty-five young men, whose work and demeanor indicate the best results, has been graduated.

The trades are carpentry, plumbing, house sign and fresco painting, and machine work; English is taught to those who are deficient; also drawing and the technical branch of each trade. There are two school terms a year, of five and a half months each. No pretence is made of turning out finished mechanics; sufficient is taught, however, to enable the graduates to become "helpers" in their respective vocations, and in most cases good positions are obtained immediately opon leaving the school. The graduates earn from $7 to $15 a week, and in proportion as their experience enables them to do better work, their compensation is increased, some of them receiving now $22.50 a week. Each graduate is given the tools of his trade. Tuition is free.

Though the school is open to any Jewish boy, preference is given to natives of Russia or Roumania.

The point of view is, that essential though it be that a boy learn a trade, it is important that his earning powers be developed as quickly as possible. Anything that helps to train his mind and hand, and promotes rapid progress, is desirable. On these thoroughly practical lines the school is conducted. On the other hand, the idea is constantly kept before the pupils, that when they become skilled mechanics they are entitled to the wages of skilled mechanics. Thus the Trade School, by exciting the ambition to excel in the minds of the pupils, tends to reduce the danger of close competition in other directions.

The aim of the school, then, is to reach the three following results:

1. To teach a boy as quickly as possible the fundamental principles of some trade, together with as much arithmetic and mechanical drawing as is indispensable in a given line of work.

2. To teach him to do well what is required of the class of help whose place he is fitted by age and attainments to fill.

3. To teach him unquestioning obedience.

To accomplish these results he is placed under the care of a skilled mechanic, who has no more pupils than he can faithfully teach, for five months and a half, eight hours a day, five days in the week, holidays excepted. A longer period would be more desirable, but it would entail a sacrifice of time, which would be difficult for pupils to bear, as no support whatever is allowed them by the fund.

IV. PRODUCTIVE WORK OF THE BARON DE HIRSCH FUND.—The Agricultural and Industrial Department of the Baron de Hirsch Fund was organized as an agency to promote the economical interests of Russo-Jewish immigrants:

1. To advise them properly in the acquisition of homesteads in rural districts all over the country.

2. To grant them loans, towards the purchase of farms, livestock and implements, in proportion to their own funds and their ability as farmers.

3. To transfer industries and those employed in them from crowded cities to agricultural districts, with a view of benefiting the wage-earners in health and comfort and at the same time creating consumers of farm products at the place of their production.

The success of the Baron de Hirsch Fund in this department has been marked. It enjoys the full confidence of immigrants intending to purchase farms as well as of owners of farm lands willing to sell. By both it is looked upon as a trustworthy bureau of agricultural and industrial information.

In the purchase of farms for an immigrant, various points are taken into consideration: his means, his ability as a farmer, the location of the homestead, the facilities it offers for cattle-breeding, its distance from a market or a creamery, etc. Each one of these is a factor determining the purchase price.

At present many favorable opportunities present themselves. Established dairy farms are offered for sale in New England at a price less than the cost of the buildings upon them. Their abandonment is due to the death or old age of their owners, whose children, attracted to the cities and to professional occupations, are willing to sell their ancestral homesteads at a great sacrifice.

Jewish immigrants coming from the villages of the Pale of Settlement in Russia are ready buyers of dairy farms, because they were accustomed to dairy pursuits in their old home. Many of them kept a smaller or larger number of dairy cattle, and raised feed for them, on leased land. On the other hand, few are skilled gardeners, and therefore they are not successful at other kinds of farming in this country.

The activity of the Baron de Hirsch Fund in its capacity as an agricultural agent, offering liberal loans, furnishing accurate information, and advising with a view to conditions and circumstances, has had the following result:

The settlement of 600 Jewish farmers on as many homesteads in New England.

In New England the farming interests of Jewish immigrants are indicated by the following figures:

1. Investment of the immigrants, $1,100,000.

2. Loans upon mortgages other than those held by the Baron de Hirsch Fund, $1,250,000.

The loans and advances made by the Baron de Hirsch Fund have substantially helped to make these investments safe and productive.

The Jewish capital invested in farming enterprises in New Jersey and other parts of the country is represented by even larger figures. Moreover, it is constantly increasing, in proportion to the spread of industrial activity in agricultural districts. As the limited means of the immigrants forbid the purchase of homesteads near large towns, which offer ready markets for farm products, the Baron de Hirsch Fund aims to remove to the more distant places in which they must settle, the industries, such as the tailoring trades, in which many of the immigrants are employed. This policy at the same time relieves the so-called Ghettos from the congestion at present endangering the social and sanitary condition of our large cities.

New York along contains 65,000 operatives who are engaged in tailoring, in the "sweat-shops," to support their families, that is, 200,000 persons, constituting a majority of the Jewish population. In other words, the tailoring trade keeps the East Side solidly Jewish, and attracts constantly newcomers from abroad and from the interior. The Baron de Hirsch Fund holds out every encouragement to these wage-earners to remove to country districts: factories on liberal terms; educational facilities, especially in the direction of trades and agriculture; and the opportunity to live in a Jewish community.

The *Woodbine Agricultural and Industrial School,* the leading educational feature of this department of the Baron de Hirsch Fund work, was opened in October, 1894, with 15 pupils. Its aim is to train up practical, intelligent farmers able to act as assistants to other farmers or prepared to work farms of their own. Applicants for admission must be at least 14 years of age, and be prepared to pass an examination equivalent to that of the third grade in the public schools of Cape May County. Tuition is free to all regular students, and board and lodging may be had at the dormitory at actual cost, but students whose parents are unable to support them while at school are boarded and lodged free of charge. These students are, however, expected to offset such expenses by labor on the School Farm. There are now 69 pupils at the school, taught by 7 instructors, one of them a graduate of the school. The course extends over three years, and the studies are divided into theoretical and practical. The studies pursued by the boys are as follows: (1) English, (2) arithmetic, (3) drawing, (4) history, (5) geography, (6) chemistry, (7) physics, (8) bookkeeping and correspondence, (9) botany, (10) experimental chemistry, (11) mathematics, (12) geometrical drawing, (13) soils and crops, (14) manures and fertilizers, (15) land measuring, (16) zoology, (17) entomology, (18) collecting of plants, (19) feeds, (20) comparative anatomy and physiology, (21) domestic animals (selection, care, etc.), (22) horticulture, (23) floriculture, (24) landscape gardening, (25) market gardening, (26) meteorology, (27) relation of forestry to agriculture, (28) dairying, (29) farm implements and machinery.

The studies for girls substitute chemistry of foods, hygiene and nursing, household economics, household sanitation, foods and preserves, foods in detail, for Nos. 10, 12, 13, 14, 15, 19, 25 and 29.

The practical work of the boys consists of care of stables, poultry yards, domestic animals, milking, and shop and field work; planting, care of crops, harvesting, work in greenhouses, cold frames, hot beds, in orchards and the blacksmith shop; care of small fruit, floriculture, and work on the nursery grounds and in the wheelwright shop.

The girls throughout the course have practical work in sewing, cooking, care of the poultry, dairy, etc., and are employed in doing the household work of the dormitory and in practical housekeeping.

The School Farms contain 240 acres, of which 30 acres are in orchards, 20 acres in berries, 6 acres in grapes, and the remainder is suitable for corn, truck and field crops in general; besides some land is in bushes and some in woods.

The buildings are: one school-house, 4 poultry houses, a barn, sheds, corn cribs, 2 greenhouses, cold frames, a boiler house, a windmill, and a storage room.

The school is provided with a small chemical laboratory, physical apparatus, Babcock's test and a library of reference books.

The school owns 5 horses, some cows, and 200 fowls.

The dormitory can accommodate 100 pupils.

Religious services are held daily; the Sabbath is devoted to divine worship, religious instruction, and rest.

Woodbine founded in 1891, now contains 1000 inhabitants, employed in 4 factories or on their farms. There are two public schools, a kindergarten, five stores, a bakery, two educational clubs, three fraternal societies, a public bath-house, an evening school, a religious school, a synagogue, and a hall.

THE JEWISH COLONIZATION ASSOCIATION

Since 1896 the Baron de Hirsch Fund has had the support of the Jewish Colonization Association, and has co-operated with it in the United States. As a result, the capacity of the Trade School has been doubled; the agricultural work, especially at the Woodbine School, has been broadened in scope and effectiveness; the American Committee has been furnished with additional means to transplant the industrial population from the great centers to the rural districts; isolated farmers in New England have been helped with loans to free their land from mortgages, so that at present more than "600 Jewish farmers are living in New England on their own land, which they themselves cultivate with the help of their families. . . . The farms are fully developed, and the farmers have commenced conscientiously to pay their debts."

The Jewish Colonization Association has also given effective support to the older colonies in South Jersey, Alliance, Carmel and Rosenhayn. The following is the report of the Association on this phase of its work:

These colonies, founded in 1882, at the time of the great exodus of Jews from Russia, have always led a precarious existence; they had not the means to support themselves, and lacked an outlet for their produce. Benevolent societies from time to time gave them assistance which enabled them to live from day to day, but without ever affording them the means to strengthen their position and assure their future. Thus, of the 300 families which these colonies comprised at their foundation there only remained 200 in 1893, and 76 at the end of 1896; all the others had returned to their miserable life in the towns. Those families who did not abandon the colonies were in a very difficult position; having contracted onerous debts, and being unable to pay the interest, they were every day threatened with being evicted and sold up.

This critical situation compelled the colonists to apply to our Association in 1897. Inquires made on the spot soon proved that neither lack of will nor the incapacity of the colonists was the cause of this state of things, but the absence of a market where they could sell their produce, which consisted expecially of potatoes and other vegetables, fruit and poultry. The nearest town, Vineland, which contains 3500 inhabitants, is in fact peopled by old farmers, who themselves produce the necessary fruit and vegetables for their own consumption. It was thus not enough to free the colonists from their debts; it was also necessary to create a market for the sale of their produce.

This double object has been achieved; our Association has granted loans to the most deserving colonists, which have enabled them to pay off their creditors. It has, besides, made loans to artisans for the establishment of factories in the center or in the neighborhood of these colonies on condition that they should employ the families of workmen on the spot, or those who were removed from New York or Philadelphia.

A new existence has thus been assured to these colonies; eight artisans have settled there; they pay weekly wages of 7500 francs to more than 250 families who have come from the centers of which we have spoken. These families occupy the houses previously abandoned by the colonists and constitute the market which was wanting. A new factory is on the eve of being established in Alliance Colony; it will permit of 40 additional families, comprising 200 persons, leaving the large cities; a hundred of them will find employment in the factory, which will likewise give work to a hundred other artisans selected from the families who are already located in the colony, and who will receive a minimum weekly wage of 2500 francs.

It is estimated that the workmen in the three colonies will annually receive more than half a million, a third of which will certainly revert to the colonists.

In South Jersey our Association has also come to the assistance of twenty-five Jewish farmers established in the neighborhood of these three colonies on isolated farms. Their position very much resembled that of the colonists of whom we have just spoken. Nineteen of them, the most deserving, have received advances, and all are profiting by the markets established in the colonies.

The three colonies, Alliance, Carmel and Rosenhayn, and the twenty-five Jewish farmers in South Jersey have been placed in a position to keep themselves; they have already paid the first instalment of the debt which they contracted towards our Association.

The number of Jewish families in this region, to whose assistance we have come, directly or otherwise, is about 600, viz.: 76 families of colonists, 25 farmers, 250 workmen from New York and the artisan population already settled in the colonies, which may be estimated at 250 families.

[1] In view of the recent organization of most Zionist Societies, it was next to impossible to reach, by means of directories and other similar agencies, such as have not affiliated with the general and local federations.

[2] The account of the Baron de Hirsch Fund activities here given, though not official, is authentic.

THE ORTHODOX JEWISH CONGREGATIONAL UNION OF AMERICA*

A convention of Orthodox Congregations met in New York, Wednesday, June 8, 1898. Lewis N. Dembitz, Esq., was called to the chair, and Mr. D. Levine acted as secretary; fifty Congregations were represented. The following provisional officers were elected: President, Rev. Dr. H. Pereira Mendes; Vice-Presidents, Dr. P. Klein, Rev. Meldola de Sola, Rev. Dr. H. W. Schneeberger, Mr. K. H. Sarasohn; Secretaries, for English, Max Cohen, for Hebrew, I. Buchhalter.

A resolution favoring Zionism was adopted.

A resolution was passed making the Orthodox Jewish Congregations in America an established society.

The principles of the convention adopted are as follows:

"This Conference of delegates from Jewish congregations in the United States and the Dominion of Canada is convened to advance the interests of positive Biblical. Rabbinical and Historical Judaism.

"We are assembled not as a synod, and, therefore, we have no legislative authority to amend religious questions, but as a representative body, which by organization and co-operation will endeavor to advance the interests of Judaism in America.

"We favor the convening of a Jewish Synod specifically authorized by congregations to meet, to be composed of men who must be certified Rabbis, and

*Cyrus Adler, ed., *The American Jewish Year Book 5660: September 5, 1899 to September 23, 1900* (Philadelphia: Jewish Publication Society of America, 1899), pp. 99-102.

a) Elders in official position (Cf. Numbers xi. 16);

b) Men of wisdom and understanding, and known amongst us (Cf. Deut. i. 13);

c) Able men. God-fearing men, men of truth, hating profit (Cf. Exodus xviii. 21).

"We believe in the Divine relation of the Bible, and we declare that the prophets in no way discountenanced ceremonial duty, but only condemned the personal life of those who observed ceremonial law, but disregarded the moral. Ceremonial law is not optative; it is obligatory.

"We affirm our adherence to the acknowledged codes of our Rabbis and the thirteen principles of Maimonides.

"We believe that in our dispersion we are to be united with our brethren of alien faith in all that devolves upon men as citizens; but that religiously, in rites, ceremonies, ideals and doctrines, we are separate, and must remain separate in accordance with the Divine declaration; 'I have separated you from the nation to be Mine.' (Lev. xx. 26.)

"And further, to prevent misunderstanding concerning Judaism, we reaffirm our belief in the coming of a personal Messiah and we protest against the admission of proselytes into the fold of Judaism without *millah* and *tebilah.*

"We protest against intermarriage between Jew and Gentile; we protest against the idea that we are merely a religious sect, and maintain that we are a nation, though temporarily without a national home, and

"Furthermore, that the restoration to Zion is the legitimate aspiration of scattered Israel, in no way conflicting with our loyalty to the land in which we dwell or may dwell at any time."

The following are extracts from the Constitution:

The organization shall be known as the Orthodox Jewish Congregational Union of America.

The objects of this organization shall be the promotion of the religious interests of the Jews in America, and the maintenance of the welfare of Orthodox Jewish Congregations in America.

All Orthodox Jewish Congregations in America shall be eligible to membership and entitled to representation in the meetings of the Union, on application for membership to the executive committee.

All questions of Orthodoxy in connection with the admission of members shall be conclusively acted upon by a sub-committee of five rabbis, to be appointed by the executive committee; said rabbis to be members of the conference.

The Union shall hold a regular annual meeting at such time and place as shall be designated by the preceding meeting. Special meetings of the Union may be called at any other time and place on the call of the executive committee, on the written request of at least ten congregations of the Union.

Each congregation affiliated with the Union shall pay as annual dues, in the following manner: congregations having fifty members or under, $5; congregations having over fifty members. $10.

The constitution may be amended by a vote of two-thirds of the delegates present at two successive meetings of the Union.

Addresses were delivered by Lewis N. Dembitz, Esq.; Dr. Schaffer, of Baltimore; Rev. Meldola de Sola, of Montreal; Rev. Dr. H. Pereira Mendes, of New York; and Rev. Dr. Joseph H. Hertz (now of Johannesburg, South Africa).

The conference organized itself permanently by the adoption of the following resolution:

Resolved, That the respesentatives of the Orthodox Jewish Congregations in America, assembled in conference in the city of New York, this 18th day of Sivan, in the year 5658, hereby express their sense of the need of the formation and maintenance of a permanent organization of the Orthodox Jewish Congregations in America to promote the religious interests of the Jews in America and to further the welfare of the Orthodox Congregations in America, and said representatives hereby agree to organize and do organize, the Orthodox Jewish Congregational Union of America; to formulate and adopt a constitution for the government of said Union; and to elect the officers to be provided for by said constitition.

And to adopt as the religious principles of the Orthodox Jewish Congregational Union of America, the declaration of principles adopted by the Conference on the 18th day of Sivan, 5658, and the said principles shall never be changed as long as three congregations shall adhere to them.

Permanent officers were elected as follows: President, Dr. H. Pereira Mendes; First Vice-President, L. N. Dembitz, Esq., of Louisville, Ky.; Second Vice-President, S. Solis Cohen, M. D., of Philadelphia; Third Vice-President, Dr. A. Friedenwald, M. D., of Baltimore; Fourth Vice-President, K. H. Sarasohn, of New York City; Treasurer, Jacob Hecht, of New York City; Secretaries, Rev. Dr. Drachman and Max Cohen; Trustees: Rev. Dr. Mendes, Rev. Dr. Klein, Rev. Dr. De Sola, Rev. Dr. Schaffer, Rabbi Bachrach, Rev. Dr. Drachman, Rev. Dr. J. H. Hertz, Rev. Dr. Schneeberger, L. N. Dembitz, Dr. A. Friedenwald, S. M. Roeder, Joseph Blumenthal, Dr. Cyrus Adler, Dr. S. Solis Cohen, K. H. Sarasohn, Jacob Hecht, L. Napoleon Levy, J. Silverman, Max Cohen, Isaac Lass and Max Deutschman.

These resolutions were adopted:

That in all towns where the number of congregations warrants, a local Union be formed, each congregation to be represented by the rabbi or minister, the president and one other lay delegate. The local Union shall organize as they deem best.

The objects of the said local Union shall be:

1st. To strengthen congregational life but not to interfere in congregational autonomy.

2d. To advance the interests of the local Judaism by the appointment of any of the following committees or others as may be deemed necessary:

Congregational membership: civil legislation; committee on Jewish presentations; city religious work (mission, circuit preaching); committee appointed to devise uniform methods in Hebrew and religious schools; Union to send out rabbis for propaganda under the direction of the Executive Committee.

AN OPEN LETTER TO THE CZAR OF RUSSIA*

[Under this title, The Independent, New York, published on September 11, 1913, the following striking arraignment of Russian misgovernment which had its culmination in the Beilis affair. The article attracted worldwide attention and elicited widespread editorial comment.]

SIRE—When you ascended the throne of the Russian Empire the expectations of your people ran high. They looked forward to a more humane reign than that which had just ended. They were yearning for reforms, for a sympathetic bond between the palace and the huts of the hungry and the homes of the oppressed. You were regarded as a young man of liberal tendencies, of advanced views. After your father's reactionary reign the Russian people longed for relief. But, alas, what an awakening was theirs!

Little by little the vision of a better day faded. Your people began to despair. Your supposed idealism failed to manifest itself in any of your acts. The evil genius of Pobyedonostseff, of the Holy Synod, reigned supreme while he lived, and still rules Russia from his grave. A long list of charlatans and mad monks and illiterate fortune-tellers, beginning with Philippe, the barber of Marseilles, and ending with the Monk Ilioder and Rasputin, have been in the ascendancy and have exerted a baneful influence at your court. Those who have counseled reform and have advocated

*Herman Bernstein, ed. The American Jewish Year Book 5675 September 21, 1914, to September 8, 1915 (Philadelphia: Jewish Publication Society of America, 1914), pp. 85-89.

liberal tendencies have become discredited and have been driven away.

The condition of the longsuffering nationalities of your Empire instead of ameliorating has become ever more tragic. Though you have special cause to be lenient with your Polish subjects, Poland has been bent under added burdens. Finland has become an autonomous government without autonomy, and it is gradually becoming converted into a Russian province. The Baptists and the Roman Catholics have suffered oppression. The Jews have experienced during your reign persecutions far more cruel than those which prevailed during the Middle Ages. New restrictions and new policies of hatred have been devised and directed against them. They have been driven from pillar to post. When the ghastly Kishineff massacres raged, the world was shocked. The civilized nations protested. It is no longer a secret that these massacres were staged, planned, organized and executed by the aid of your Government. Your former director of the Secret Police Department of the Russian Empire, M. Alexander Lopukhin, who investigated the cause of the massacres, reported to the late Premier Stolypin that the anti-Jewish proclamations inciting the populace against the Jews were printed on presses owned by the Police Department and were distributed by members of the Police Department.

Then you were drawn into a war with Japan by Admiral Alexeyeff and others of your advisers—men who sought the personal gain of power and wealth, and who led Russia headlong to ruin. The army and navy proved so demoralized by graft and debauchery that in her struggle Russia revealed herself as a colossus upon feet of clay. Humiliated on land and sea, it was only by the ingenious statesmanship of Count Witte at Portsmouth that Russia was saved from utter disgrace.

On October 17 (Russian style), 1905, you signed the manifesto granting a constitution to Russia. You signed that document under pressure. You were frightened by the sweeping wave of revolution that was rising over the Russian land. You were informed that only such a measure could save your throne. By adopting it your throne has, for a time, been saved. On the day after the manifesto was issued, a counter-revolution was organized. Massacres broke out in hundreds of towns in various parts of Russia at the same hour and upon the same signal. Jews and intellectuals were attacked, plundered and killed. The gallows was revived in Russia. Men, women and children were hanged for offenses punishable in civilized countries by a few months, imprisonment only. The prisons became overcrowded. The best of the Russian people were thrown into dungeons, or exiled to forsaken and pest-ridden regions to die there of starvation.

The story of the first and second Dumas is well known to the whole world. Every aspiration for liberty and justice that found vent in those national assemblies was withered in the bud. Every manifestation of independence was penalized. The voice of the people was silenced. The causes of the dispersion of the Russian parliaments, and of the falling of the ceiling where the Duma assembled upon the seats of the opposition deputies, the imprisonment of the signers of the Viborg manifesto, the murder of the distinguished Jewish Duma deputies, Professor Herzenstein and M. Yollos, by the Black Hundred organization, with the aid of Dr. Dubrovin, who is still one of your favorites—all these are no longer secrets to the outside world.

The restrictions directed against the Jews of Russia assumed shocking forms. Jewish soldiers who fought bravely in the Russo-Japanese war were driven from Moscow upon their return from the battlefield as soon as they could leave the hospital. They had no rights of domicile there. The Governor-General of Moscow, Hershelman, ordered the expulsion of a twenty-month-old Jewish boy, stating in his official order that "the boy may be dangerous to the constituted regime of the Russian Empire."

Your father, Alexander III, once said to Count Servius Witt:

"Is it true that you are fond of the Jews?"

Count Witte replied:

"Permit me to answer you by another question. Suppose that you gather all the Jews of Russia, place them in ships on the Black Sea and then sink the ships. You would not do that, would you? The Jews must live among us, with us. Therefore we must give them the opportunity to live as we do. In my opinion, the only way of solving the Jewish question is to give the Jews equal rights."

Alexander III was silent for a while and then remarked:

"Perhaps you are right."

You have gone much further than your father in your anti-Jewish policies. If you do not know, you should know that the Jews have contributed much to the development of Russia. Rubinstein may be said to have founded the Russian school of music. Antokolsky has made Russian sculpture to rank high. Levitan, a Jewish landscape painter, has taught the Russian people how to admire the landscapes of their own country. Prof. Elie Mechnikoff, head of the Pasteur Institute in Paris, the greatest living biologist, who exiled himself from Russia, ascribed his love for science to the influence of his Jewish mother. He has declared that Russia has lost through the persecution of the Jews some of the greatest scientists. The literature, art and music of Russia have been popularized and made accessible in many lands outside of Russia by Jews.

Many of the Jews whom you have cruelly oppressed have come to America. They have adapted themselves here to the American conditions. They are making remarkable progress in every field of human activity. They have added to the wealth of the nation by their manufactures, their skill in innumerable trades which they practise here but were forbidden to practise in their native land. They have widened the spheres of commerce. They have become patriotic and law-abiding citizens. They and their adopted land have profited marvelously by the avidity with which they have availed themselves of the educational opportunities extended to them. Russia has lost and is suppressing forces which, if utilized, would develop her tremendous resources beyond the power of belief. How the Jews are regarded in this country may be surmised from the impressive manner in which Congress expressed it protest against the dishonor by Russia of American passports when borne by Jews. The violation of the Treaty of 1832 by Russia, by her discrimination against Jews, was regarded an affront to the American people. The unanimous voice of America should have convinced you that the Jews have made good as American citizens.

Your advisers are misleading you with regard to the Jews in Russia. That is the most charitable view to take. To divert your attention from their own incompetency, they are pointing to the Jews as the cause of all the troubles that exist in Russia. To divert the attention of the Russian people from their real enemies, the officials are inciting the bestial passions of the mob against the Jews.

The best Jews of Russia are either in exile, in prison, or have been stifled into stupefaction. Though you prevent the best of them from serving Russia, you are employing the worst to serve you. You have engaged Jewish outcasts as spies and provocateurs. You have chosen as your agents the Azeffs and teh Bogrovs, the assassins of your uncle, the Grand Duke Sergius, of Von Plehve and of the late Premier Stolypin.

Your advisers have misled you and you are now drifting to your your ruin, a plunging Russia into anarchy. You have become known as the "Pardoning Czar," but you have limited your pardons to those who have participated in the massacres of the Jews. You are now striking a new blow at the Jews of your Empire by depriving them of the last opportunity to secure an education, and are attempting to carry out the diabolical plans of your reactionary advisers. Your laws are being so cunningly administered that the Jewish prostitute enjoys extensive rights, while the Jewish student girl has none. The yellow passport of prostitution gives a Jewish girl the right to live in your capital. The Jewish girl with the highest aspirations who seeks an education in St. Petersburg is driven out by the police.

And now, to add the crown of infamy, your Minister of Justice has staged a "ritual murder" case. Russia is here moving backward. Your own great-grandfather, Alexander I, by an official decree prohibited ritual murder accusations against the Jews. But that was a hundred years ago. Papal bulls have been issued against them. The entire civilized world has declared their falsity. The Pogrom policy can no longer be pursued effectively. The civilized nations have but recently protested against it in thunder-tones. Hence your advisers have revived an ancient and exploded falsehood to discredit the Jews, to stir the passions of the unthinking mob against them.

A Christian boy was murdered in Kieff. A Jew, Mendel Beilis, was found in the neighborhood and arrested, and has been imprisoned now for more than two years, awaiting trial. He is charged with having killed the boy to secure his blood for ritual purposes. For more than two years the manufacture of the most absurb evidence against him has been in progress. The head of the Kieff Detective Bureau, M. Mistchuk, who reported that he could find no incriminating evidence and that he was convinced it was not a case of ritual murder, has been cast into prison for weakening the case of the Government against the Jew. All sorts of difficulties are being placed in the way of the defense. Beilis is denied the privilege of calling witnesses. It seems as though Russia is determined to strike at all the Jews through this infamous proceeding. She has closed her ears to the verdict of science. The impressive protest of the International Medical Congress, which has just concluded its session in London, passes unobserved.

This is not the letter of one who hates Russia, but of one who admires the Russia that has produced a great literature, that has given birth to great men and women, that is struggling for emancipation, that possesses marvelous possibilities in her industries and natural resources. It is the expression of one who, though he loves the land, shudders at these manifestations of medieval bigotry and cruelty for which you are responsible in the eyes of the world and before God's throne.

How can you, the man who suggested the establishment of universal peace at The Hague, tolerate, in the land in which you hold absolute sway, such refinement of barbarity and brutality, and yet venture to face the rulers of civilized powers, as their equal? How can you permit the revival of long-exploded myths and superstitions? How, in short, do you expect to meet your Maker with such a burden upon your soul? Open you eyes! Observe the fruits that freedom bears under other skies! Drive from your land the dark spirits of intolerance and despotism which have made of it a charnel-house and a prison! Then a new light will dawn upon your vast domain and you can yet bring to its millions happiness and prosperity.

GOVERNOR MOSES ALEXANDER OF IDAHO*

We take great pleasure in presenting to our readers—and especially to the young men—His Excellency, Moses Alexander, Governor of the State of Idaho, United States of America.

We want you to know this gentleman because he is a Jew, a real Jew, president of Cong. Beth Israel, member of St. Joseph Lodge, No. 73, Independent Order B'nai B'rith.

Isn't he an interesting individual, this Governor of Idaho—this first Jew to be elected anywhere in the United States to that high office? And isn't he even more interesting—more worth knowing—because he is a real Jew! So many of us are apt to imagine that by being Jews we are burdened with a terrible responsibility. That being a Jew handicaps us, defeats our ambitions, thwarts our careers and puts obstacles in the paths of our progress. Well, then, here is one Jew who didn't find this faith a handicap, whose career was not blighted because of it. He was elected because he is a real Jew. He did not hold himself aloof from Jewish interests, and yet—he was elected Governor of the sovereign State of Idaho.

Who elected him? The Jews of Idaho? There is only one Jewish congregation in the entire State, that of Boise City, of which he is president. He was therefore not elected by the Jewish vote. But he was elected by the men and women of Idaho because they felt that the affairs

*Mordecai Soltes, *The Yiddish Press: An Americanizing Agency* (New York: Teachers College, Columbia University, 1924), pp. 211-212.

of their State would be safest in the hands of Moses Alexander statesman, synagogue leader—Jew!

Here, indeed is something for everyone who thinks that being a Jew is somehow harmful to him, to think about.

But—yes, there is a "but." If Mr. Moses Alexander had not done one thing which most Jews in America will not do, he might never have been heard of. He had the good sense to get away; away to the West, where a man who is a man, has elbow-room, where he can display his true qualities without being hampered by the cramping condition of the tumultuous city. Many young men are wasting themselves away in the big cities of the East who have the same qualities as this Jewish Governor, except perhaps his courage. Perhaps none of them imitating Mr. Alexander's example, would attain his rank, but they would reach a higher rung on life's ladder than they will ever reach in the crowded, cold, and indifferent cities.

Two lessons stand out clearly when we think of Governor Alexander. They are: (1) Go West, young Jew! (2) If you go West, be proud and frank, and above all, be a Jew like the Governor of the State of Idaho. (*Tageblatt*, English Page, November 23, 1914, NN, 63, 37.)

THE KEHILLAH OF NEW YORK *

I

A BRIEF HISTORY OF THE KEHILLAH

By HARRY SACKLER
Administrative Secretary of the Kehillah

1. The Kehillah Idea

The Kehillah idea—that is, orangized Jewish life with a Jewish community as its basis—is deeply rooted in Jewish tradition and in Jewish experience. During the many centuries of national disintegration, the result of persecution and dispersion, the Jews still managed to maintain their community life—the last vestige of autonomous existence. Wherever a group of Jews found refuge, even if it were only a temporary respite, they immediately began to look after the communal needs; a place to pray for the living and a place to rest for the dead.

But while the primary functions of the traditional Kehillah were of a religious nature, it also took upon itself to care for many of the social and economic, as well as the political, needs of the Jewish group. Charity—or more properly "Justice" (Zdokoh)—was one of its main tasks; and whenever the peace of the community or of any of its members was threatened by the powers that be, it developed upon the leaders of the Kehillah to avert the blow or, at least, to mitigate its severity. And so, in the course of centuries, the Kehillah became the stronghold of the individual Jew, and "Kahal" came to be looked upon by the non-Jewish world as the authoritative representative of Jewish interests.

It would, indeed, have been rather strange and disconcerting if a tradition so deeply rooted in Jewish life and in Jewish experi-

*Kehillah (Jewish Community) of New York City, ed. *The Jewish Communal Register of New York City 1917-11918.* 2d ed. (New York: Kehillah (Jewish Community of New York City, 1918), pp. 45-58.

ence, would have been discontinued in the new haven which the Jews found in the Western hemisphere. For a long time it looked as if American Jewry—and particularly in its greatest point of concentration, in the City of New York— would break with the old tradition and be content to remain a conglomeration of isolated, small congregations. For many years it looked as if there were small hope that the greatest Jewish aggregation in the world would make an effort to unite on a common platform and thus make possible a solution of both its external and internal problems. There were, indeed, many difficulties in the way of such an organization. The heterogeneous character of the Jewish population; its unprecedented growth, due to a constant influx of immigrants; the new-comers' natural distrust of the older settlers, who looked upon them from on high; the strained relationship that existed for many years between "Uptown" and "Downtown"; the economic adjustment which absorbed the entire attention of the vast majority of the new settlers and left little room for the higher, more spiritual needs; the "Landsmannschaft" tendency to segregation—all these represented, and in a measure still represent, the forces that kept the Kehillah idea in abeyance. But, fortunately, none of these difficulties was insuperable. The "Melting Pot" process within the Jewish community has been going on slowly, but steadily, and the sporadic outbursts of external pressure greatly helped to weld Jewish interests and develop community consciousness.

Beginning with the mass immigration of Eastern European Jews, one generation ago, the problem of organizing the Jewish community in New York City became more acute from year to year. But the formative forces making for such an organization were continually gaining strength, and it required only some external impetus to bring these forces into play and to precipitate the formation of a Kehillah or Jewish Community in this city. This external impetus was supplied by the Bingham incident, in the fall of the year 1908. General Bingham, who was then the Police Commissioner of New York, made a statement that the Jews contributed 50% of the crimimals of New York City. This statement was afterwards retracted as the result of many meetings held by

Jewish organizations, which protested vehemently against this unfounded accusation. While probably undue importance was attached to this incident at the time, it is certain that it sufficed to
arouse community consciousness to a degree where the organization of the Kehillah became feasible.

2. Organization and Programme

The preliminary steps leading to the organization of the Kehillah were taken during the fall and winter of 1908-1909. The conference held at Clinton Hall on October 11 and 12, 1908, decided
that an attempt be made to form a central organization of the
Jews of New York City. The breaking of the trail was entrusted to
a Committee of Twenty Five, and after four months of preparation, the call for the "Constituent Convention of the Jewish Community of New York City" was issued.

On February 27, 1909, three hundred delegates, representing
two hundred and twenty-two organizations, convened in the audi-
torium of the Hebrew Charities Building. The convention was
called to order by Dr. J. L. Magnes, who was elected chairman.

In his keynote speech, the chairman outlined the reasons for the
calling of the convention and stated the aims of the contemplated
organization. He emphasized the fact that "at the present time
there is no representative, authoritative, permanent organization
that dare speak for the Jewish people" and that "any individual or
any organization can claim to be the spokesman of the Jews, and
as a result there is confusion worse confounded." He called attention to the chaos prevailing in our religious affairs, to the sorry
plight in which Jewish education found itself then, to our social
and charitable problems and to the utter lack of Jewish statistics,
as the prerequisite of any ameliorating effort. The remedy, he saw
in the creation of a Jewish public opinion. "There is no such thing
at present, and a central organization like that of the Jewish Community of New York City is necessary to create a Jewish public
opinion."

The Constituent Convention held sessions on February 27, 28;
March 6, 27 and April 10. Ultimately it adopted a constitution

and proceeded to elect an executive committee consisting of twenty five members and an advisory council of seventy members.

The constitution adopted gave sufficient latitude to the work of the new organization by declaring that the purpose of the Jewish Community of New York is "to further the cause of Judaism in New York City and to represent the Jews of the city with respect to all local matters of Jewish interest." The apparent limitation to "local matters" was, in fact, a purely legalistic provision. The relationship of the new organization to the American Jewish Committee gave the former ample scope for making its voice heard and its opinion felt in all questions affecting the Jews the world over. This broad field of endeavor was secured through the constitutional provision that "the twenty five members elected by the Jewish Committee of New York City as the Executive Committee thereof, shall, at the same time, constitute District XII of the American Jewish Committee."

The proceedings of the Constituent Convention were followed with eagerness by the Jews of New York and the new Kehillah attracted a great number of followers. It is true, there were those who doubted the ultimate success of this new venture in Jewish organization. They based their lack of belief on the fact that no govermental authority could possibly be secured; in other words, that the Kehillah of New York could not hope to wield the same power, based on governmental coercion, as the Kehillahs of the old world. But the enthusiastic sponsors of the Kehillah felt that this apparent weakness was really a source of strength. They gloried in the fact that the new Kehillah would ultimately derive its stength from the purely moral and spiritual powers inherent in the Jewish people.

The first year of the Kehillah was crowded with many experiences. "Each day has brought us new proofs of the need of a Kehillah," declared the Chairman of the Executive Committee, in his report to the first annual convention. The magnitude of the internal problems first revealed itself. New problems were cropping up continually, clamoring for immediate attention.

Meanshile, the Vaad Horabbonim or the Board of Authoritative Rabbis was established for the regulation of Kashruth, of Marriage and Divorce, Circumcision and Ritual Bath. The Board was also to cope with the problem of Sabbath Observance and to establish a Beth Din or Court of Arbitration.

The problems of education and of social and philanthropic work received particular attention. A report on the educational situation, embodying the findings of a comprehensive investigation, was laid before the first convention, simultaneously with the announcement that a fund of $75,000 had been given by Jacob H. Schiff and the New York Foundation for the purpose of promoting and improving Jewish education. The establishing of an Employment Bureau for handicapped Jews was recommended. The regulation of the collections for Palestinian poor, known as "Chalukah," the repudiation of "White Slave" charges made by an unfriendly magazine, intercession in behalf of Jewish employees in the various Muncipal departments who wished to be excused for the High Holidays, and the conducting of four model provisional synagogues for the New Year and the Day of Atonement, were the more important of the numerous activities which engrossed the attention of the Kehillah during its first year of existence.

3. The Kehillah at Work

The founders of the Kehillah showed foresight, when they defined its main task to be the formulation of our communal problems and the coordination of the existing communal instruments in order to call into being a conscious, organized and united community. The Kehillah would surely have followed this clear-sighted policy, were it not for the fact that many of the vital needs of the community had been entirely neglected. A careful survey of the field disclosed the imminent necessity of creating several new communal agencies, simultaneously with the coordination of those already existing. The Kehillah then set to work with unparalleled determination and perseverance, and the next seven years saw the birth of several of the most important communal instruments.

In 1910, the Bureau of Education was organized, for the purpose of standardizing the methods of Jewish education. This Bu-

reau was also to find ways and means of providing Jewish training
for all the Jewish children of school age in this city. In the seven
years of its existence, this Bureau has grown to astonishing propor-
tions, and its activities, as an educational factor, have long since
extended beyond the city limits. The work is conducted through
nine departments, a description of which will be found elsewhere
in this volume.

The work of surveying and charting the communal assets of
New York Jewry was undertaken in 1911 and the results published in the Jewish Communal Directory, the first attempt of its
kind in this city.

The Employment Brueau for the Handicapped began its activities in November, 1911, and has since helped to find employment
for thousands of Jews suffering from disabilities of many sorts.

The work of securing employment for handicaped Jews,
brought the Kehillah face to face with one of the industrial problems affecting Jewish life, and it was inevitable that ere long many
other phases of the industrial problems would present themselves.
The leaders of the Kehillah were frequently called upon to settle
labor disputes, where both sides were Jews. The record of the
organization abounds with many successful arbitrations of big
strikes. This gave rise to the idea that the Kehillah ought to establish permanent machinery looking to the adjustment of all industrial disputes in the Jewish community. This idea was realized in
1914, when the Bureau of Industry was established. Its scope was
defined as an "endeavor, on the basis of a comprehensive knowledge of industrial conditions, to direct vocational training, to provide employment for the handicapped, as well as for the highly
skilled, and to work out methods for the maintenance of peace in
industries where Jews preponderate."

The supression of improper moral conditions, so far as they
affect the Jews in this city, was undertaken by the Welfare Committee of the Kehillah as early as 1912, following certain shocking
revelations which had cast a sinister shadow on the good name of
our people. A discreet but effective activity was carried on to
stamp out the shame from our house, and the work met with
unusual success. Judge Gaynor, who was then Mayor of New

York, expressed his approbation in a letter in which he said, "nobody has done so much work to better moral conditions in this city, during my time, as you have done."

An attempt to supply the dire want of scientifically trained communal workers was made through the establishment of the School for Communal Work, while the Bureau of Philanthropic Research—having as its aim, the scientific study of the charity problem of New York Jewry, from a communal point of view—was organized by the Council of Jewish Communal Institutions in conjunction with the Kehillah.

The maintenance of these communal agencies was a source of constant anxiety to the leaders of the Kehillah. The great mass of the people was not sufficiently alive to its obligations and failed to supply the necessary funds. But the Kehillah was undaunted. Neither indifference nor open hostility, could deflect it from the determined goal, to arouse the Jews of New York to a full realization of their communal needs and their communal responsibilities.

4. Democratization

Intensive work, carefully planned and well directed, marked the first seven years of the Kehillah's existence. In the annals of the organization, this its first period, may well be designated as one where the use of the so-called "scientific" method was in the ascendency. This method was summed up by the Chairman of the Executive Committee in his statement to the Eighth Annual Convention, as an effort "first, to secure exact, systematic, comprehensive knowledge concerning the Jewish Community of New York City, and the Jewish problem in all of its phases; second, to engage upon as many experiments as possible through first-hand experience of the various phases of the problem; and, third, to point out the paths along which the community might develop in order to become in fact a conscious, organized, united community."

But aside from the creation of this communal machinery, and the work of specialization that this entailed, the Kehillah has rendered a far greater service to the Jews of this city, by emphasizing the fact of the existence of the community. Its sheet existence had been a constant reiteration of this fact. Its activities have shown the way leading to the ultimate development of an organized community.

The work of coordinating the existing comminal agencies was in many instances successfully carried out, in spite of heated opposition. It was quite evident that whatever opposition there was would ultimately give way before an awakened Jewish public opinion. Moreover, the opposition was never organized and never advanced a communal theory differing from the one held by the Kehillah. It is safe to say that it was generally actuated by the simple motive of protecting its "vested interests" lest they come to harm in an enlightened, well organized community. To be sure, there was also honest opposition. But this may be traced to the innate distrust that many people have for everything new and unusual. One of the greatest gains of the Kehillah in the eight years of its existence was the dissipation of this distrust, of this Kehillah-phobia. The complexion of the Jewish community has materially changed during these years, and all Jewish work is now carried on on a much higher plane than it was carried on prior to 1910. The Federation for the Support of Jewish Philanthropic Societies, a project insistently advocated by the Kehillah, may fairly be pointed out as an example of the awakening communal consciousness.

However, one phase of the Kehillah's work receded into the background, owing to the all-absorbing activity of communal experimentation; namely, the expansion of the Kehillah organization from the point of view of numbers. The great mass of New York Jewry, while tacitly approving the work of the Kehillah, has not displayed an active interest in the formation of its policy and of its programme. This indifference on the part of the Jewish mass may be traced to a somewhat defective system or representation which considered the Jewish society as the only unit from which representation was allowed to the annual convention. The distribution of the Jewish population in Greater New York, creating densely populated Jewish districts at points widely remote form each other, was another contributing factor. As a central organization, the Kehillah was too far removed from the simpler elements of our population, who are impressed only by a concrete, visible fact. Many of them had only heard of the existence of the Kehillah and most likely ocnsidered it as "one of many good organizations."

At the last annual convention, this phase of the problem was carefully gone into and the thorough-going democratization of the Kehillah decided upon. To afford the Kehillah an opportunity for doing the work of democratization without let or hindrance, it was deemed best to sever the Bureaus from the Kehillah and to give them an independent existence, so that all the energy of the Kehillah could be devoted to its main task: namely, the formulation of our communal problems and the coordination of the existing communal agencies which will bring about a conscious, organized and united community.

The plan of representation, appended to this review, was the result of a careful study of the various constituencies which would make the Kehillah representative of New York Jewry in the widest sense. It is based on the experience of the Kehillah since 1908, in addition to a careful and searching survey which extended over six months of investigatiom, from July, 1917, to January, 1918. The compilation and the interpretation of these facts are submitted in this volume.

II
AN ACT

To Incorporate the Kehillah of New York City.

The People of the State of New York, represented in Senate and Assembly, do enact as follows:

Section 1. Judah L. Magnes, William Fishman, Joseph Barondess, Louis Borgenicht, Samuel Dorf, Bernard Drachman, Israel Friedlaender, Harry Fischel, Samuel I. Hyman, Morris Jarmulowsky, Philip Klein, Leon Kamaiky, Adolph Lewisohn, Moses Z. Margolies, Louis Marshall, H. Pereira Mendes, Solomon Neumann, Jacob H. Schiff, Bernard Semel, Joseph Silverman, Pierre A. Siegelstein, Solomon M. Stroock, Cyrus L. Sulzberger, Israel Unterberg and Felix M. Warburg, and their associates and successors, are hereby constituted a body corporate in perpetuity, under the name of the Kehillah of New York City, and by said name shall possess all of the powers which by the general corporation law are conferred upon corporations, and shall be capable of taking, holding and acquiring, by deed, gift, purchase, bequest, devise or by judicial order or decree, any estate, real or personal, in trust or otherwise, which shall be necessary or useful for the uses and purposes of the corporation, to the amount of three million dollars; and to act as one of the constituent bodies of and to cooperate with the American Jewish Committee, a corporation organized under chapter sixteen of the laws of nineteen hundred and eleven.

Sec. 2. The objects of said corporation shall be, to stimulate and encourage the instruction of the Jews residing in the city of New York in the tenets of their religion and in the history, language, literature, institutions and traditions of their people; to conduct, support and maintain schools and classes for that purpose; to publish and distribute text-books, maps, charts, and illustrations to facilitate such instruction; to conduct lectures and classes in civics and other kindred subjects; to establish an educational bureau to further the foregoing pruposes; to conduct religious services and support, maintain and establish temporary as well as permanent synagogues; to adjust differences among Jewish residents or organizations located in said city, whenever thereunto requested by the parties thereto, by arbitration or by means of boards of mediation and conciliation; to maintain an employment bureau; to collate and publish statistical and other information concerning the Jewish inhabitants of said city and their activities; to study and ameliorate their social, moral and economic conditions, and to cooperate with the various charitable, philanthropic, educational and religious organizations and bodies of said city for the promotion of their common welfare.

Sec. 3. The business and affairs of said corporation shall be conducted by a board of twenty-five members to be known as the executive committee, and the persons named in the first section of this act as incorporators shall constitute the first executive committee of said corporation. At the first meeting of said executive committee held after the passage of this act, the members thereof shall be divided into three classes, the first of which shall hold office until the installation of their successors, who shall be elected at a convention held by the members of said corporation as herein provided, and such successors shall hold office for a period of three years from date of their installation; the second class shall hold office for two years after the holding of said convention, and the third for one year thereafter, or until their respective successors shall be elected. At the expiration of the term of any member of the executive committee his successor shall be elected for a term of three years. All vacancies which may occur in said committee shall be filled until the ensuing election by said committee. An annual election for members of said committee shall take place at a convention of the members of said corporation to be held at such time and in such manner as shall be fixed by the by-laws to be adopted by said executive committee, or by the members of said corporation in convention assembled. At all meetings of the executive committee one-third thereof shall constitute a quorum for the transaction of business, but no by-law shall be adopted, amended or repealed without the presence of a majority of the members of said committee for the time being.

Sec. 4. The members of said corporation shall consist of the persons who shall be designated and chosen as delegates to the annual convention of said corporation by such method or methods and by such organizations, societies, nominating and constituent bodies as shall be provided in by-laws to be adopted for that purpose by the executive committee, such by-laws being, however, subject to alteration, revision or amendment at any regular convention of said corporation or at a special convention called for such purpose, provided that thirty days' notice be given of the proposed change.

Sec. 5. This act shall take effect immediately.

This act was signed by the Governor April 5, 1914.

F LANDSMANNSCHAFT ORGANIZATIONS THE VERBAND MOVEMENT IN NEW YORK CITY*

By S. MARGOSHES
President, The Federation of Galician and Bucovienan
Jews of America

I. Rise and Development

The origin of the six Federations or "Verbands" now existing in New York City, embracing hundreds of societies with a membership running into the tens of thousands, can be traced back to two fundamental human emotions: first, the feeling of kinship and, second, the sense of grievance. In the absence of a strong Jewish communal consciousness in New York City, it was only natural for the Jews coming from the same country to develop a high degree of consciousness of kind, extending in the main only to the members of their own group of countrymen. So the Spanish and the Portuguese Jews found it difficult in the first half of the last century to admit whole-heartedly the German Jews to a close kinship with them—a difficulty which the German Jews experienced almost half a century later with the Jews hailing from Russia, and the Russian Jews in their turn only a decade later with the Jews coming from Galicia and Roumania. Because of this clannishness, several Jewish communities sprang up practically side by side in New York City—a Spanish Portuguese Community, a German Community, a Russian Community, an Oriental Community and a Galician, a Hungarian and a Roumanian Community. Almost every one of these Communities was self-sufficient with its own synagogues, charitable and educational institutions, and, what was inevitable, with its own politics. Under such conditions, the least

*Kehillah.(Jewish Community) of New York City, ed. *The Jewish Communal Register of New York City 1917-1918*. 2d ed. (New York: Kehillah (Jewish Community of New York City, 1918), pp. 1328-1339.

untoward act, fancied or real, on the part of one group led inevitably to strong separatistic tendencies in the other groups. So, for instance, did the ascendency of the German Community result in the struggle of the so-called Down Town against Up Town, a struggle in which the combatants were mainly Russian and German Jews. In the same way did the sense of grievance which the Galician, Roumanian, Russian-Polish and Bessarabian Jew felt against the ascendency of the Russian Jewish Community, find its outlet in the formation of separate Verbands. For the Verbands, in spite of their voluble protestations of good intentions, were invariably organized as offensive and defensive alliances—a sort of Verein zur Abwehr des Anti-Galizianerismus or Anti-Rumanierismus, as the case might be. Only subsequent conditions changed their original plans and induced a new course of development.

Through the sheer fact of organization, the Federations had generated a great social energy. What were they to do with it? Keeping this energy idle until an opportunity presented itself for spending it in warding off attacks meant dissipating it. The next best thing to do was to harness it in the work of philanthropy— work always sure to make the strongest appeal to the East European Jewish imagination. Hence the sudden metamorphosis from a bellicose organization into a charitable society. The Galician Federation, the first and foremost among the federations, led with its Har Moriah Hospital, and the other Federations quickly followed: the Federation of Russian-Polish Hebrews of America with its Beth David Hospital; the Federation of Roumanian Jews with its Jewish Home for Convalescents and the Bessarabian Jews with the Hebrew National Orphan House. In the very nature of the case, this change had to have very far reaching effects on the Federations. In the first place, as charitable societies the Federations had to lose their separartistic characteristics, since, for legal and practical purposes, it was not feasible to run a charitable institution for Galicians, Roumanians, or Bessarabians exclusively; in the second place, as charitable societies the Federations could not manage to keep the clannish enthusiasm at that degree of white heat peculiar only to purely separatistic organizations. The result was that with their claims on the purely "local" interests greatly impaired, the

Federations, now saddled with charitable institutions, invariably found themselves in financial straits, out of which they could be saved only by the aid of rich and philanthropically inclined individual members. The handing over, however, of the management of these institutions to the rich and influential members became everywhere a signal for a struggle of the "masses" against the "rich,"—a struggle which when it did not end in utter bankruptcy as a consequence of the withdrawal of the rich, resulted in the institutions practically becoming the private property of a few individuals, over which the Federations had hardly any control. The latter is the state of affairs now obtaining in most of the charitable institutions established by the Federations.

II. Aims and Purposes

The mere transition from a sort of tribal organization to a charitable society would in itself have amply sufficed to bring in its train a re-statement of the aims and purposes of the Federations, had not even greater changes outside the Federations taken place, which profoundly modified the function of a Landsmannschaft organization. At the time when the Federations took shape, the chaos in Jewish communal life was so great that the Federations, organizing as they did into single units hundreds of isolated Jewish bodies, represented a tremendous step forward in Jewish communal organization in New York City. Paradoxical as it may sound, it is nevertheless a fact that it is these very Federations, born out of a sense of grievance and distrust of one Jewish group to another, which have made Jewish communal organization, as we know it to-day in New York City, at all possible. They were the first simple and primitive forms of community organization—the indispensable antecedents of the higher forms of Jewish communal life that were to come later. But as with all early forms of development, so with the Federations; the arrival of higher forms meant their very doom. The Federations could and did perform a necessary function in the days when there was no unified Jewish community; but with a Jewish community established in New York that is city-wide in scope and that conceives of the entire Jewish communal work of the city as a unit, what are Landsmannschaft organizations if not vestiges of a rude and discordant past, to be discarded as soon as possible in the interests of the harmony of the future? For there is no denying that the very physical fact of grouping large masses of Jews along sectional lines of cleavage, is bound to produce a psychological effect, not entirely favorable to a complete fusion of all Jewish elements in the Melting Pot of the larger Jewish Community of Greater New York.

Much as the foregoing conclusion would seem to point to dissolution, rather than to the advisability of a restatement of aims on the part of the Federations, the Federations themselves, even at this late hour, still have aims other than nirvana. To be sure, they have to give up a good many of their pretensions in favor of the new power that has arisen in the last decade—the organized Jewish Community. The defence of Jewish group-interests in America which was the main purpose of the Federations at their inception, is no more the same vital issue which it was fifteen years ago, when one Jewish group was set against the other. One can confidently look to the ever increasing Jewish communal consciousness and Jewish communal intelligence to do away with any need for such defence. On the other hand, the Federations can no more be said to represent separate Jewish communities. Unlike the days gone by, New York City represents no more a mosaic of Jewish communities, there is only one Jewish communal organization, which is getting stronger from year to year, and which is bound to prevail. It is also clear by this time that the great Jewish problems of New York City, such as those of religious authority, Jewish education, philanthropy, recreation, correction and industry are community wide, transcending all Landsmannschaft boundaries, and that because of it, the Jewish institutions in New York City, built and maintained for the purpose of coping with just those communal problems, must be operated as community plants with the entire community in mind, rather than any single group. This the Federations, which, until now thought in terms of Landsmannschaften and their interests, must fully appreciate. They must learn to speak of themselves as a part of a single community. They must understand that here in New York City, there are only Jew-

ish Communal interests and that there are no Galician, Roumanian, Russian-Polish or Bessarabian interests in America that are
different from those of the entire Jewish community. Once this is
admitted, the aim of the Federations becomes clear. Within the
community they have no interests that are not shared by all Jews
alike, but in addition, their main concern is with those of their
Jewish brethren in Europe in whose welfare and development all
other Jewish groups in America cannot be expected to have the
same high degree of interest. While the Jewish community as a
whole can be counted upon to be interested in the fate of, say, the
Galician Jews now still in Galicia, it is the Galician Jews in America, who have left behind their fathers, mothers, sisters and brothers in Galicia, who have a special interest in what is happening to
the Jews of Galicia. Thus the Federation of Bucovinean and Galician Jews of America must consider it as its first function to
utilize the energy and interests of the entire Jewish community of
New York City for the purpose of ameliorating the conditions of
the Galician Jews on the other side of the Atlantic. This is the
main reason for its existence. Only as secondary tasks can the
Federation, as the expression of the will of the Galician Jews in
America,—endeavor to integrate the Galician Jews in New York
City in the larger Jewish comminity and to use the social force
generated by the organization as a power for good in the furtherance of the interest of the Jewish people the world over. The same
is true of all other Federations existing in New York City—the
Oriental, the Roumanian, the Russian-Polish and the Bessarabian.
In the measure that they restate and carry out these aims, they
form a valuable asset in Jewish communal organizations; similarly,
in the measure that they continue to draw the old line of cleavage
between one Landsmannschaft and the other, they constitute a
hindrance to the growth of Jewish communal consciousness and
the sooner they are overcome the better.

III. Present Status

Of all Federations, it is the Galician Federation, the largest and
the strongest of the six existing in New York City, that was first to

fall in line with the new idea of what a Federation should be. By giving up its control over the Har Moriah Hospital, which it had founded and which it had maintained for years, the Federation of Galician and Bucovinean Jews of America gave up its character as a charitable society. Through a new formulation of its purposes, and a thorough re-organization of its departments, following its convention in the fall of 1917, the Galician Federation put itself squarely on a new basis,—on the basis of a large organization working for its purposes within the framework of an organized Jewish community. The other Federations meanwhile still continue to consume all their energy in the maintenance of small charitable institutions, which from the point of view of community work, are either negligible or altogether out of place. Of the Roumanian Verbands,—for there are two, the Federation of Roumanian Jews of America and the American Union of Roumanian Jews,—the latter conceives its aim in terms of help to the Jews in Roumania, while the former is still busy attending to those Roumanian Jews in America who are in need of its Home for Convalescents. The present plight of the Jews in Roumania and the presence of a Jewish commission from Roumania in the United States, was instrumental in bringing about an understanding between the two Roumanian Verbands, only however, to give way, a short time later, to new dissensions based mainly on strictly personal grievances. The Federation of Russian-Polish Hebrews confines its activity to the Beth David Hospital, and is not heard from save on very rare occasions, such as, for instance, a quarrel on the American Jewish Congress. The Bessarabian Federation is still too young to have struck out on any definite program. Its activities are mainly charitable, though it is claimed that its Orphan House is a dubious proposition from the point of view of Jewish community needs. The Federation of Oriental Jews in America is successfully fulfilling its task of introducing the Oriental Jews in America to the rest of the Jewish community. Of all Landsmannschaft organizations, the Oriental Federation was the first to appreciate the fact that though a Federation is based on sectional lines, its greatest contribution lies in wiping out these lines in the higher interests of the very Jews that it represents. The Jewish group last to be heard from in connection with the Federation Movement is the Hungarian. But it, too, now has a Federation of Hungarian Jews of America. The organization is now going through the early stages of infancy and, it can only be hoped, that benefiting by the experiences of the older Landsmannschaft federations, it will bring fresh vision to its task.

AMERICAN UNION OF ROUMANIAN JEWS, 44 7th St. President, Dr. P. A. Siegelstein, 220 E. 12th St.; Secretaries, Edward Herbert, Dr. Jos. E. Braunstein, A. L. Kalman; Chairman Executive Committee, Leo Wolfson. Established and incorporated 1916. Membership, 68 organizations.

PURPOSE: "To defend the interests of the Jews in Roumania, to work for their civic and political emancipation and for their economic reconstruction and rehabilitation; and to represent and further the interests of the Roumanian Jews in the U. S. and Canada."

Siegelstein, Pierre A., President American Union of Roumanian Jews (44 East 7th St.), since 1916. Term 1 year. Born 1870 in Roumania. Came to U. S. 1885. Received College Education. Physician. Res. 220 East 12th St.

FEDERATION OF BESSARABIAN ORGANIZATIONS, 52 St. Marks Place. Pres., Leo Lerner, 116 Nassau Street; Secretary, M. Feldman, 941 Simpson Street. Established 1911, Incorporated 1912. Membership over 3000.

PURPOSE: To organize the Jews coming from the provinces of Bessarabia and the Southern part of Russia for cooperative social effort.

ACTIVITIES: Maintains the Hebrew National Orphan House.

Lerner, Leo. President Federation of Bessarabian Organizations (52 St. Marks Pl.) Also Pres. Hebrew National Orphan House (52 St. Marks Pl.) Born 1859 in Russia. Came to U.S. 1891. Graduated N.Y.U. Law School. Lawyer 116 Nassau St.

FEDERATION OF GALICIAN AND BUCOVINEAN JEWS OF AMERICA. 82 Second Avenue. President, Dr. Samuel Margoshes,

1223 Union Avenue; Vice Pres. S., Thau, 21 E. Houston St. Treas., F. Baron, 128 Rivington St. Rec. Sec'y., M. Baden, 2 E. 113th St. First Landsmannschaft Organization in New York City. Organized in 1903—has 300 branches in New York City, with a few branches dispersed all over the country. Membership—60,000.

PURPOSE: To study the political, economic and social conditions of the Jews in Galicia and Bucovina, and to devise ways and means for ameliorating those conditions thru the exercise of the collective influence and energy of the Galician Jews of America.

To work towards the fusion of Galician Jews of America into the larger Jewish community in this country, thus making possible the solution of communal problems that affect Galician Jews equally with the Jews hailing from other countries.

To further the interests of the Jewish people the world over.

ACTIVITIES: The Federation does its work thru the following departments:

1. Department of Data and Information, whose function is the collection of data bearing on Galician Jews here and in Galicia.

2. Departments of Publicity—which distirbutes information on various phases of Jewish life in Galicia as well as all the activities of the Federation thru special pamphlets, bulletins and by means of the public press.

3. Department of Co-operation with Galicia and Bucovina, whose function it is to secure for our brethren in those provinces the rights necessary for their protection as an ethnic group.

4. Department of Communal Education—which conducts educational work in the Galician quarter.

5. Department of Communal Welfare—doing civic and relief work for immigrants in close co-operation with the existing agencies and institutions primarily interested in these phases of communal activity.

6. Department of American Jewish Affairs—dealing with matters affecting all Jews in America.

7. Department of Universal Jewish Affairs—dealing with general Jewish affairs affecting the Jews the world over.

Margoshes, Samuel, was born in Galicia in 1887. Received his Jewish education in Cheder and Yeshivah and subsequently attended the Gymnasium at Tarnow, Galicia. Came to U.S. in 1905 and entered the Jewish Theological Seminary of America in 1907, from which he graduated as rabbi in 1911. Studied philosophy and sociology at Columbia University from 1908 to 1911; receiving the degree of M.A. in 1910. Studied education at Teachers' College, Columbia University. In 1917 he received the degree of Doctor of Hebrew Literature from the Jewish Theological Seminary. He contributed to the Hebrew and Yiddish press. He was elected to the American Jewish Congress in 1917, and in the fall of 1917 became president of the Federation of Galician and Bucovinean Jews of America. Since 1912, he has been affiliated with the Bureau of Jewish Education.

FEDERATION OF ORIENTAL JEWS OF AMERICA, 356 Second Ave. Officers: President, Joseph Gedalecia, 320 2nd Ave.; Secretary, A. J. Amateau, 40 W. 115th St. Established 1911. Incorporated 1912.

PURPOSE: "To create a forum where communal problems are discussed and presented to the Oriental Community for solution."

Gedalecia, Joseph, Pres. Oriental Jewish Community of N.Y.C. (12 E. 119th St.), since 1913. Term 1 year. Born 1876 in Turkey. Came to U. S. 1887. Received a high school education. Social Worker, 356 Second Ave. Res. 320 Second Avenue.

FEDERATION OF ROUMANIAN JEWS OF AMERICA, 185 Forsyth Street. President, Samuel Goldstein, 955 Prospect Avenue; Secretary, Charles L. Ornstein, 299 Broadway. Established and Incorporated 1908.

PURPOSE: To work for the securing of equal civil and political rights for the Jews in Roumania and to participate in all movements of a Jewish national character.

ACTIVITIES: Maintains a Jewish Home for Convalescents at Grand View, on the Hudson.

Goldstein, Samuel, Pres. Federation of Roumanian Jews of America (185 Forsyth St.); elected 1917. Term 1 year. Born 1875 in Roumania. Came to U. S. 1889. Received general Jewish education. Leather Merchant, 234 E. 35th St. Res. 955 Prospect Ave.

FEDERATION OF RUSSIAN-POLISH HEBREWS OF AMERICA, 1822 Lexington Avenue. President, Jacob Carlinger, 299 Broadway; Secretary, David Trautman, 36 W. 113th St. Established and incorporated 1908. Membership, about 40,000 in 251 branches.

PURPOSE: To assist Jews arriving to this country from Russian Poland.

ACTIVITIES: Maintains the Beth David Hospital.

INDEX

MAIN ENTRY INDEX

References are to entry numbers

Abelow, Samuel P., 46
Abernathy, Arthur T., 658
Adar, Zevi, 470
Adler, Cyrus, 103, 139, 177, 227, 228, 325, 471
Adler, Frank J., 417
Adler, Seig, 47
Agresti, Olivia R., 229
Alexander, Hartley B., 1
Algemeiner, Zhurnal, 700
Alper, Michael, 472
Alt, Herschel, 326
Alter, Robert, 570
Altfeld, E. Milton, 48
Altman, Sig, 571
America, La, 776
American Academy for Jewish Research. *Proceedings of the AAJR,* 789
American Association for Jewish Education, 823
American Hebrew and Jewish Tribune, 701
American Israelite, 702
American Jewish Archives, 703
American Jewish Historical Quarterly, 704
American Jewish Year Book, 705
American Jews: Their Lives and Achievements, 230

American Zionist, 706
Amerikaner, Der, 715
Angoff, Charles, 572
Antin, Mary, 178
Apshtein, Avraham, 573
Apsler, Alfred, 452
Asmonean, The, 707
Aufbau, Der, 716

Bailin, I. B. 179
Bailyn, Bernard, 602
Baker, Liva, 231
Baker, Max, 30
Band, Benjamin, 49
Baron, Salo W., 2, 143
Barron, Milton L., 622
Baruch, Bernard M., 180
Bauer, Yehuda, 104
Belsky, Joseph, 534
Belth, Nathan C., 141, 659
Benderly, S., 473
Beh-Horin, Meir, 519
Benjamin, I. J., 142
Bentwich, Norman, 232, 233
Bercovich, Shlome, 520
Berkson, Isaac B., 474
Berman, Louis, 623
Bernard, Jacqueline, 327
Bernheimer, Charles S., 181, 372, 597
Bernstein, Philip S., 418

Bigman, Stanley K., 328
Birmingham, Stephen, 234, 235
Bisgyer, Maurice, 182, 292
Bitzaron, 708
Black Anti-Semitism and Jewish Racism, 660
Blake, Peter, 419
Blau, Joseph L., 143, 346, 420
Bloch, Josef S., 144
Bloch, Joshua, 819, 820
Bloom, Sol, 183
Blumenfield, Shmuel M., 475
Blumenthal, L. Roy, 145
Blushtein, M., 476
B'nai B'rith Messenger, 709
Bogen Boris D., 184, 329
Bookbinder, Hyman H., 535
Bos del Pueblo, La, 777
Brandes, Joseph, 598
Brav, Stanley R., 330
Breck, Allen D., 50
Bregstone, Philip P., 51
Britt, George, 661
Britt, Steuart H., 675
Broches, S., 52
Bronshtein, M., 520
Brotz, Howard, 624
Broun, Heywood, 661   Burgin, Hertz, 536
Butwin, Frances, 3
Byars, William U., 146

Cahan, Ab, 185
California Jewish Voice, 710
Campbell, Monroe, Jr., 331
Campus 1966, Change and Challenge, 477
Carlson, John R., 662
Carmin, Itzhak J., 238
Carvalho, Solomon Nunes, 186
Celler, Emanuel, 187
CCAR Journal, 711
Chaikin, Jr., 105

Changing Patterns of Jewish Life on the Campus, 478
Chertoff, Mordecai S., 537
Chipkin, Israel S., 479, 480
Chyet, Stanley F., 188, 236
Clark, Ronald W., 237
Cohen, Bernard, 574
Cohen, George, 4
Cohen, Harry, 238
Cohen, Henry, 663
Cohen, Jack J., 481
Cohen, Morris Raphael, 189, 332
Cohen, Naomi W., 106, 239
Coit, Margaret L., 240
Coleman, Edward D., 821
Commentary: A Jewish Review, 712
Conan, Abraham P., 219
Congress Bi-Weekly, 713
Connolly, Thomas E., 47
Conservative Judaism, 714
Cooperman, Jehiel B., 575
Cooperman, Sarah H., 575
Cowen, Philip, 190
Critical Studies in American Jewish History, 5

Daly, Charles P., 107
David, Jay, 191
Davidson, Gabriel, 108
Davie, Maurice R., 599
Davis, Moshe, 6, 7, 8, 422, 423
Davis-DuBois, Rachel, 9
Davison, Lynn, 219
Deborah, Die, 725
DeHaas, Jacob, 241
Deinard, Ephraim, 822
Dimensions in American Judaism, 726
Dinin, Samuel, 483, 484
Dinnerstein, Leonard, 53, 664
Directory of Day Schools in the

United States, Canada and Mexico, 482

Doherty, Beka, 356

Doroshkin, Milton, 334

Drachman, Bernard, 242

Dresner, Samuel H., 424

Drury, Betty, 600

Duffus, Robert L., 243

Duggan, Stephen, 600

Duker, Abraham G., 823

Dushkin, Alexander M., 485, 486

Echo des Judenthums, 728

Edelstein, Menachem, 487

Edidin, Ben M., 335

Educational Alliance, Reports of, 166

Educational Research Council of America, 824

Egert, B. P., 538

Eglyen Elet, 729

Ehrenfried, Albert, 54

Einhorn, David, *Memorial Volume,* 421

Eisenberg, Azriel, 576

Eisenstein, Ira, 425

Eisenstein, Judah D., 192

Elovitz, Mark H., 55

Elzas, Barnett A., 56, 57, 426

Encyclopaedia Judaica, 731

Engelman, Uriah Z., 86, 486, 488

Epstein, Benjamin R., 666, 669, 670, 671

Epstein, Melech, 244, 539, 540

Ezekiel, Herbert T., 58, 59

Falk, Louis A., 12

Feibelman, Julian B., 60

Fein, Isaac M., 61

Feingold, Henry L., 541

Feinstein, Marnin, 109

Feldman, Abraham J., 110

Fels, Mary, 245

Felsenthal, Bernhard, 489

Felsenthal, Emma, 246

Fermi, Laura, 601

Fierman, Floyd S., 147

Fifty Years of Social Service: The History of the United Hebrew Charities of the City of New York, now *The Jewish Social Service Association, Inc.,* 336

Fifty Years' Work of the Hebrew Education Society of Philadelphia, 490

Fineberg, Solomon A., 667

Fink, Reuben, 148

Fish, Sidney M., 247

Fisher, Galen, 652

Fishman, Hertzel, 625

Fishman, Priscilla, 337

Fitzpatrick, Donovan, 248

Fleming, Donald, 602

Flexner, Abraham, 193

Foner, Philip S., 11

Forster, Arnold, 666, 668, 669, 670, 671

Fortune, Editors of, 665

Forverts (Jewish Daily Forward), 732

Frank, Fedora S., 62

Frank, Waldo, 338

Franzblau, Abraham N., 491

Fredman, J. George, 12

Freeman, Moses, 63

Freid, Jacob, 339, 340

Freie Arbeiter Shtimme, 733

Freiheit, 734

Freund, Michael, 384

Freund, Miriam K., 111

Friedlaender, Israel, 341

Friedman, Lee M., 13, 14, 64, 112

Friedman, Murray I., 502
Friedman, Saul S., 542
Friedman, Theodore, 342
Fuchs, Lawrence H., 543
*Future of the Jewish Communi-
ty in America, The,* 408

Gale, Joseph, 343
Gannes, Abraham O., 492
Gartner, Lloyd P., 95, 97, 149
Gay, Ruth, 15
Gelbart, Gershon I., 493
Geltman, Max, 672
Gilbert, Arthur, 626
Ginsberg, Louis, 65, 66
Ginsberg, Eli, 249, 344, 345
Gladstone, J., 113
Glanz, Rudolf, 67, 68, 577, 578,
603, 627, 628, 629, 630, 825
Glassman, Leo M., 250
Glazer, Nathan, 346, 427, 631
Glock, Charles Y., 632, 673
Glushakow, A. D., 69
Gold, Herbert, 194
Gold, Michael, 604
Goldberg, Abraham, 251
Goldberg, Isaac, 252
Goldberg, S. P. 347
Golden, Harry, 16, 70, 348, 349,
544, 674
Goldhurst, Richard, 349
Goldman, Alex J., 428
Goldscheider, Calvin, 350
Goldstein, Herbert S., 253
Goldstein, Israel, 429, 494, 545
Goldstein, Leonard J., 407
Goldstein, Margaret F., 430
Goldstein, Sidney, 350
Gompers, Samuel, 195
Goodman, Abram V., 114
Goodman, Philip, 150
Goodman, Saul, 495
Gordis, Robert, 342
Gordon, Albert I., 351, 352

Goren, Arthur A., 71
Graeber, Isacque, 675
Green, Ber, 254
Greenblum, Joseph, 400, 401
Grinstein, Hyman B., 72
Groiser Kundes, Der, 717
Gross, Theodore L., 579
*Group-Life in America: A Task
Force Report,* 633
Grusd, Edward E., 115
Gumpertz, Sydney G., 116
Gutstein, Morris A., 73, 74, 255,
431
Guttmann, Allen, 580

Haber, Julius, 196
Hadassah Magazine, 735
Hadoar, 736
Ha-Ivri, 737
Halpern, Ben, 634, 635
Handlin, Mary F., 346, 676
Handlin, Oscar, 17, 18, 346, 676
Hapardes, 738
Hapgood, Hutchins, 605
Harofe Haivri, 739
Harris, Louis, 636
Hartstein, Jacob I., 19
Ha-Toren, 740
Ha-Tzofeh b'Ertz Ha-Hadashah,
741
*Hebrew Sheltering and Immi-
grant Aid Society of America,
Annual Reports of,* 140
Hebrew Union College, The, 175
Hecht, Ben, 197, 677
Heckelman, A. Joseph, 117
Heller, James G., 256
Hellman, George S., 257
Hendrick, Burton J., 353
Herberg, Will, 637
Hershkowitz, Leo, 151, 152
Hertz, Emanuel, 153
Hertz, J. S., 354, 546
Hertz, Richard C., 496

Higham, John, 678, 679, 680
Hillquit, Morris, 198
Hindus, Maurice, 199
Hindus, Milton, 154
Hirsh, Joseph, 355, 356
Hirshler, Eric E., 606
Historia Judaica, 742
Hoenig, Sidney B., 258
Hoffman, B., 547
Hoffmann, Banesh, 259
Holmes, John H., 681
Honor, Leo L., 497
Horeb, 743
Horwich, Bernard, 200
Huhner, Leon, 20, 75, 118, 260
Hurwitz, Henry, 498
Hurwitz, Maximilian, 119
Hyman, Joseph C., 548

Ideas: A Journal of Contemporary Jewish Thought, 744
Igazság, 745
Inglehart, Babette F., 826
Intermarriage and the Future of the American Jew, 638
Intermountain Jewish News, 746
International Jew, The, 697
Isaacs, Stephen F., 549
Israel Honorarium, The, 314

Jacob, H. E., 261
Jacobs, Joseph, 827
Jacobs, Paul, 550
James, Edmund J., 607
Janowsky, Oscar J., 358, 359, 360, 499
Jew, The, 747
Jew and Gentile, 639
Jewish Advocate, 748
Jewish Book Annual, 749
Jewish Chronicle, 750
Jewish Communal Register of New York City, The, 409
Jewish Communal Survey of

Greater New York, 361
Jewish Community Voice, The, 751
Jewish Education, 752
Jewish Encyclopedia, 753
Jewish Evangelist, 754
Jewish Exponent, 755
Jewish Frontier, 756
Jewish Heritage, 757
Jewish Horizon, 758
Jewish Leader, 759
Jewish Life, 760
Jewish Observer, 761
Jewish Parent, 762
Jewish Post and Opinion, 763
Jewish Press, 764
Jewish Quarterly Review, 765
Jewish Social Studies, 766
Jewish Spectator, 767
Jewish Telegraphic Agency Community News Reporter, 768
Jewish Telegraphic Agency Daily News Bulletin, 769
Jewish Telegraphic Agency Weekly News Digest, 770
Jewish Veteran, 771
Jick, Leon A., 500
Joseph, Samuel, 608, 609
Jospe, Alfred, 501
Journal of Jewish Communal Service, 772
Judaism, 773
Jude, Der, 718
J.W.B. Circle, The, 774

Kabakoff, Yaakov, 581
Kagan, Solomon R., 262, 263
Kahn, Roger, 362
Kallen, Horace M., 363
Kaminetsky, Joseph, 502
Kampf, Avram, 432
Kaplan, Benjamin, 364, 365
Kaplan, Mordecai M., 433, 434
Karp, Abraham H., 21, 435

Karp, Deborah, 264
Karpf, Maurice J., 366
Karpman, I. J. Carmin, 265
Katsh, Abraham I., 503, 504, 551, 552
Katz, Irving I., 76, 436
Katz, Shlomo, 640
Katzoff, Louis, 505
Kayserling, M., 120
Kazin, Alfred, 201
Kertzer, Morris N., 367
Kibitzer, Der, 719
Kiell, Norman, 368
Kirbatch Americano, El, 730
Kirshenboim, Yakov, 369
Kisch, Guido, 610
Klaperman, Gilbert, 506
Knortz, Karl, 682
Knox, Israel, 266
Kohler, Kaufmann, 202, 437
Kohler, Max J., 121, 267
Kohn, Eugene, 22, 425
Kohn, S. Joshua, 77
Kohut, Alexander, 438
Kohut, George A., 155
Kohut, Rebekah, 203
Konovitz, Israel, 507
Kopelyov, Y., 370, 582
Koppman, Lionel, 456
Korn, Bertram W., 78, 79, 80, 122, 123, 124, 268, 439
Kraft, Louis, 371, 372
Kramer, Judith R., 373
Kranzler, George, 374, 375
Krock, Arthur, 204
Kultur un Dertziung, 775

Lachs, Samuel T., 514
Landau, David, 269
Landesman, Alter F., 81
Landman, Isaac, 641
Lasker, Bruno, 642
Learsi, Rufus, 23
Lebeson, Anita L., 24, 125

Leiser, Joseph, 440
Lenn, Theodore I., 441
Leroy-Beaulieu, Anatole, 611
Lesser, Allen, 270
L'Estrange, Hamon, 643
Leventman, Seymour, 373
Levin, Alexandra L., 271, 272
Levin, Meyer, 572
Levine, Allan E., 828
Levine, Louis, 553
Levinger, Elma E., 25
Levinger, Lee J., 26, 44, 442, 508, 683, 684
Levinthal, Israel H., 443
Levitan, Tina, 273, 274, 376
Levy, Beryl H., 444
Lewis, Jerry D., 583
Lewisohn, Ludwig, 205, 206, 377
Lichtenstein, Gaston, 58, 59
Liebman, Charles S., 445, 446
Lifson, David S., 126
Linfield, Harry S., 378, 379
Linzer, Norman, 829
Lipman, Eugene J., 644
Lipsky, Louis, 554
Liptzin, Sol, 380, 584, 585
Lisitzky, Ephraim E., 207
Litman, Simon, 275
Livingston, Sigmund, 685
London, Hannah R., 276, 277, 278
Lotz, Philip H., 279
Lowenthal, Marvin, 280
Lozowick, Louis, 281
Lyons, Eugene, 282

Mack, Julian W., 555
Madison, Charles A., 283
Makover, A. B., 284
Makovsky, Donald I., 285
Malin, Irving, 586
Mangione, Anthony R., 826
Mann, Arthur, 447

Manners, Ande, 612
Manuel, Frank E., 556
Manuscript Catalog of the American Jewish Archives, 830
Manuscript Collections in the American Jewish Historical Society: Catalogued Jan. 1968-Jun. 1969, 831
Marans, Hillel, 82
Marcus, Jacob R., 27, 28, 127, 156, 157, 158, 159, 208, 832, 833, 834, 835
Margalith, Aaron M., 103
Margolis, Isidor, 509
Mark, Yudel, 520
Markens, Isaac, 29, 160
Marmor, Kalman, 587
Masliansky, H., 209
Maslow, Will, 382
Mason, Alpheus T., 286
Masserman, Paul, 30
May, Max B., 287
Mayer, John E., 645
Mayerberg, Samuel S., 210
Mayzel, Nachman, 588
McCall, Samuel W., 31, 383
McKenna, M. J., 613
McWilliams, Carey, 686
Meade, Robert D., 288
Meisel, A., 32
Meites, Hyman L., 83
Mendelson, Wallace, 289
Menkus, Belden, 448
Menorah Journal, 779
Merriam, Eve, 290
Mersand, Joseph, 589
Metzker, Isaac, 161
Meyer, Isidore S., 8, 128, 153, 836, 837
Michigan Jewish History, 780
Midstream, 781
Miller, Alan W., 449
Mintz, Alan L., 464
Moïse, L. C., 291

Monsky, Mrs. Henry, 292
Morais, Henry S., 84, 293
Morgan Zhurnal, 782
Morris, Robert, 384
Morse, Arthur D., 557
Moynihan, Daniel P., 631
Myers, Gustavus, 687

Nasza Trybuna, 783
National Jewish Weekly, 784
Negro-Jewish Relations in the United States, 646
Neusner, Jacob, 450, 451
New Frontiers for Jewish Life on the Campus, 510
Newman, Louis I., 511
Newmark, Marco R., 211
Newmark, Maurice H., 211
Niger, S., 113, 512
Nizer, Louis, 558
Nodel, Julius J., 452
Nulman, Louis, 513

Occident and American Jewish Advocate, The, 785
Olson, Bernhard E., 647
Ordens Echo, 786
Ormian, Haim, 533
Osherowitch, M., 294
Osterweis, Rollin G., 295

Palsson, Mary D., 53
Parzen, Herbert, 296
Passow, Isidore D., 514
Pawlikowski, John T., 648
Pedagogic Reporter, 787
Penn, Ascher, 385, 453
Perlmutter, Sholem, 297
Peters, Madison C., 33, 129
Philipson, David, 162, 163, 212, 454, 515
Pickus, Manuel, 395
Pilch, Judah, 516, 517, 518, 519
Pitt, James E., 649

Plaut, W. Gunther, 85, 164
Potohoretz, Norman, 213
Polier, Justine W., 165
Poll, Solomon, 386
Pomerantz, J. Chaim, 520
Pool, David de Sola, 298, 455
Pool, Tamar de Sola, 455
Postal, Bernard, 456
Poupko, Bernard A., 521
Prais, G. M. [George M. Price,] 614
Present Tense, 788
Proceedings of the Rabbinical Assembly of America, 789
Proskauer, Joseph M., 214
Publications of the American Jewish Historical Society, 791

Rabbinical Assembly of America, Proceedings of, 790
Rabbinical Council Record, 792
Rabinowicz, Harry M., 590
Rabinowitz, Benjamin, 130
Radkau, Joachim, 615
Raisin, Mordechai Zev, 34, 299
Rappaport, Israel B., 522
Rawidowicz, Simon, 387
Reconstructionist, 793
Record, The, 794
Response: A Contemporary Jewish Review, 795
Reznikoff, Charles, 86, 167
Rhode Island Jewish Historical Notes, 796
Ribalow, Harold U., 215, 300
Ribalow, Menachem, 591, 592, 797
Riis, Jacob A., 616
Ringer, Benjamin B., 401, 650
Rischin, Moses, 87, 357, 838
Rivkin, B., 593
Robison, Sophia M., 388
Rogoff, Abraham M., 131

Rogoff, H. çHarry, Hillel,' 113, 301, 302
Rogow, Arnold A., 168
Rogow, Sally, 303
Rose, Peter I., 389
Rosen, Bernard C., 457
Rosenbach, A. S. W., 839
Rosenbach, Hyman P., 88
Rosenbaum, Jeanette W., 216
Rosenberg, Stuart E., 89, 458
Rosenblatt, Samuel, 304
Rosenbloom, Joseph R., 305
Rosenfeld, Leonora C., 169
Rosenstock, Morton, 306
Rosenthal, Frank, 90, 840
Rosenthal, Gilbert S., 459
Rosenzweig, Gershon, 390
Roskolenko, Harry, 217
Ross, B. Joyce, 307
Roth, Cecil, 798
Rothblatt, H. M. 523
Rothkoff, Aaron, 524
Routtenberg, Max J., 460
Roy, Ralph L., 688
Rubin, Israel, 391
Rubinger, Naphtali J., 132
Ruderman, Jerome L., 35
Russell, Charles E., 308
Rywell, Martin, 16

Sachs, A. S., 133
St. John, Robert, 36
Sanders, Ronald, 617
Saphire, Saul, 248
Schaber, Will, 170
Schachner, Nathan, 134
Schappes, Morris U., 37, 171, 172
Scharfstein, Zevi, 525, 526, 527, 796
Schechtman, Joseph B., 559
Schiff, Alvin I., 528
Schindler, Solomon, 91
Schneiderman, Harry, 392

Schoener, Allon, 173

Schulman, Eliahu çElias,' 594

Schweppe, Emma, 9

Sefer ha-shanah l'Yehudei Amerikah, 595

Segal, Charles M., 38

Selzer, Michael, 174

Selznick, Gertrude J., 632, 689

Sentinel, 799

Shapiro, Yonathan, 560

Sharfman, I. Leo, 498

Shatzky, Yakov, 135

Sherman, C. Bezalel, 394, 651

Sheviley Hahinuch, 800

Shiloh, Ailon, 218

Shindeling, Abraham I., 92, 93, 395

Sh'ma, 801

Shpall, Leo, 94

Sidorsky, David, 396

Silber, Mendel, 841, 842

Silberman, Lou H., 461

Silcox, Edwin C., 652

Silver, Samuel M., 462

Silverberg, Robert, 136

Simonhoff, Harry, 137, 309, 310, 397

Simons, John, 311

Sklare, Marshall, 398, 399, 400, 401, 463

Sleeper, James A., 464

Sloan, Irving J., 39

Snetsinger, John, 561

Snyder, Charles R., 402

Sokolsky, George E., 690

Solis-Cohen, Elfrida C., 843

Solomon, Barbara S., 403

Soltes, Mordecai, 404

Southern Israelite, 802

Spaeth, Joe L., 632

Spargo, John, 691

Spivak, John L., 692

Stark, Rodney, 673, 693

Stein, Arthur, 657

Stein, Herman D., 346

Stein, Leon, 219

Steinberg, Stephen, 529, 689, 693

Stember, Charles H., 694

Stern, Elisabeth G., 220

Stern, Horace, 405

Stern, Malcolm H., 313

Stern, Norton B., 844

Stock, Ernest, 695

Stolberg, Benjamin, 562

Straus, Oscar S., 221

Strober, Gerald S., 406, 653

Strong, Donald S., 696

Suhl, Yuri, 40

Sulman, Esther, 407

Sura, 803

Swanson, Bert E., 636

Swichkow, Louis J., 95

Szajkowski, Zosa, 563

Talpioth, 804

Tartakover, Arie, 533

Tcherikover, Elias, 564, 565

Teller, Judd L., 138

Tercentenary Issue, *Jewish Quarterly Review*, 41

Thomas, Helen S., 315

Thomashefsky, Boris, 222

Thorowgood, Thomas, 654, 655

To Bigotry No Sanction: A Documented Analysis of Anti-Semitic Propaganda, 698

Tog, Der, 720

Trachtenberg, Joshua, 96

Tradition, 805

Truax, Rhoda, 316

Tumin, Melvin M., 845

Two Hundred and Fiftieth Anniversary of the Settlement of the Jews in the United States, The, 42

Uchill, Ida L., 410

United Synagogue Review, 806
Universal Jewish Encyclopedia,
806
Unterman, Isaac, 530
Urofsky, Melvin I., 317

Van den Haag, Ernest, 411
Vara, La, 778
Varheit, Di, 722
Vorspan, Albert, 318, 531, 644
Vorspan, Max, 97
Voss, Carl H., 176, 656

Wald, Lillian D., 223, 618
Walden, Daniel, 596
Waldman, Morris D., 412
Waskow, Arthur I., 465
Watters, Leon L., 98
Waxman, Mordecai, 466
Weinberger, Moshe, 467
Weinstein, Jacob J., 319
Weintraub, Ruth G., 699
Weisbord, Robert G., 657
Werner, M. R., 320
Wessel, Henry N., 99
*Western States Jewish Historical
Quarterly,* 808
Weyl, Nathaniel, 567
White, Lyman C., 619
Whiteman, Maxwell, 321
*Who's Who in American Jewry,
1926,* 322; *1938,* 323
Wieder, Arnold A., 100
Wiener, Norbert, 224
Wiernik, Peter, 43
Winter, Nathan H., 532
Wirth, Louis, 413
Wirtz, William, 331

Wischnitzer, Mark, 620, 621
Wischnitzer, Rachel, 468
Wise, Isaac M., 225
Wise, James W., 44, 324
Wise, Stephen, 226
Wolf, Edwin, 2d, 101, 846
Wolf, Simon, 45, 393
Wolfe, Jack, 102
Wyman, David S., 568

Yaffe, James, 414
*Yearbook of the Central Confer-
ence of American Rabbis,*
809
Yedies fun YIVO [News of the
YIVO], 810
Yiddishe Heim, Di, 723
Yiddishe Kultur, 811
*Yiddishe Landsmanshaften fun
New York, Di,* 333
Yiddishe Vort, Dos, 727
Yiddishe Zeitung, 812
Yiddisher Kemfer, 813
Yiddisher Puck, Der, 721
Yiddishes Tageblatt, 814
Yidishe Sprakh, 815
*YIVO Annual Jewish Social Sci-
ence,* 816
YIVO Bleter, 817
Young Israel Viewpoint, 818

Zaar, Isaac, 569
Zafren, Herbert C., 847
Zagat, Samuel, 415
Zarchin, Michael M., 416
Zeitlin, Joseph, 469
Zohori, Menahem, 533
Zukunft, Di, 724